ABBY LUCHSINGER
COZY QUILTS
• FOR THE MODERN HOME •
16 Seasonal Projects
stashBOOKS
an imprint of C&T Publishing

Publisher: Amy Barrett-Daffin

Creative Director: Gailen Runge

Senior Editor: Roxane Cerda

Editor: Madison Moore

Technical Editor: Kathy Patterson

Cover/Book Designer: April Mostek

Production Coordinator: Zinnia Heinzmann

Illustrator: Kirstie Pettersen

Front cover photography by Kate Longley

Other photos by Kate Longley on pages 5, 7, 9, 13, 36, 37, 41, 56, 57, 89, 106, 111, and 127.

Photography by Abby Luchsinger, unless otherwise noted

Published by Stash Books, an imprint of C&T Publishing, Inc., P.O. Box 1456, Lafayette, CA 94549

Library of Congress Cataloging-in-Publication Data
Names: Luchsinger, Abby, 1987- author
Title: Cozy quilts for the modern home : 16 seasonal projects / Abby Luchsinger.
Description: Lafayette, CA : Stash Books, [2026] | Summary: This modern quilt collection offers sixteen stunning seasonal projects, featuring spring blooms, summer stars, fall migration, and winter snowflakes—perfect for creating beautiful quilts year-round"-- Provided by publisher.
Identifiers: LCCN 2025026966 | ISBN 9781644036099 trade paperback | ISBN 9781644036105 ebook
Subjects: LCSH: Patchwork quilts | Quilting--Patterns | House furnishings
Classification: LCC TT835 .L785 2026 | DDC 746.46/041--dc23/eng/20250806
LC record available at https://lccn.loc.gov/2025026966

Printed in the USA

10 9 8 7 6 5 4 3 2

DEDICATION

For Gloria and Robin—Grama and Mom: the first two generations of my quilting legacy.

For Robbie, Henry, Cora, Audrey, and Charlotte: five pieces of my heart.

Acknowledgments

First of all, thank you to my Grama, Gloria, for sharing your love of quilting with me and for patiently teaching me to sew starting at a very early age. I am so grateful for all the time we have spent making quilts and sweet memories together. To my Mom, Robin, thank you for continuing to share a love of quilting with me and for encouraging me as I have grown to cherish this craft.

To my husband, Robbie: You are my biggest cheerleader and my soft place to land. You make me laugh and always stand by my side. Thank you for encouraging me to chase my dreams and for helping in so many ways to make that possible. You were my best friend at 5 years old and you are my favorite forever. I love you, babe!

My precious kids, Henry, Cora, Audrey, and Charlotte: I love you more than you will ever know. You are truly the joys of my life, and I am so thankful for the gift of being your mom every day. I am so proud of the unique and amazing person each of you is, and I adore getting to watch you grow into who you are becoming.

David and Robin and Kerry, Dad and Mom and Stepdad, you have loved and supported me my entire life and every step of the way as I have grown a hobby into a business, balanced with the cherished roles of wife and mother, daughter and friend, and I am so thankful for you.

To my life long best friend, Melissa, and my dear friends that make up the Nine Patch Quilt Collective, Tamara, Heather, Ann, Dana, Rachel, Megan, Emily, and Kristina: you are my sounding board, first-ask for advice, comic relief, and the most amazing cheerleaders. I am so thankful for each of you and your sweet friendship.

Also, a huge thank you to two of the most generous and talented friends and long-arm quilters: Tamara Darragh of Remi Vail Studio and Sandy Saengsuk of Thai Charm, LLC. Your beautiful quilting makes these designs shine, and I am so grateful for your nimble hands and generous hearts!

Thank you to the team at C&T Publishing for the opportunity to create a book of my own, and especially to my patient and skilled editor, Madison Moore, for expertly guiding me through this process.

To Art Gallery Fabrics and their incredible staff: thank you so much for your support and for providing all the beautiful fabrics used in the projects in this book. Pat and Walter Bravo, thank you also for believing in me as a designer, giving me the dream opportunity to design fabric of my very own, and for your continued mentorship. I am so grateful.

And finally, thanks to God, my creator. The beauty of your creation is an endless source of inspiration. Thank you for the gifts of imagination and artistry, and for my family, friends, and quilting community that are all part of the journey that has brought this opportunity to fruition. Most of all, thank you for the gift of your son, Jesus, and his atoning sacrifice. Your love pursues, transforms, restores, and is so much greater than I can ever imagine or understand. To you be all the glory forever and ever.

For we walk by faith, not by sight.—2 Corinthians 5:7

Contents

INTRODUCTION

My very first memories of sewing were sitting on my Grama's lap as a toddler, her hands over mine as she gently guided the fabric through her sewing machine. I watched, mesmerized, as the needle zipped up and down, up and down, and a neat row of tiny stitches formed behind it. My favorite part was when we reached the end of a seam. Grama would raise the foot and the needle and pull the fabric away from the machine while I picked up her sewing snips and very carefully cut the thread tails. Handling sewing snips was a big responsibility, and I took it very seriously.

Grama continued to teach me by allowing me to do more and more on my own as I grew older. I cut dozens of little heart templates out of her scraps so she could appliqué them onto a quilt for her bed. I learned to sew straight seams all by myself and piece scraps into baby doll sized quilts and pillows. And most fun of all, I was able to start choosing projects for us to do together. We made stuffed animals, doll clothes and accessories, nightgowns and skirts, whole cloth quilts for my close friends, and even my high school prom dress. My high school graduation gift was a sewing machine of my very own, an older Singer that was also my mom's first sewing machine.

After stepping away from my job in higher education to focus on raising my four young children in 2020, I stumbled into the quilting community on social media and was so inspired by the modern styles of quilting I saw there. I became a frequent pattern tester but quickly realized that my heart wanted to create designs of my own. I launched my pattern design business, Abby Maed, with a vision of preserving the rich legacy of quilting passed down through generations of my family, creating quilt designs that felt fresh but also cozy and nostalgic—modern, heirloom-quality quilts.

As a designer, I am most inspired by the beauty right outside my window. Both in the soft earthy colors that have become my signature palette, and in the seasonally inspired motifs in my designs, I am continually drawn to bringing the beauty of nature and the changing seasons into my own home to cozy up with, savor, and enjoy. The chapters and projects in this book follow nature's comforting rhythm of changing seasons, from the soft pinks and greens that herald new life in the budding plants and flowers of spring, to the warm yellows and oranges of sun-drenched summer days, to the rich reds and browns of changing leaves and fall harvests, and finally to the sweet creams and soft blues of a slumbering world tucked away under winter snow. I hope you enjoy making these cozy modern quilting projects and using them in your home just as much as I do!

Tools & Materials

FABRIC

The projects shown in this book are all made with high-quality quilting cotton, which is the most widely used fabric for quilting projects. I use all Art Gallery Fabrics, often from the Pure Solids line. Specific prints and colors are listed in each project. It is possible to use other types of fabrics (linen blends, flannels, or wovens) to achieve different looks and textures in your quilts, however, this may change the yardage needed and the amount of expected shrinkage—especially if you're mixing fabric types within a project.

BATTING

There are many kinds of batting available to use in quilted projects. They offer different levels of warmth, loft, and drape. The batting used in the projects in this book is Hobbs Heirloom 100% cotton batting unless otherwise noted.

Gütermann
Polyester
Gütermann
100 % Polyester

SEWING MACHINE & BASIC TOOLS

A domestic sewing machine is an invaluable tool for constructing quilts. Sewing machines come with many different features and price points, but a basic sewing machine with a standard straight stitch will have all the necessary functionality. I sew on a Bernina 770QE, but I started out on a reliable entry level machine and made many quilts with it before eventually investing in a larger machine. Start each project with a fresh universal needle in the sewing machine for the best results.

I recommend using a high quality 50-weight cotton or polyester quilting thread as that can be used for both piecing and quilting. You may choose to use heavier thread weights for quilting to achieve more visibility and texture in the quilting design. I used Aurifil or Gutermann 50-weight 100% cotton thread to piece all the projects. Your sewing toolkit should also always include straight pins, fabric clips, a small pair of scissors or thread snips, and a seam ripper. Make sure you have an iron and ironing mat for pressing seams.

ROTARY CUTTER AND CUTTING MAT

A 45mm rotary cutter is a staple tool for precise cutting. Start each project with a fresh blade and always cut with a self-healing mat underneath the fabric.

ACRYLIC QUILTING RULERS

There is an endless variety of sizes and shapes of quilting rulers. I suggest having one longer ruler for cutting yardage and squaring up your quilts, and a small ruler or two for trimming blocks. I highly recommend using a suction cup handle on your most used rulers to keep your fingers safely away from the sharp rotary blade.

FABRIC MARKER

Having a reliable way to mark fabric both for piecing and quilting is imperative. When marking lines that will later be cut, I often use a regular pencil. However, when the mark is in a visible location, like the top of a quilt sandwich, a hera marker that simply creases the fabric or a temporary fabric marker are great choices. My favorite removable marking tool is the heat erasable Pilot Frixion pen. I use it to write labels on my fabrics and mark quilting lines.

SAFETY PINS OR BASTING SPRAY

Once a quilt top is finished and you are ready to make a quilt sandwich, you need safety pins or basting spray to hold the layers of fabric and batting in place for quilting. Safety pins are reusable and mess-free, but also more time consuming and trickier to quilt around. Alternatively, basting spray is a consumable, and you need to have a large flat area that is well ventilated to use it. However, it's very efficient and effective at keeping the layers secure.

Project-Specific Supplies

Zippers: There are three projects in the book that use zippers. The required length and type are specified in each project, though they all use #5 size zippers. If you plan to make several zipper projects, consider ordering a coil of zipper tape that you can cut the exact length needed for each project.

Foam Interfacing and Fusible Fleece: For projects that benefit from more structure, like the Sweetberry Market Tote (page 56), foam interfacing is a great alternative to traditional batting to add texture and dimension to the quilting. Similarly, fusible fleece adds more structure than batting, but with more flexibility and less loft than foam. The Cabin Game Board pattern (page 94) recommends fusible fleece.

Abbreviations, Definitions & Best Practices

FE: Fat eighth; a cut of fabric measuring 9″ × 21″

FQ: Fat quarter; a cut of fabric measuring 18″ × 21″

WOF: Width of fabric; the usable width of quilting cotton, which is assumed to be 42″ in this book

RST: Right sides together

WST: Wrong sides together

HST: Half-square triangle

QST: Quarter-square triangle

FG: Flying geese

Seam Allowance: Use a ¼″ seam allowance unless otherwise specified.

Scant Seam Allowance: A seam allowance that is very slightly less (approximately 1 thread-width less) than the standard seam allowance.

Backing Overage: The backing yardage includes a 4″ overage on all sides of the quilt top to ensure compatibility with longarm quilting services.

Labels: Letter and number labels are listed for each cut of fabric in each project. As you cut pieces out, label them with this letter/number combination to keep track of them during construction.

Basic Techniques

You'll use these basic piecing techniques across many of the projects. This chapter does not include any cutting lists or dimensions, so when a project refers you to one of the piecing techniques found here, use the cut pieces specified by that project.

Half-Square Triangles

2-AT-A-TIME HALF-SQUARE TRIANGLES

1. Pair 2 squares of the same size. Mark a line, corner-to-corner, on the wrong side of the lighter colored square. Place the squares RST.

2. Sew ¼″ away from both sides of the marked line.

3. Cut on the marked line, and press both seams open (or toward the darker fabric). Trim as instructed.

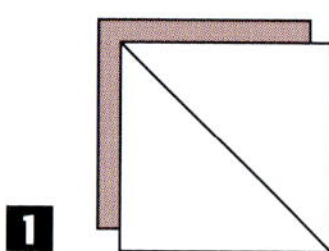

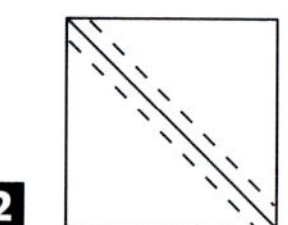

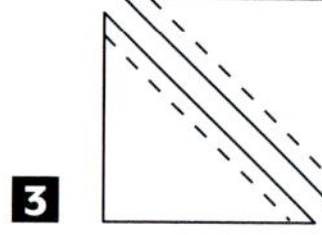

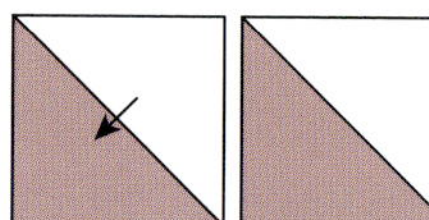

4-AT-A-TIME HALF-SQUARE TRIANGLES

1. Pair 2 squares of the same size. Mark diagonal lines, corner-to-corner in both directions, on the wrong side of the lighter fabric square. Place the squares RST.

2. Sew a ¼″ seam around the perimeter of the squares.

3. Cut on both diagonal lines and press the seams open (or toward the darker fabric) on all 4 pieces. Trim as instructed.

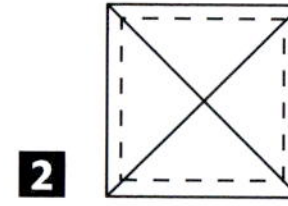

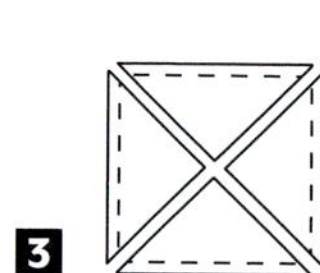

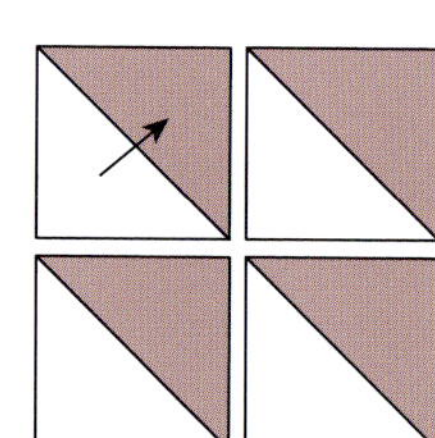

GEORGIA PEACH
MARMALADE
MANDARIN
SUMMER SUN
SWEET TANGERINE
BURNT ORANGE
TIGERLILY
DRIED CARROT
SEDONA
AUTUMNAL
DESERT DUNES
CINNAMON
GRAPEFRUIT
MIAMI SUNSET
CORAL REEF
HIBISCUS
FLAMINGO
UNDENIABLY RED
RUBY
LONDON RED
AURORA RED
TERRACOTTA TILE
COTTON CANDY
CRYSTAL PINK
QUARTZ PINK
CACTUS FLOWER
CHERRY LIPGLOSS
DRAGON FRUIT
SPICEBERRY
WEATHERED BRICK
CANDIED CHERRY
DRIED ROSES
BOUGAINVILLEA
VERY BERRY
ROCK CANDY
COSMOS
VERVE VIOLET
PURPLE WINE
CABERNET
PLUM PRESERVE
BEWITCHED
SWEET FIG
MAUVELOUS
SUGAR PLUM
FIELD OF LAVENDER
WISTERIA
PURPLE PANSY
AMETHYST
HYDRANGEA
ROYAL COBALT
BLUEBERRY ZEST
ATMOSPHERIC
PERIWINKLE
AERO BLUE
SLATE
SPRUCE
SWIMMING POOL
OCEAN WAVES
OCEAN FOG
CRYSTALLINE
TRANQUIL WATERS
PARISIAN BLUE
DENIM BLUE
NIGHT SEA
HEART OF THE OCEAN
NOCTURNAL
ZAMBIA STONE
TILE BLUE
MALDIVES
COZUMEL BLUE
FRESH WATER
MIRAGE BLUE
TENDER GREEN
MEDITATION
WARM WAVE
ICY MINT
MORNING FROST
JADE CREAM
EMERALD
PEACOCK
SECRET LAGOON
FOREST NIGHT
ROSEMARY
ASPARAGUS
HUNTER FIELDS
EUCALYPTUS
PATINA GREEN
PACIFIC
DARK CITRON
LIGHT CITRON
LEMONADE
PARROT
OLIVE OIL
EMPIRE YELLOW
PINEAPPLE
BANANA CREAM
AURUS
FRESH SAGE
SIENNA BRICK
GINGERBREAD
RAW GOLD
HONEY
LEMON TART
TURMERIC
CANARY
HONEYDEW
GOLDEN BRONZE
DRIED MOSS
GARDEN FERN
TOASTY WALNUT
VANILLA CUSTARD
MACCHIATO
VINTAGE WALNUT
SANDSTONE
LATTE
PAMPAS
WHITE LINEN
CREME DE LA CREME
LIGHT GREY
SNOW
CELESTIAL
VAPOROUS
MYSTIC GREY
NEBULA
POTTER'S CLAY
GENTLE FEATHER
MUSHROOM
SMOOTH PEBBLE
MINK
COCONUT MILK
MAGNETISM
LAVA ROCK
CAVIAR
DEEP BLACK
TRUFFLE PES919
COFFEE BEAN
THISTLE PES903
SPICED PES905
POPPY PES904
QUEEN BEE PES906
MATCHA PES915
CERULEAN PES912
SNAPDRAGON PES 908

Flying Geese

4-AT-A-TIME FLYING GEESE

1. Gather 4 small squares and 1 large square per pattern instructions. Mark a diagonal line, corner-to-corner, on the wrong side of the 4 small squares.

2. Place 2 small squares RST on opposite corners of the large square. Make sure the marked lines align diagonally. Sew ¼″ away from both sides of the marked line.

3. Cut on the marked line. Press the seams toward the small triangles making 2 heart-shaped pieces.

4. Place 1 of the 2 remaining small squares on the corner of each Step 3 unit, the diagonal line aligned as shown. Sew ¼″ away from both sides of the marked lines.

5. Cut on the marked lines. Press the seams toward the small triangles and trim as instructed.

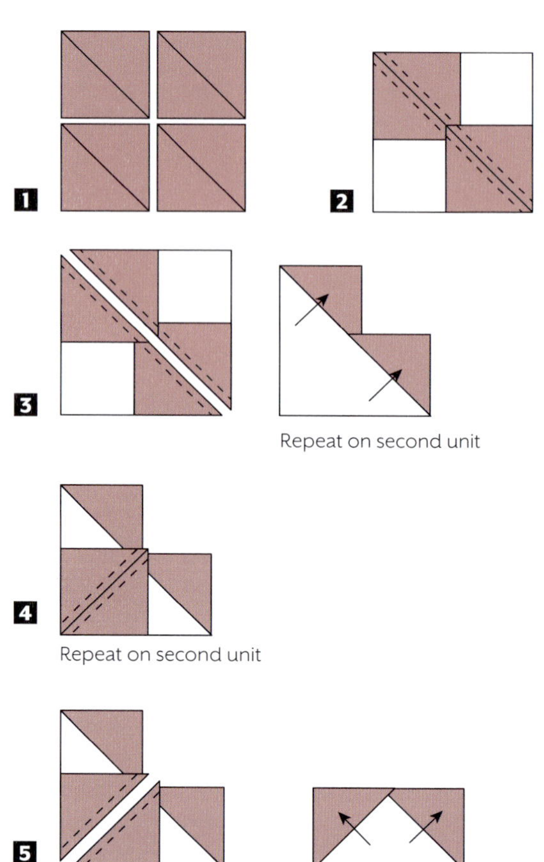

Curves

Access all the curved piecing patterns in Templates (page 127). Each project will note which template(s) to use.

1. Trace or print the template onto cardstock or paper, making sure it is at 100% scale. Trace the template onto the fabric, then cut it out.

2. Pair a convex piece with the corresponding concave piece. Fold each in half to mark the centers.

3. Place the pieces RST with the curves in opposite directions. Match up the center points of both curves, and pin together.

4. Bring the curves together, matching up the raw edges. Pin generously. Be sure to pin at the beginning and end of the curve.

5. Slowly and carefully sew around the curve. Stop to adjust the fabric as needed to avoid puckers. Press the seam as instructed in the project. Trim as instructed.

CURVES

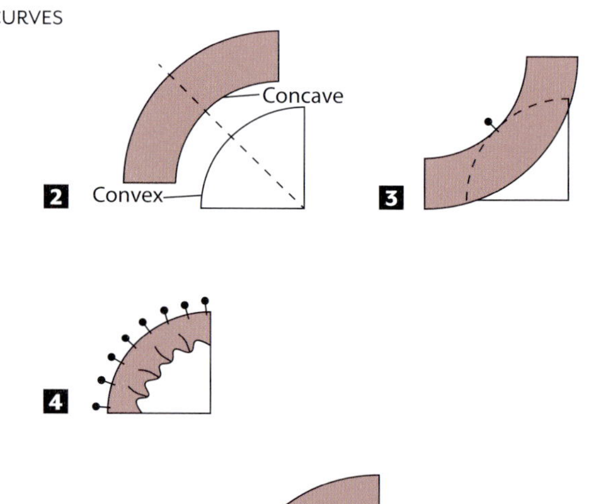

Binding

CONTINUOUS BIAS BINDING

Bias binding is binding cut from the fabric at a 45-degree angle (on the bias). It differs from straight-grain binding, the most used modern quilt binding. Bias binding involves a little more effort to calculate and make, but it has more give and stretch than straight-grain binding. This makes it a great choice for binding projects that have a curved edge such as the Signs of Spring Bunting (page 22) and the Rainglow Pouch (page 36). Continuous bias binding is a speedy method of making bias binding that minimizes the number of seams to sew.

Calculating Fabric Square Size

Continuous bias binding is made from a square of fabric.

Start by determining how much and what size binding you need, plus a few inches extra. The Signs of Spring Bunting (page 22) calls for 7 strips of 2˝-wide binding that are each 24˝ in length, or a minimum of 168˝ of binding plus a little extra. I recommend adding 12˝ or so onto your calculated length, which would be a total of 180˝ of binding needed for this example.

Keep in mind that square size must be divisible by the width of the binding strip you're making. So, for 2˝ binding, the square's dimensions must be an even number (divisible by 2).

Calculate the square dimension by first multiplying the total length of binding by the width of the binding.

Example: 180 × 2 = 360

Then take the square root of the answer and round up to the nearest number divisible by the binding width to determine the square size needed.

Example: √360= 18.97. 18.97˝ rounds to a 20˝ square of fabric needed to make 180˝ of bias binding.

Another approach is to test usable square sizes in reverse to see what size will yield the needed amount of binding. To test a 20˝ square size in reverse, first multiply the square size by itself: 20 × 20 = 400

Then divide that number by the width of binding needed to get the approximate length of binding that will be made: 400 / 2 = 200˝ bias binding from a 20˝ square of fabric, which is more than enough.

Assembly

1. Cut the binding fabric square diagonally, corner to corner.

2. Match the left edge of the top/left triangle to the right edge of the bottom/right triangle, RST. Pin.

3. Sew together with a ¼″ seam allowance. Press the seam open.

4. On the wrong side of the fabric, mark parallel lines running alongside the longest edge every 2″ (or the desired width of the binding).

5. Bring the 2 short ends of the fabric RST, lining up the corner of one end with the first drawn line on the other end. Pin. Match the drawn lines together across the raw edges, pinning. Offset the final line with the other corner, as shown. Sew with a ¼″ seam. Press the seam open.

6. Starting at one offset corner, use scissors to carefully cut along the continuous drawn line, creating one continuous strip of bias binding.

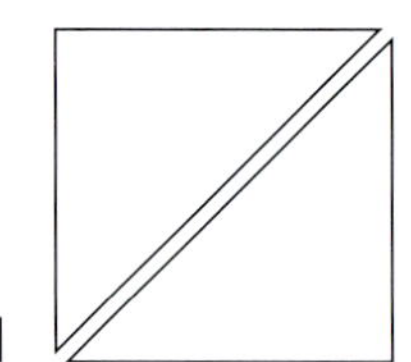

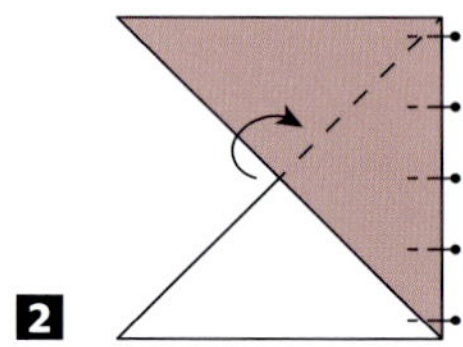

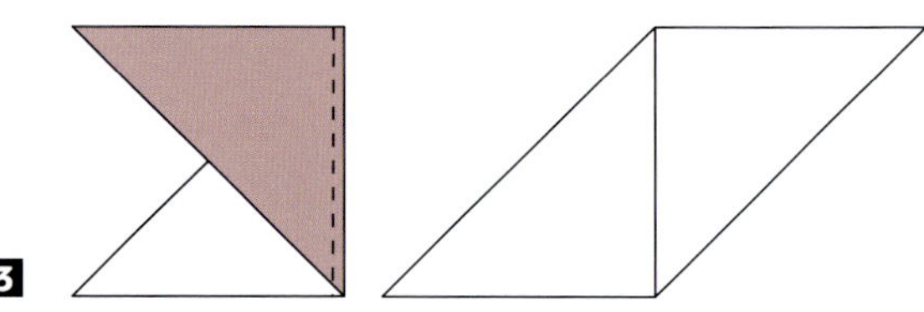

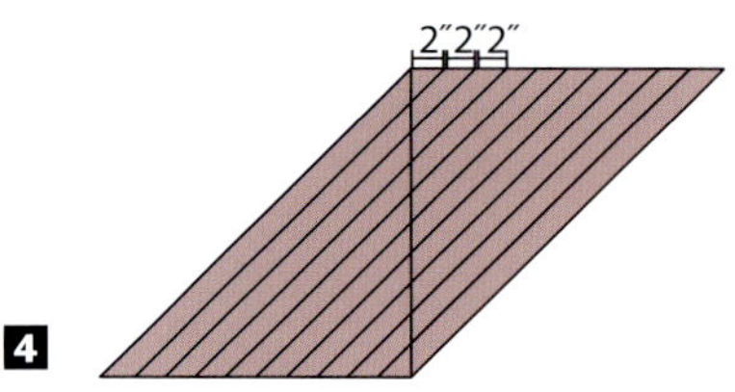

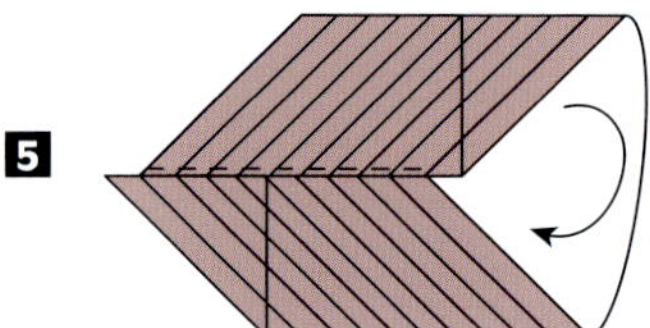

STRAIGHT-GRAIN BINDING

1. Cut strips of fabric WOF × desired width of binding (as specified in the project instructions).

2. Place the short ends of 2 binding strips RST at a 90-degree angle. Mark a diagonal line from the top left corner of the top binding strip to the bottom right corner of the bottom binding strip.

3. Sew on the marked line. Cut off the excess corner fabric ¼″ from the seam. Press the seam open.

4. Repeat Steps 2–3 until all the strips are sewn together. Press the binding in half lengthwise, WST.

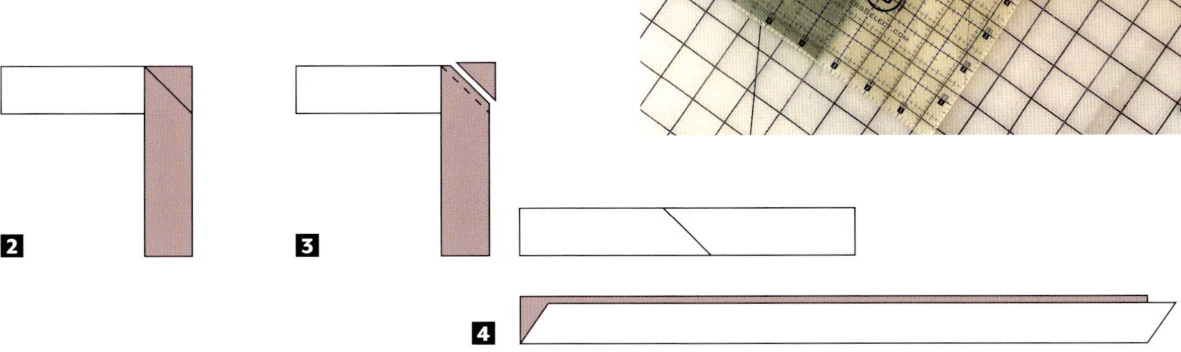

Quilt Finishing

BACKING

Piece together fabric for the backing so that it is 8″ longer and wider than the quilt top (4″ of overage on each side). This is the minimum required overage needed for most longarm quilting, but if you plan to quilt on a domestic machine, a couple of inches on each side may be sufficient.

QUILT SANDWICH

Lay out the backing fabric, wrong side up. Layer the batting on top, and then the quilt top, right side up to make a quilt sandwich.

BASTING

Lay the quilt sandwich on a flat surface (e.g. a clean, hard floor) and baste the layers together using safety pins every few inches or by using an adhesive basting spray between the layers. It's very important to ensure that the layers are flat and smooth to avoid any puckers during quilting.

QUILTING

Plan out a quilting design, making sure the distance between quilting lines is no more than 4″ for cotton batting. Mark the quilting design using a hera marker or temporary fabric marking pen. If you're working with a longarm quilter, they can often help you plan a design.

If quilting on a domestic machine, quilt the marked design using a walking foot or a free motion foot. It is also helpful to wear quilting or gardening gloves with grip to make it easier to guide the quilt through the machine. Be sure to spread the weight of the quilt over the sewing table as much as possible to avoid creating uneven tension in the quilting.

TRIM AND SQUARE UP

Once the quilting is complete, use a long acrylic ruler and rotary cutter to trim the excess batting and backing fabric away from the edge of the quilt top. Trim so all the corners are square, and the edges are even.

BINDING

TIP Binding can be sewn to either the back or front of the quilt first and then folded over the raw edge and secured on the opposite side. The method described here suggests the binding be attached to the back of the quilt first, but the steps are interchangeable whether the binding is initially sewn to the front or back of the quilt.

Make or gather continuous bias binding or straight-grain quilt binding.

1. Start by aligning the raw edge of the binding strip with the raw edge of the quilt backing. Leave a 4″–6″ tail unsewn at the start. Pin or clip in place around the perimeter of the quilt. Begin sewing the binding in place with a ¼″ seam allowance along one of the straight edges. When you approach a corner, stop sewing ¼″ from the edge and back stitch to secure.

2. Fold the binding away from the corner at a 90-degree angle, as shown. Then fold back on itself and align the binding strip with the next raw edge of the quilt backing. Start sewing ¼″ away from the corner on the next side of the quilt.

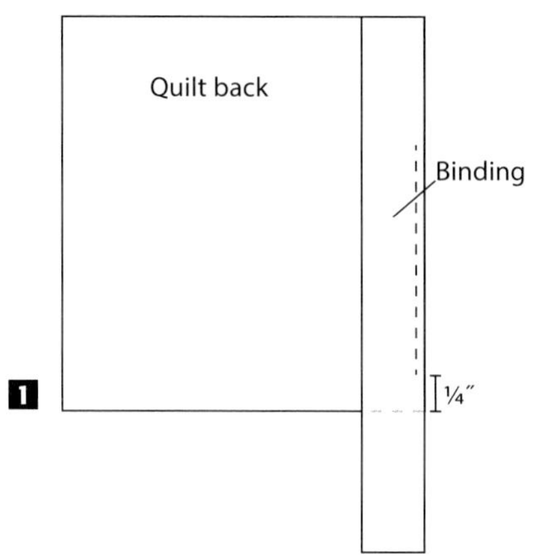

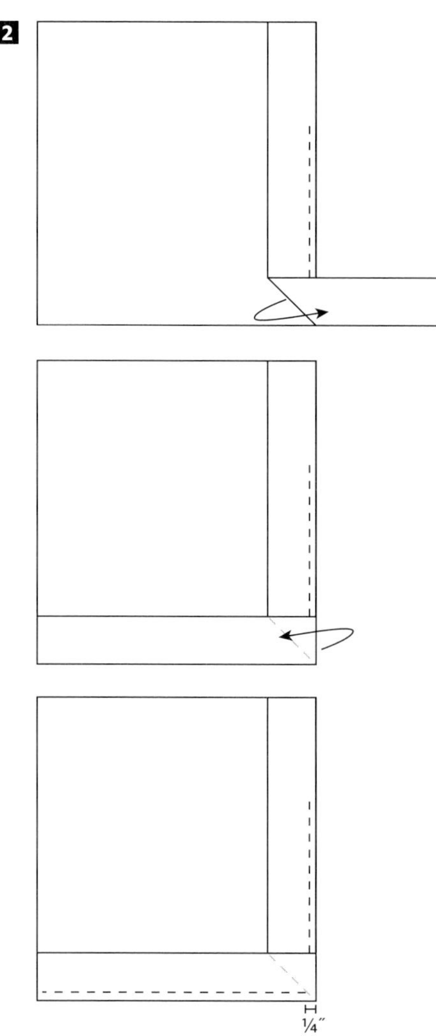

3. Continue sewing around the perimeter of the quilt to attach the binding in place. Stop sewing approximately 8″ from where you started sewing. Overlap the binding tails and measure the overlapping portion to be exactly 2½″ (or the width of the binding if it differs). Trim off any excess overlap.

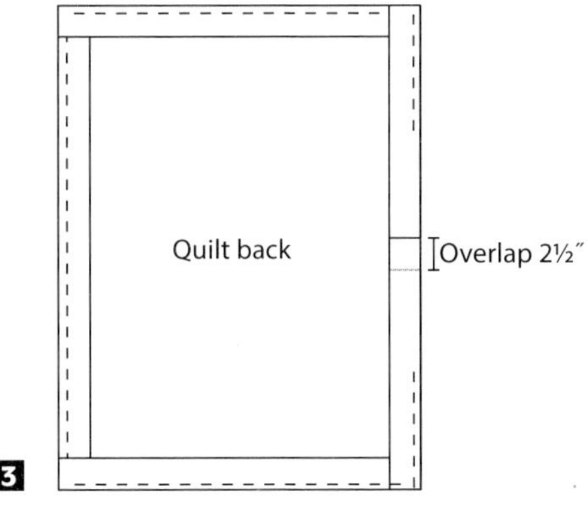

4. Place the ends of the binding strips RST at a 90-degree angle and repeat Steps 2–3 in Straight-Grain Binding (page 17) to sew the ends together and trim the excess fabric. Make sure the binding is not twisted. Finger-press the seam open, then refold the binding, clip in place on the edge of the quilt, and sew the rest of the binding to the quilt backing.

5. Fold the edge of the binding over to the opposite (front) side of the quilt, and clip in place, enclosing the raw edge. At each corner, continue folding over the binding past the edge of the quilt in one direction. Then fold it back on itself from the other direction to create a mitered corner, as shown. Clip in place.

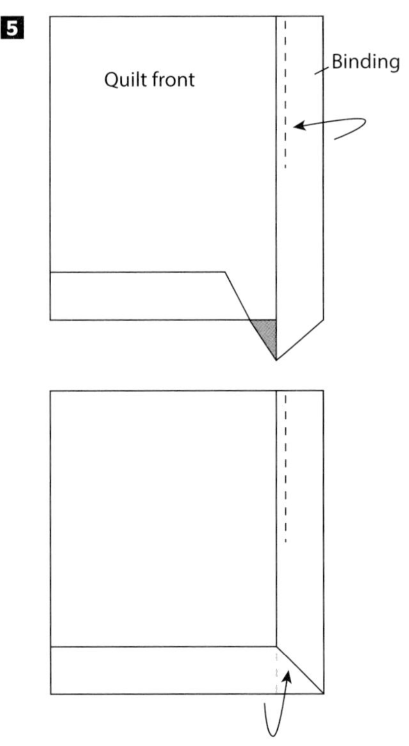

TIP Use an iron to press the binding away from the backing before folding it over for an extra crisp finish.

6. Start sewing the binding to the front of the quilt along one of the sides by sewing ⅛″ from the folded edge of the binding all the way around the perimeter of the quilt. If you prefer an invisible finish, hand sew with a ladder stitch. If you prefer a more decorative finish, hand sew with the stitch of your choice.

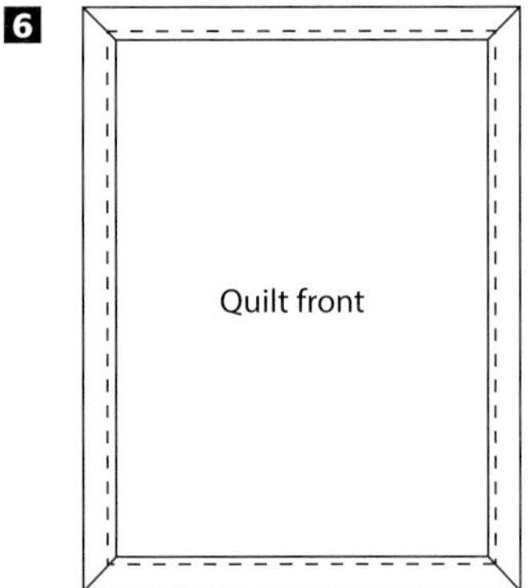

SPRING

Spring ushers forth a season of new life, abundant growth, and fresh possibility. The world moves from the soft shades of unfurling leaves and budding branches into a celebration of color as the flowers and trees start to bloom. The projects in this chapter celebrate this season of transition in the delicate flowers of the Signs of Spring Bunting (page 22), the soft greens of a sweet clover patch in the Cloverly Quilt (page 32), the promise of the beauty that follows spring rains in the darling Rainglow Pouch (page 36), and the delight of cheery tulips welcoming the return of sunshine and warmer weather in the Fleuriste Quilt (page 42).

SIGNS OF SPRING BUNTING

Finished Block Size: 6˝ × 9˝ || **Finished Bunting Length:** 48˝

This sweet, decorative bunting features three different spring flower designs to make a fresh, floral décor piece and welcome home the new season. This bunting would be darling in a nursery or a child's bedroom, strung across a mantle, or decorating a sewing room! Be sure to share your project online with the hashtag **#signsofspringbunting**

FABRICS & SUPPLIES

Yardages are based on 42˝ wide fabric and 90˝ wide batting.

Purple (Fabric A): ⅛ yard

Peach (Fabric B): ⅛ yard

Dark orange (Fabric C): ⅛ yard

Pink (Fabric D): ⅛ yard

Blue (Fabric E): ⅛ yard

Cream (Background Fabric F): ½ yard

Purple floral (Backing and Binding Fabric): 1⅛ yards

Batting: ¼ yard

Bunting Template (see Templates, page 127)

Material Notes

This bunting uses Art Gallery Fabrics in Sweet Fig, Apricot Crepe, Dried Carrot, Quartz Pink, Ocean Fog, Melodic Blooms Sweet, and Calico Days Lavender.

CUTTING INSTRUCTIONS

Prepare the Bunting Template for this project (see Templates, page 127). Label each piece as specified in parenthesis in the cutting lists.

Fabric A

Cut 1 strip 2½˝ × WOF; subcut into:

- 8 squares 2½˝ × 2½˝ (A1)

Fabric B

Cut 1 strip 2½˝ × WOF; subcut into:

- 8 squares 2½˝ × 2½˝ (B1)
- 8 squares 1½˝ × 1½˝ (B2)

Fabric C

Cut 1 strip 1¼˝ × WOF; subcut into:

- 8 squares 1¼˝ × 1¼˝ (C1)

Fabric D

Cut 1 strip 3½˝ × WOF; subcut into:

- 3 rectangles 3½˝ × 4½˝ (D1)
- 12 squares 1½˝ × 1½˝ (D2)

Fabric E

Cut 1 strip 2¼˝ × WOF; subcut into:

- 6 rectangles 2¼˝ × 3½˝ (E1)
- 4 rectangles 2¼˝ × 2˝ (E2)
- 4 rectangles 2¼˝ × 1½˝ (E3)

Cut 1 strip 1˝ × WOF; subcut into:

- 7 rectangles 1˝ × 3½˝ (E4)

Background Fabric F

Cut 1 strip 2¼˝ × WOF; subcut into:

- 6 squares 2¼˝ × 2¼˝ (F1)
- 2 rectangles 2¼˝ × 2˝ (F2)
- 8 rectangles 2¼˝ × 1½˝ (F3)
- 6 rectangles 2¼˝ × 1˝ (F4)

Cut 6 strips 1½˝ × WOF; subcut into:

- 14 rectangles 1½˝ × 7½˝ (F5)
- 14 rectangles 1½˝ × 6½˝ (F6)
- 6 rectangles 1½˝ × 2½˝ (F7)
- 12 squares 1½˝ × 1½˝ (F8)

Cut 2 strips 1¼˝ × WOF; subcut into:

- 52 squares 1¼˝ × 1¼˝ (F9)
- 4 squares 1˝ × 1˝ (F10)

Backing and Binding Fabric

Cut 1 strip 20˝ × WOF; subcut into:

- 1 square 20˝ × 20˝ for Continuous Bias Binding (page 15)
- 2 rectangles 8˝ × 11˝ for backing

Cut 1 strip 11˝ × WOF; subcut into:

- 5 rectangles 8˝ × 11˝ for backing

Cut 3 strips 2˝ × WOF; sew together end-to-end, and press the seams open for chain binding

Batting

Cut 7 rectangles 8˝ × 11˝

Block Assembly

Seam allowances are ¼″ unless otherwise noted. Pressing direction is indicated by the arrows in the diagrams.

PRIMROSE BLOCK

Repeat all the steps in this section to sew a total of 2 Primrose blocks.

Flower

1. Mark a diagonal line, corner-to-corner, on the wrong side of 2 F9 squares and 1 B2 square.

2. Pin the F9 squares RST to the top two corners of an A1 square, as shown.

3. Sew on the marked lines. Cut away excess corner fabric ¼″ away from the sewn lines. Press the seam toward the F fabric.

4. Pin the B2 square RST to the bottom left corner of the A1 square as shown.

5. Sew on the marked line. Cut away excess corner fabric ¼″ away from the sewn line. Press the seam toward the B fabric to complete 1 petal.

6. Repeat Steps 1–5 to make a total of 4 Primrose petals.

7. Arrange the 4 petals so that the Fabric B corners are all pointed toward the center, as shown. Sew the top two petals together and press the seam toward the right petal. Sew the bottom two petals together and press the seam to the left petal.

8. Sew the top petal row to the bottom petal row and press the seam open to complete 1 Primrose flower.

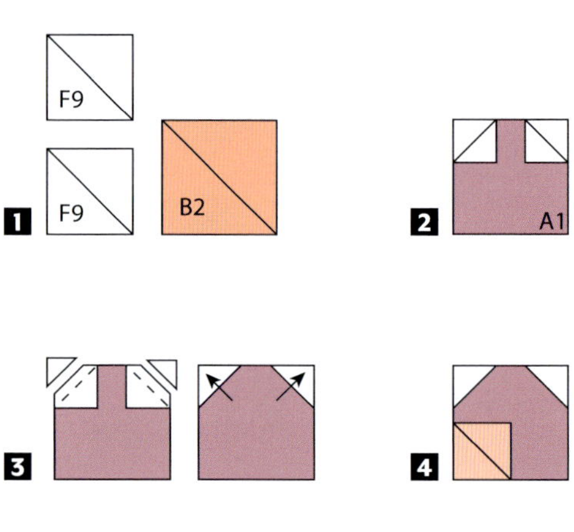

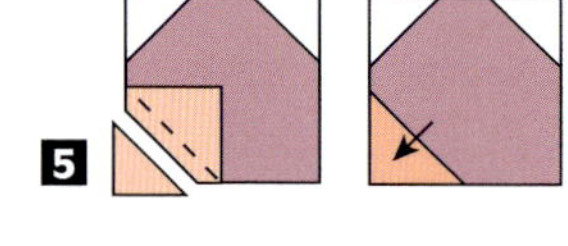

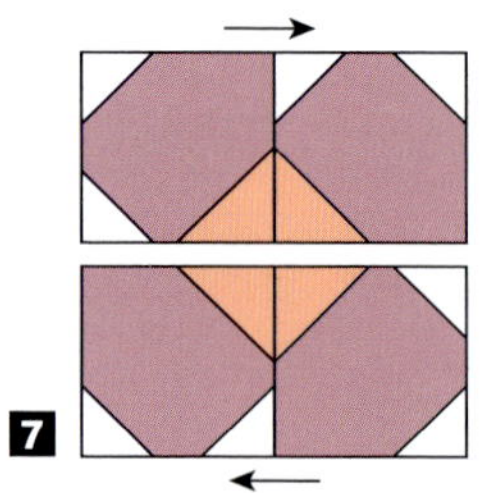

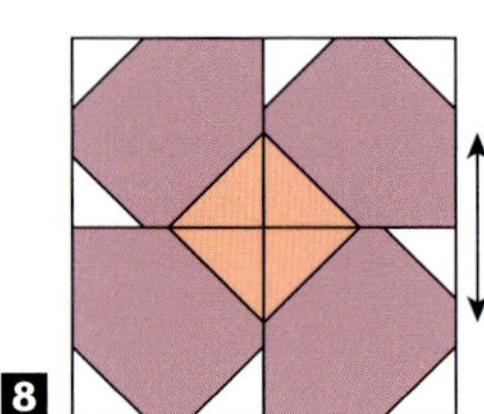

Leaves & Stem

1. Mark a diagonal line, corner-to-corner, on the wrong side of 2 F9 squares and 2 F10 squares.

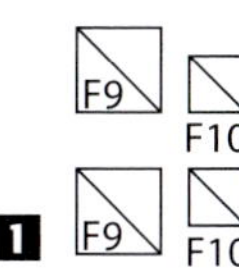

2. Pin 1 F9 and 1 F10 square on opposite corners of 1 E3 rectangle, as shown. Repeat with the remaining F9 and F10 squares on the opposite corners of another E3 rectangle. Mirror the orientation of the squares between the two E3 rectangles.

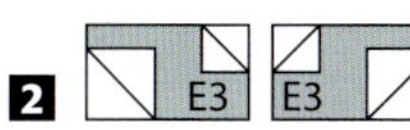

3. Sew on all marked lines. Cut away the excess corner fabric ¼˝ away from the sewn lines and press the seams toward the F fabric to complete 2 Primrose leaves.

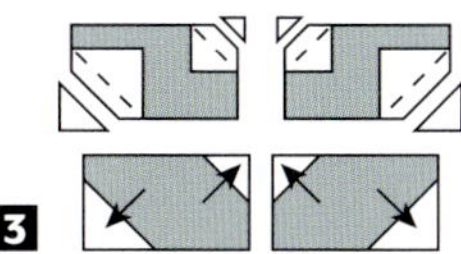

4. Sew 1 F4 rectangle to the top of the left leaf and 1 F2 rectangle to the bottom of the left leaf, as shown. Press the seams toward the Fabric F rectangles.

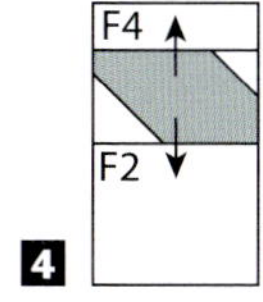

5. Sew 1 F3 rectangle to the top of the right leaf and 1 F3 rectangle to the bottom of the right leaf, as shown. Press the seams toward the Fabric F rectangles.

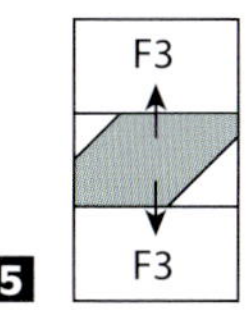

6. Arrange 1 E4 rectangle between the leaf units. Sew the left leaf unit to the left side of the E4 rectangle. Sew the right leaf unit to the right side of the E4 rectangle. Press the seams toward the E4 rectangle.

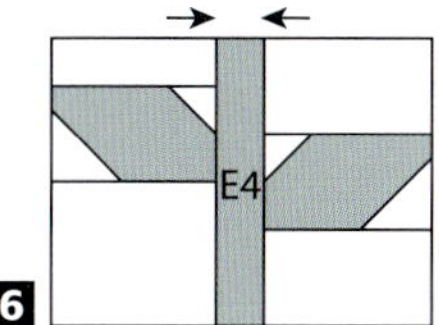

Assembly

1. Sew the flower unit to the leaves and stem unit and press the seam open.

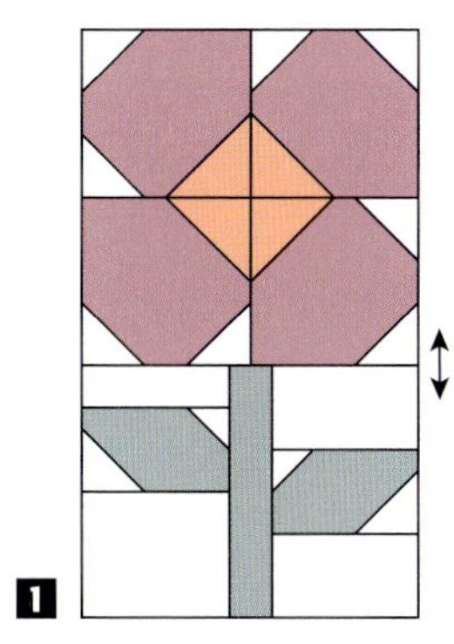

2. Sew an F5 rectangle to the left and right sides of the Step 1 unit. Press the seams toward the Fabric F rectangles.

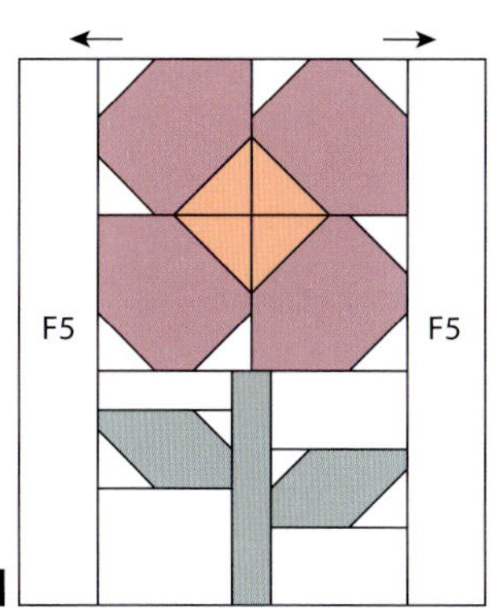

3. Sew an F6 rectangle to the top and bottom of the Step 2 unit. Press the seams toward the Fabric F rectangles to complete the Primrose block.

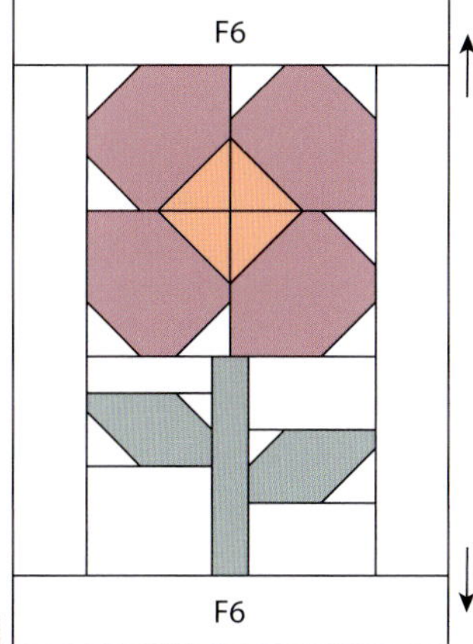

POPPY BLOCK

Repeat all the steps in this section to sew a total of 2 Poppy blocks.

Flower

1. Mark a diagonal line, corner-to-corner, on the wrong side of 3 F9 squares and 1 C1 square.

2. Pin the 3 F9 squares RST to 3 adjacent corners of a B1 square. Pin the C1 square to the remaining corner, as shown.

3. Sew on the marked lines. Cut away excess corner fabric ¼˝ away from the sewn lines. Press the seams toward the corner triangles to complete 1 petal.

4. Repeat Steps 1–3 to make a total of 4 petals.

5. Arrange the 4 petals so that the Fabric C corners are all pointed toward the center. Sew the top 2 petals together and press the seam toward the right petal. Sew the bottom 2 petals together and press the seam to the left petal.

6. Sew the top petal row to the bottom petal row. Press the seam open to complete 1 Poppy flower.

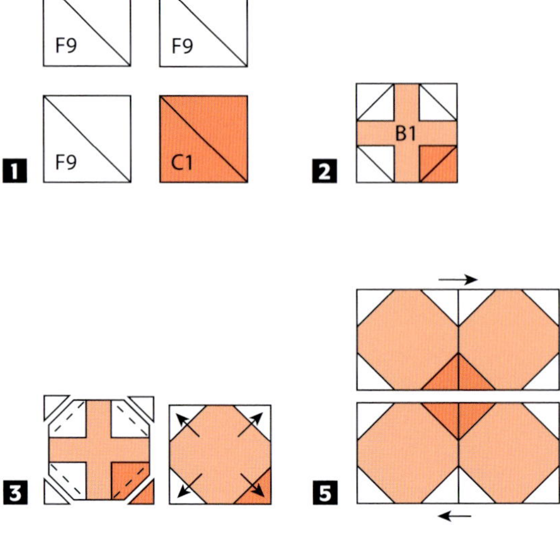

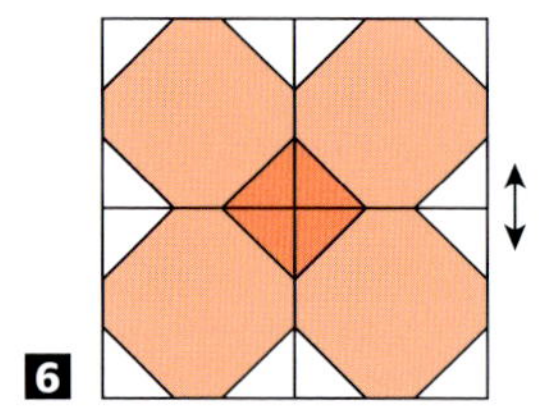

Leaves & Stem

1. Mark a diagonal line, corner-to-corner, on the wrong side of 4 F9 squares.

2. Pin 2 F9 squares on opposite corners of 1 E2 rectangle, as shown. Repeat with the remaining 2 F9 squares on the opposite corners of another E2 rectangle, as shown. Mirror the orientation of the squares between the two E2 rectangles.

3. Sew on all marked lines. Cut away excess corner fabric ¼˝ away from the sewn lines. Press the seams towards the F fabric to complete 2 Poppy leaves.

LEAVES & STEM

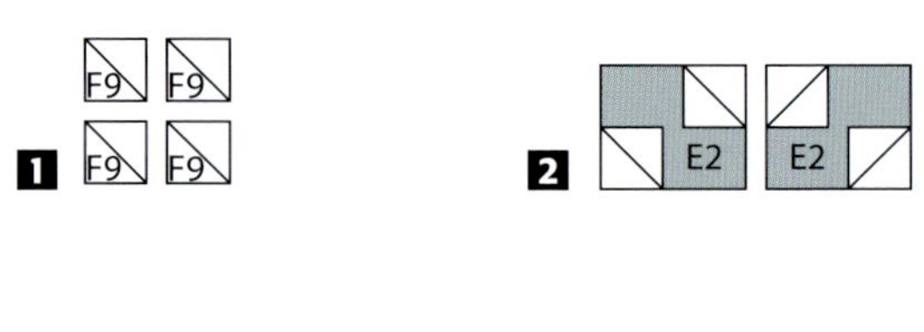

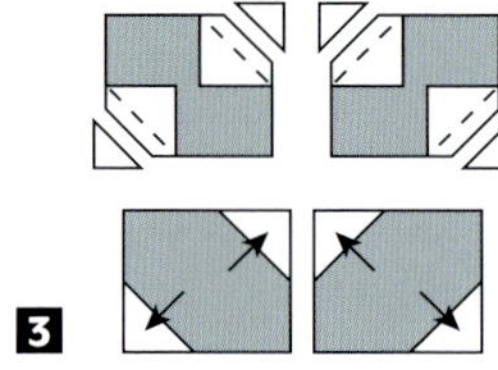

4. Sew 1 F4 rectangle to the top of each leaf. Sew 1 F3 rectangle to the bottom of each leaf. Press the seams toward the Fabric F rectangles.

5. Arrange 1 E4 rectangle between the mirrored leaf units. Sew the left leaf unit to the left side of the E4 rectangle. Sew the right leaf unit to the right side of the E4 rectangle. Press the seams toward the E4 rectangle.

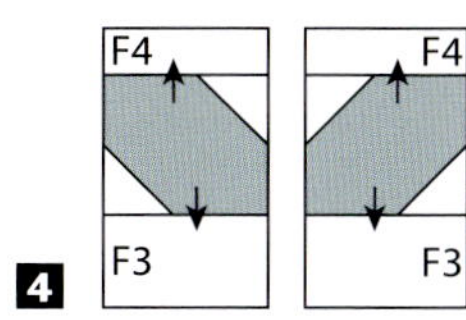

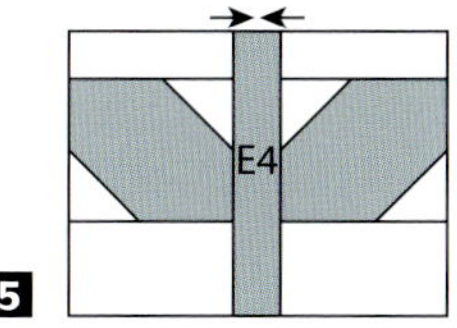

Assembly

1. Sew the flower unit to the leaves and stem unit. Press the seam open.

2. Sew 1 F5 rectangle to the left and right side of the Step 1 unit. Press the seams toward the Fabric F rectangles.

3. Sew 1 F6 rectangle to the top and bottom of the Step 2 unit. Press the seams toward the Fabric F rectangles to complete 1 Poppy block.

ASSEMBLY

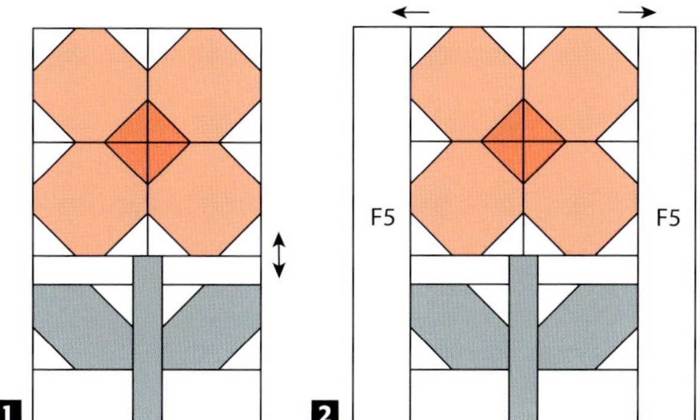

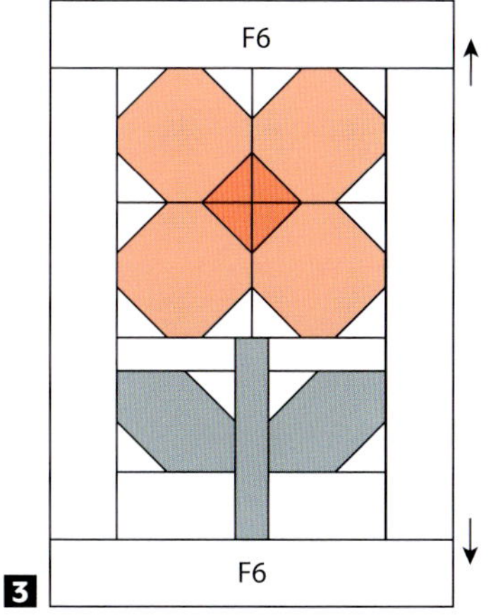

TULIP BLOCK

Repeat all the steps in this section to sew a total of 3 Tulip blocks.

Flower

1. Mark a diagonal line, corner-to-corner, on the wrong side of 2 F8 squares.

2. Pin the 2 F8 squares RST to 2 adjacent corners on the long 4½˝ side of a D1 rectangle.

3. Sew on the marked lines. Cut away excess corner fabric ¼˝ away from the sewn lines. Press the seams toward the F fabric.

FLOWER

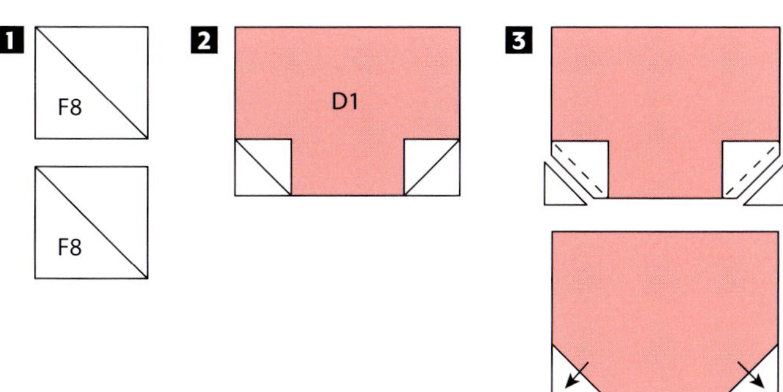

4. Mark a diagonal line, corner-to-corner, on the wrong side of 4 D2 squares.

5. Pin 2 D2 squares RST to the right side of 2 F7 rectangles, as shown.

6. Sew on the marked lines. Cut away excess corner fabric ¼″ away from the sewn lines. Press the seams toward the D fabric.

7. Pin the remaining 2 D2 squares RST to the left side of the Step 6 units.

8. Sew on the marked lines. Cut away excess corner fabric ¼″ away from the sewn lines. Press the seams toward D fabric to complete 2 flying geese.

9. Sew the 2 flying geese together, oriented the same direction, along the short side of the rectangle. Press the seam open.

10. Sew the flying geese unit to the top of the D1 rectangle, as shown. Press the seam toward the D1 rectangle to complete 1 Tulip flower.

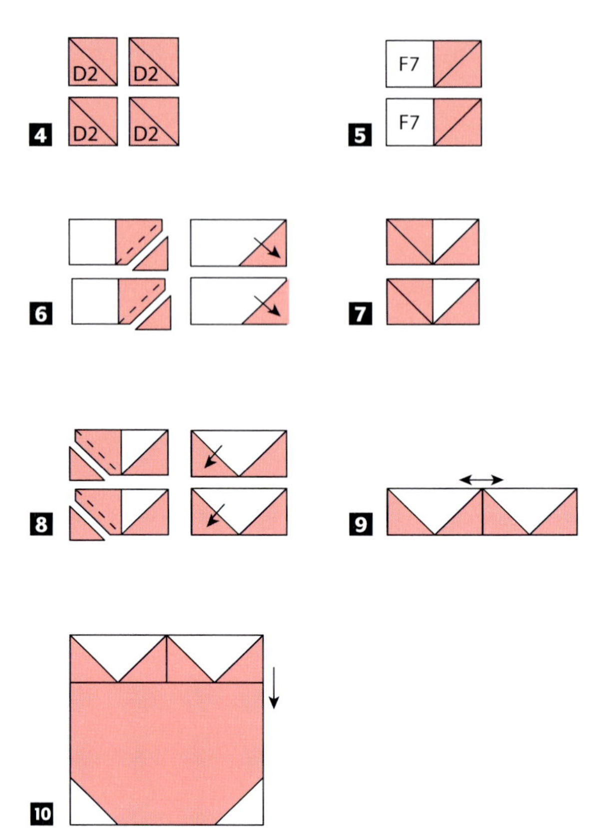

Leaves & Stem

1. Mark a diagonal line, corner-to-corner, on the wrong side of 2 F1 and 2 F8 squares.

2. Pin 1 F1 square on the top of 1 E1 rectangle as shown. Repeat with the remaining F1 on the top of another E1 rectangle as shown. Mirror the orientation of the marked diagonal lines between the two E1 rectangles.

3. Sew on both marked lines. Cut away excess corner fabric ¼″ away from the sewn lines. Press the seams toward the F fabric.

4. Pin 1 F8 square to the bottom left corner of a Step 3 unit, opposite the corner where the F1 square was sewn. Repeat with the remaining F8 square on the bottom right corner of the other Step 3 unit. Mirror the orientation of the square between the two E1 rectangles.

LEAVES & STEM

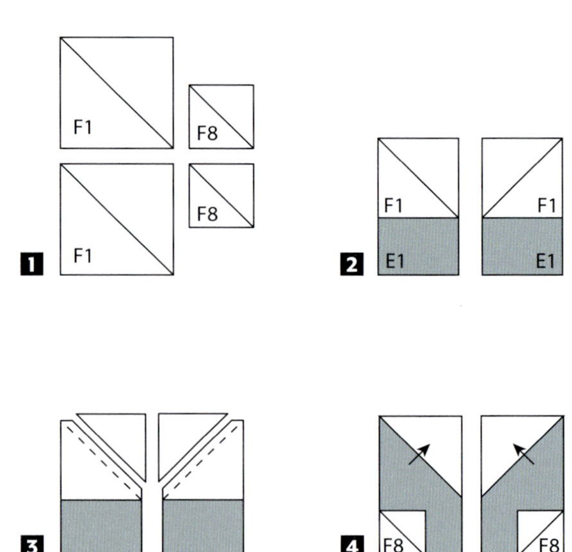

5. Sew on both marked lines. Cut away excess corner fabric ¼˝ away from the sewn lines. Press the seams toward the F fabric to complete 2 Tulip leaves.

6. Arrange 1 E4 rectangle between the mirrored leaf units. Sew the left leaf unit to the left side of the E4 rectangle and sew the right leaf unit to the right side of the E4 rectangle. Press the seams towards the E4 rectangle.

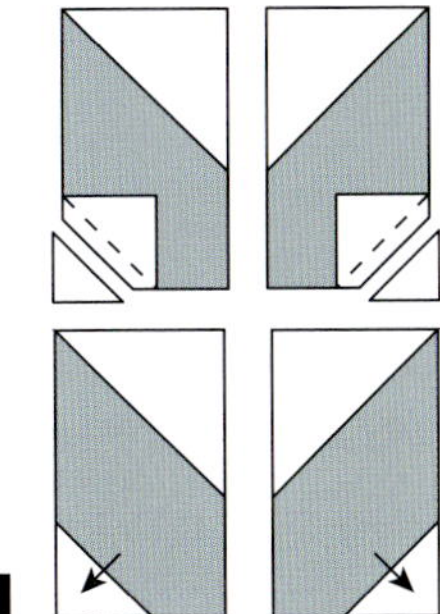

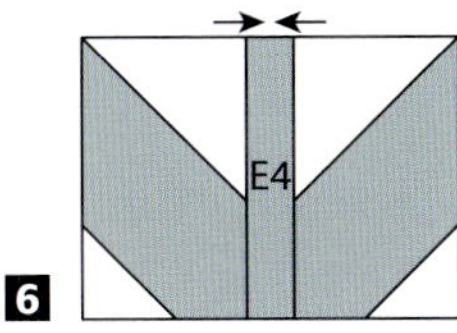

Assembly

1. Sew the flower unit to the leaves and stem unit. Press the seam open.

2. Sew an F5 rectangle to the left and right sides of the Step 1 unit. Press the seams toward the Fabric F rectangles.

3. Sew 1 F6 rectangle to the top and bottom of the Step 2 unit. Press the seams toward the Fabric F rectangles to complete 1 Tulip block.

ASSEMBLY

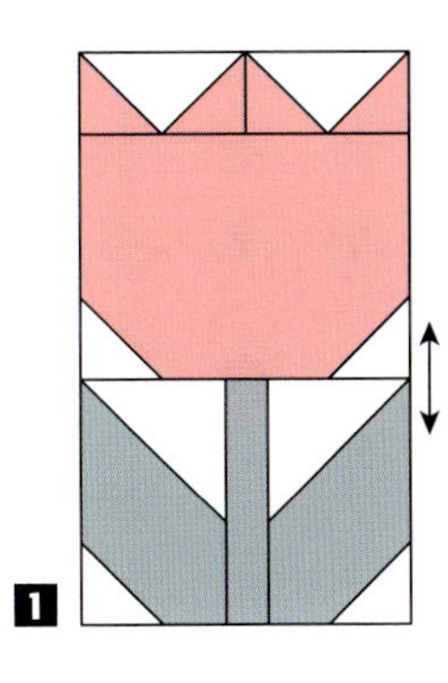

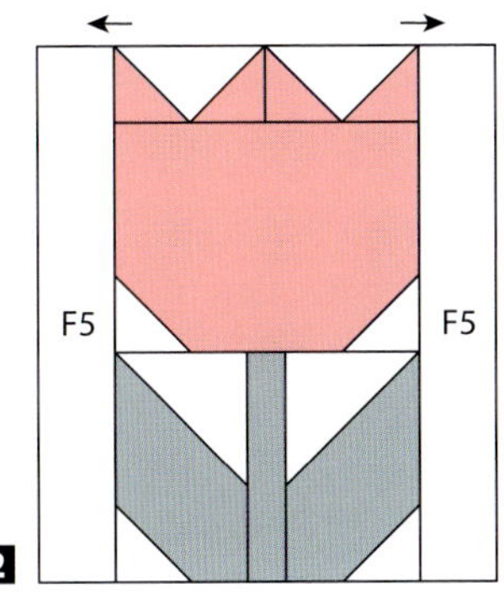

Bunting Assembly

1. Make a quilt sandwich with each of the 7 flower blocks by layering an 8˝ × 11˝ backing rectangle right side down, a batting rectangle, and finally a flower block, right side up. Center the block on the batting and backing.

2. Baste the layers together with safety pins or basting spray and quilt all 7 flower blocks as desired. Trim away excess batting and backing from the perimeter of the blocks after quilting.

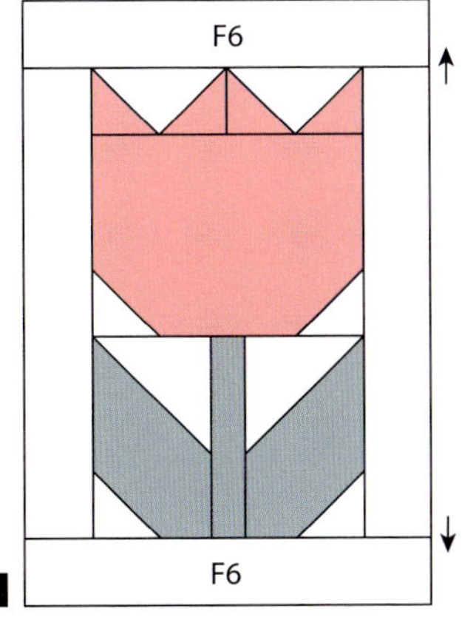

BUNTING ASSEMBLY

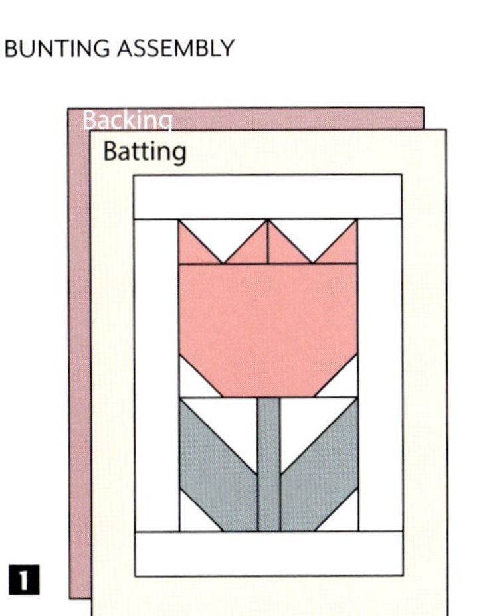

3. Center the prepared Bunting Template along the bottom edge of each quilted block, aligning the center of the block with the center marked on the template. Trace the curve of the template from where it meets the right edge of the block to where it meets the left edge of the block.

4. Cut on the marked line to round the bottom corners of each quilted flower block.

5. Follow instructions for Continuous Bias Binding (page 15) to make approximately 180˝ of 2˝-wide binding from the 20˝ × 20˝ square.

6. Subcut the binding into 7 strips, each 24˝ long, and press each strip in half lengthwise, WST.

7. Align the raw edges of 1 binding strip with the raw edge of the backing of 1 quilted flower block, RST. Starting in the top right corner, pin or clip the binding in place down the right side, around the bottom, and up the left side of the block. Leave approximately 1˝ of binding overhanging both top corners. Sew the binding in place with a scant ¼˝ seam.

8. Fold the binding over the raw edge of the backing to the front side of the block, so that the binding just covers the stitching from Step 7. Top stitch the binding ⅛˝ from the folded edge. Carefully trim the excess binding overhanging the top corners.

9. Repeat Steps 7–8 for all quilted flower blocks.

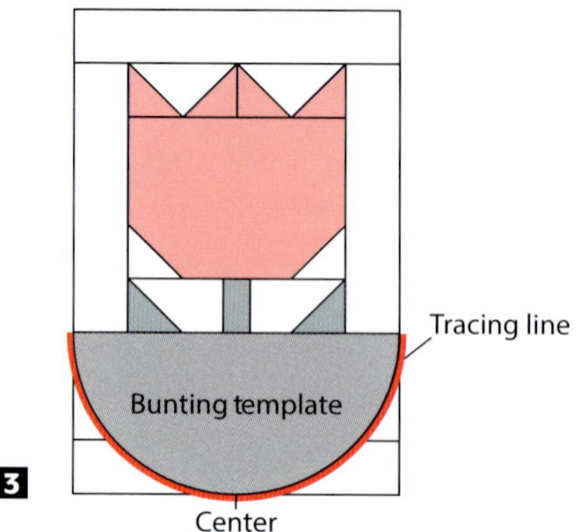

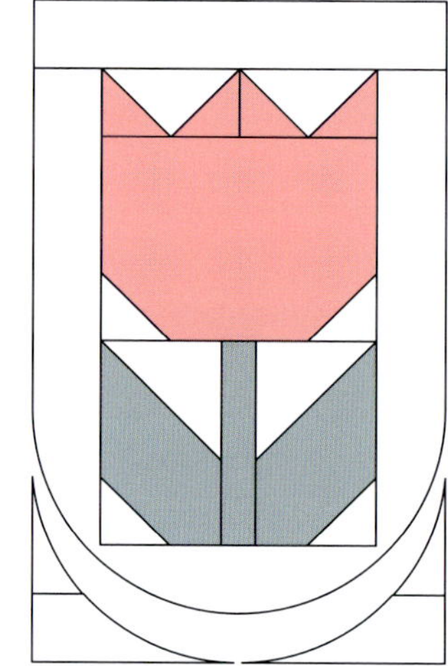

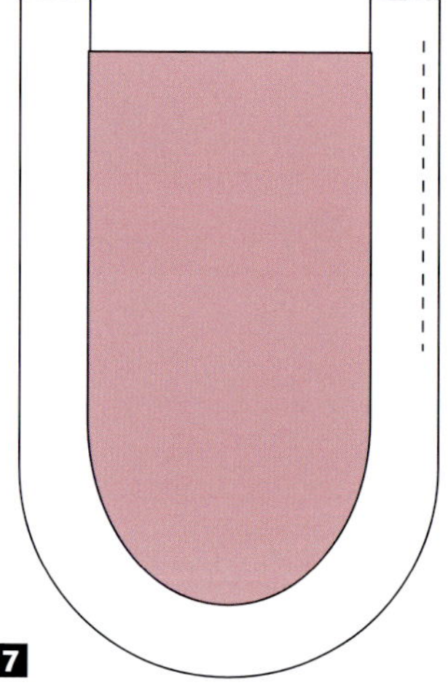

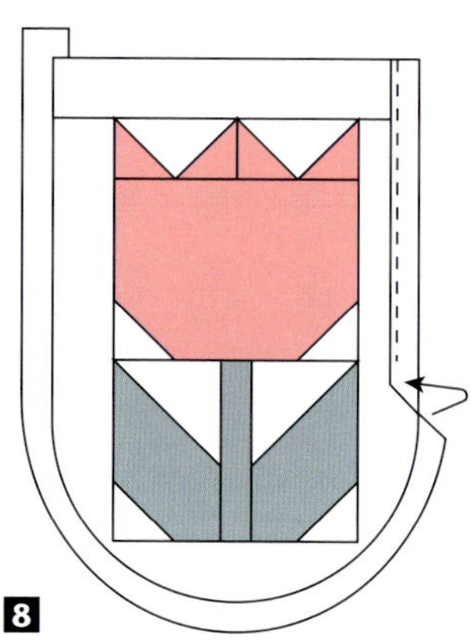

10. On the remaining 2″-wide binding sewn together from 3 WOF strips, fold the 2 short raw edges to the wrong side by ¼″. Press and sew ⅛″ from the raw edge.

10

11. Fold the Step 10 binding in half lengthwise WST, and press. Fold in half, short ends together, and mark the center point.

11

12. Arrange the quilted blocks in your preferred order, right sides up. The order shown here is: primrose, tulip, poppy, tulip, primrose, tulip, poppy.

12

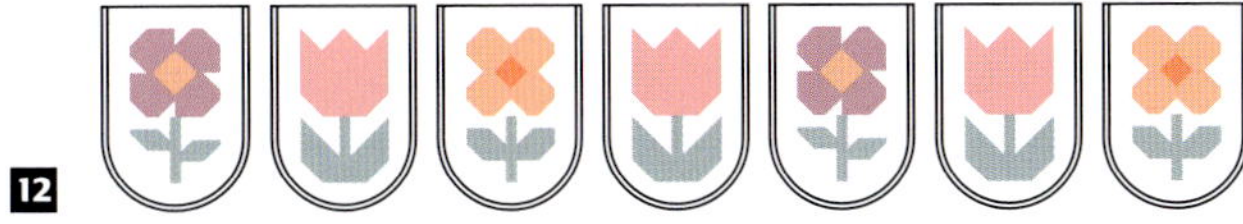

13. Line up the center of the middle flower block with the mark on the binding, raw edge of the block aligned to the raw edge of the binding (block should be on top of binding). Pin in place. Align and pin the remaining blocks to the binding, leaving approximately 1″ between blocks.

13

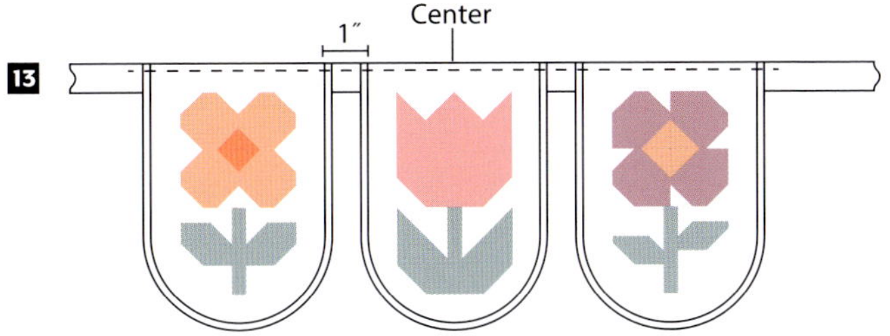

14. Sew the binding to the center block, going through both layers of the binding. Sew the binding to the remaining blocks, continuing the seam in both directions, ¼″ from the raw edges.

15. Fold and press the edge of the binding over to the right side of the bunting. Sew ⅛″ from the folded edge along the entire length of the binding to secure it in place and complete the Signs of Spring Bunting.

15

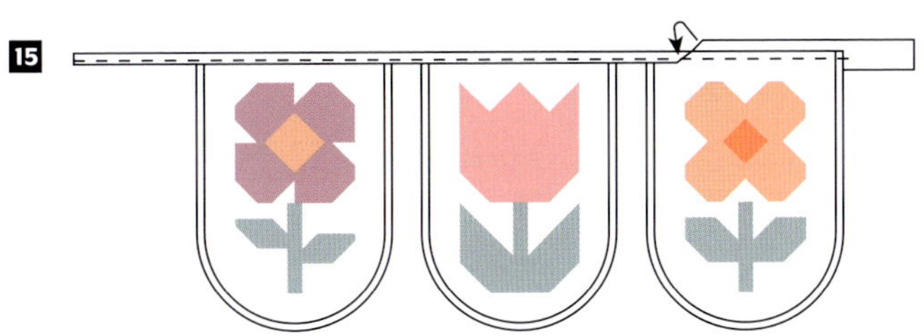

CLOVERLY QUILT

Finished Block Size: 13″ × 13″ || **Finished Quilt:** 60″ × 70″

The Cloverly Quilt is inspired by patches of tiny sweet clover that blanket the ground and herald the arrival of spring. This fresh and playful design uses fat quarters and background yardage in a cool, early spring palette. Be sure to share your project online with the hashtag **#cloverlyquilt**

FABRICS & SUPPLIES

Yardages are based on 42″ wide fabric.

Light dusty green (Fabric A): 1 fat quarter

Medium dusty teal (Fabric B): 1 fat quarter

Dark dusty teal (Fabric C): 1 fat quarter

Dark dusty green (Fabric D): 1 fat quarter

Light dusty purple (Fabric E): 1 fat quarter

Medium dusty purple (Fabric F): 1 fat quarter

Dark dusty purple (Fabric G): 1 fat eighth or ⅛ yard

Cream (Background Fabric H): 3⅛ yards

Binding: ⅝ yard

Backing: 4 yards (using a horizontal seam)

Material Notes

The fabrics used in this quilt are Art Gallery Fabrics Northern Waters, Spruce, Ocean Fog, Pacific, Mauvelous, Sweet Fig, Bewitched, Expressions Vert, and Blooms & Stems.

CUTTING INSTRUCTIONS

Label each piece as specified in parenthesis in the cutting lists. For each fat quarter, label the pieces with the fabric color letter and the number in parenthesis. For example, a 4½″ × 6½″ rectangle from Fabric B should be labeled B2.

Fabrics A–F

Cut from each FQ:

- 8 rectangles 4½″ × 6½″ (2)
- 8 rectangles 4½″ × 2½″ (1)

2	2	1	1	
2	2	1	1	
2	2	1	1	
2	2	1	1	

18″ × 21″

Fabric G

Cut 1 strip 1½″ × WOF; subcut into:

- 12 squares 1½″ × 1½″ (G1)

Background Fabric H

Cut 4 strips 7½″ × WOF; subcut into:

- 12 rectangles 7½″ × 13½″ (H5)

Cut 2 strips 6½″ × WOF; subcut into:

- 48 rectangles 6½″ × 1½″ (H4)

Cut 7 strips 3″ × WOF; sew together and subcut into:

- 4 strips 3″ × 60½″ (H8)

Cut 3 strips 3″ × WOF; subcut into:

- 6 rectangles 3″ × 20½″ (H7)

Cut 3 strips 2½″ × WOF; subcut into:

- 48 squares 2½″ × 2½″ (H3)

Cut 5 strips 2″ × WOF; subcut into:

- 96 squares 2″ × 2″ (H2)

Cut 8 strips 1½″ × WOF; subcut into:

- 9 rectangles 1½″ × 20½″ (H6)
- 96 squares 1½″ × 1½″ (H1)

Binding Fabric

Cut 7 strips 2½″ × WOF

Quilted by Tamara Darragh of Remi Vail Studio

Leaf Assembly

Seam allowances are ¼˝ unless otherwise noted. Pressing direction is indicated by the arrows in the diagrams.

1. Mark a diagonal line, corner-to-corner, on the wrong side of 2 H1 squares and 2 H2 squares.

2. Pin 1 H1 square to the top right corner of 1 A1 rectangle on the 4½˝ edge. Pin 1 H2 square to the top left corner of the same A1 rectangle.

3. Sew on both marked lines. Cut away excess fabric ¼˝ away from the sewn lines. Press the seams toward the corner triangles.

4. Sew 1 H3 square to the right side of the Step 3 unit. Press the seam toward the H3 square.

5. Pin 1 H1 square to the top left corner of 1 A2 rectangle on the 4½˝ edge. Pin 1 H2 square to the top right corner of the same A2 rectangle.

6. Sew on both marked lines. Cut away excess fabric ¼˝ away from the sewn lines. Press the seams toward the corner triangles.

7. Sew the Step 4 unit to the left side of the Step 6 unit. Press the seam toward the Step 6 unit to complete 1 clover leaf.

8. Repeat Steps 1–7 with all remaining H1, H2, and H3 squares paired with the A1-F1 rectangles and A2-F2 rectangles (from all fat quarter fabrics) to create a total of 48 clover leaves.

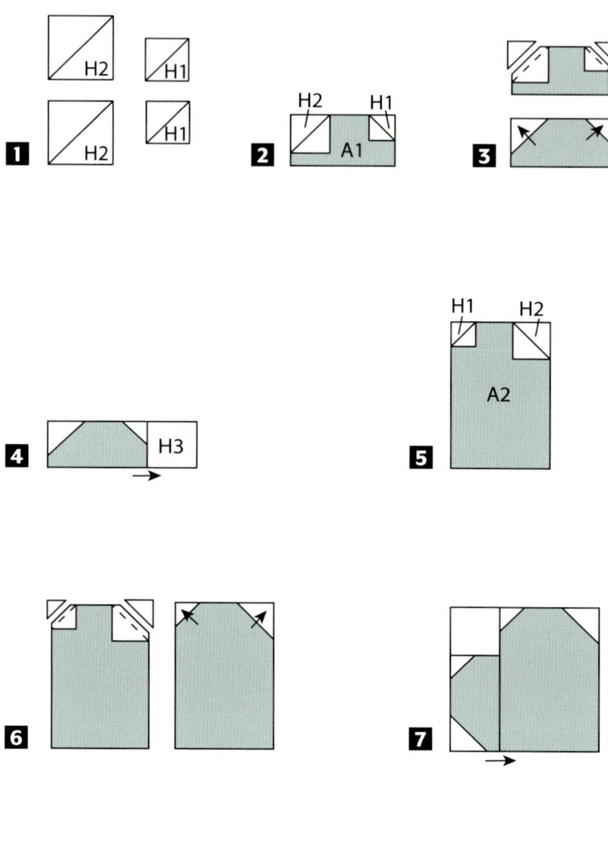

Clover Block Assembly

1. Gather 1 G1 square, 4 H4 rectangles, and 4 different color clover leaves. You can use the sample quilt for guidance on combining colors within each Clover block or simply randomize the colors you choose to ensure each block has 4 different color leaves. Arrange the pieces as shown and sew into 3 rows. Press all seams toward the H4 rectangles.

CLOVER BLOCK ASSEMBLY

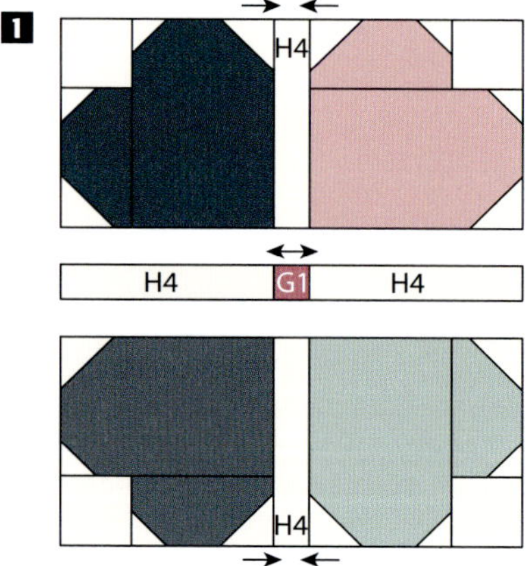

2. Sew the rows together. Press the seams open or toward the center row to complete 1 Clover block.

3. Sew 1 H5 rectangle to the bottom of the Clover block. Press the seam toward the H5 rectangle to complete a Clover section.

4. Repeat Steps 1–3 to make a total of 12 Clover sections.

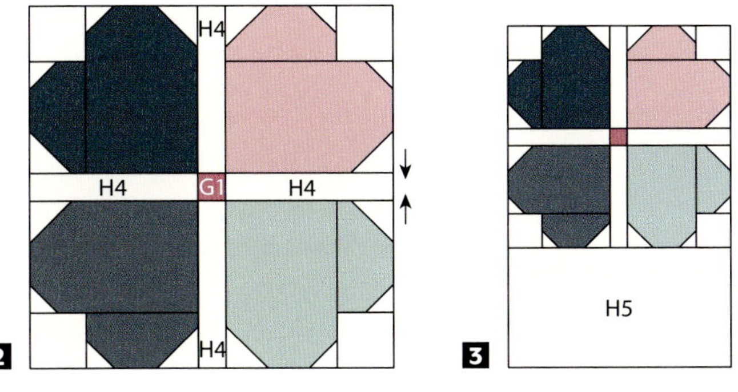

Quilt Assembly

1. Arrange 4 Clover sections in a row, alternating the orientation of each section as shown. Place H6 sashing strips between the sections. Place an H7 sashing strip at the start and end of the row. Sew the row together. Press the seams toward the H6 and H7 sashing strips.

2. Repeat Step 1 to make a total of 3 rows.

3. Arrange the rows with the H8 sashing strips between them. Place an H8 strip at the top and bottom as well. Sew the rows and sashing strips together. Press the seams toward the H8 sashing strips to complete the Cloverly quilt top.

4. Finish the quilt as desired (see Quilt Finishing, page 17).

QUILT ASSEMBLY

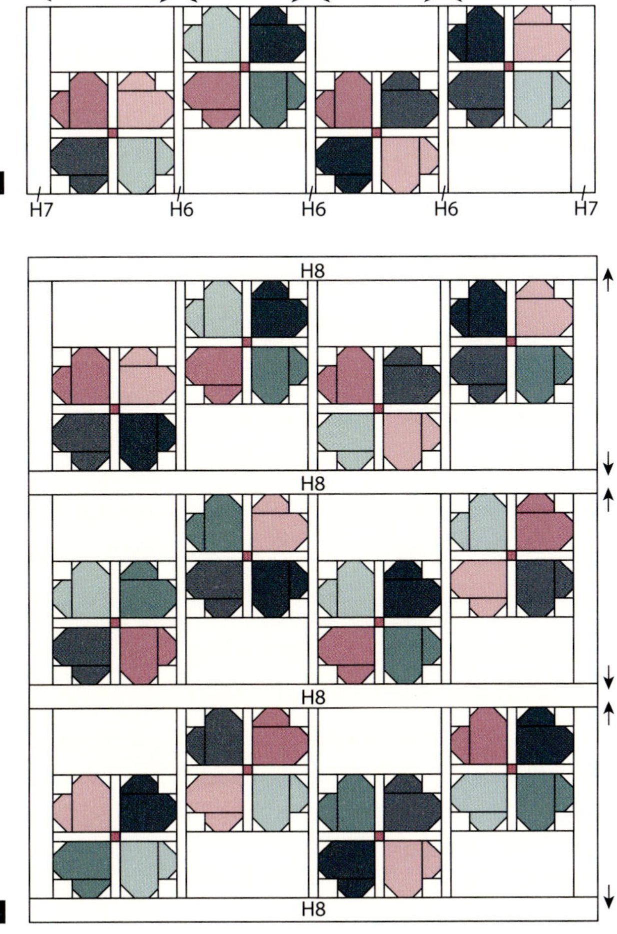

RAINGLOW POUCH

Finished Block Size: 10″ × 10″ || **Finished Pouch:** 5″ × 10″

The Rainglow Pouch features a darling rainbow motif and unzips to lay flat when open. It is sized just right to stash your favorite sewing notions, art supplies, toys, makeup, or purse essentials, and small enough to easily take on the go. Share your finished pouch online with **#rainglowpouch**

FABRICS & SUPPLIES

Yardages are based on 42″ wide fabric.

Light pink (Fabric A): ⅛ yard

Dark pink (Fabric B): ⅛ yard

Yellow (Fabric C): ⅛ yard

Blue (Fabric D): ⅛ yard

Floral print (Lining Fabric E): ⅓ yard

½″ double-fold bias binding: 1⅛ yards*

Batting: ⅓ yard

#5 Nylon coil handbag zipper: 36″ (or a 36″ #5 separating zipper)

Zipper sewing machine foot

Rainglow Pouch Templates (see Templates, page 127)

*You can use a leftover 10″ × 10″ square from the lining fabric yardage to make continuous bias binding in lieu of using premade binding (see Continuous Bias Binding, page 15). If doing so, make sure to press folds into the binding before beginning to assemble.

Material Notes

The fabrics used in this pouch are Art Gallery Fabrics Crystal Pink, Quartz Pink, Honeyed Tunes, Ocean Fog, and Fiori di Salerno.

CUTTING INSTRUCTIONS

Prepare Rainglow Pouch Templates 1–4 for this project (see Templates, page 127). Label each piece as specified in the parenthesis in the cutting lists.

Fabric A

Cut 4 Template 1 (A1)

Fabric B

Cut 4 Template 2 (B1)

Fabric C

Cut 4 Template 3 (C1)

Fabric D

Cut 4 Template 4 (D1)

Cut 1 rectangle 2″ × 2½″ (zipper tab)

Lining Fabric E

Cut 1 square 12″ × 12″ (E1)

Batting

Cut 1 square 12″ × 12″

Clover
GOLD EYE EMBROIDERY
NEEDLES (NO. 3 - 9)

Assembly

Seam allowances are ¼″ unless otherwise noted. Pressing direction is indicated by the arrows in the diagrams.

BLOCK ASSEMBLY

1. Gather 4 A1 pieces and 4 B1 pieces. Sew each B1 concave side to an A1 convex side to make 4 AB units (see Curves, page 14). Press 2 AB unit seams inward toward A1 and press 2 AB unit seams outward toward B1.

2. Gather 4 C1 pieces. Sew each C1 concave side to an AB unit to make 4 ABC units. Press 2 ABC unit seams inward toward B1 and press 2 ABC unit seams outward toward C1. Be sure to press the same two units inward and outward as in Step 1.

3. Gather 4 D1 pieces. Sew each D1 concave side to an ABC unit to make 4 quarter circle units. Press 2 quarter circle unit seams inward toward C1 and press 2 quarter circle unit seams outward toward D1. Be sure to press the same two units inward and outward as in Steps 1 and 2. Minimally trim the straight edges to 5½″ × 5½″ if needed.

4. Sew 1 quarter circle unit with the seams pressed inward to 1 quarter circle unit with the seams pressed outward, taking care to align and nest seams. Press the seam open. Repeat to make a total of 2 half circle units.

5. Sew the 2 half circle units together, again taking care to align and nest seams. Press the seam open to make 1 Circle block.

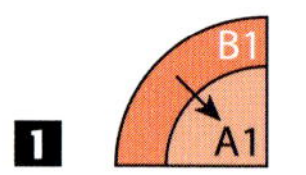

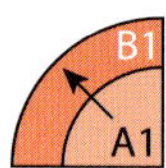

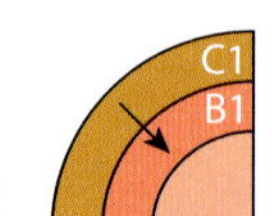

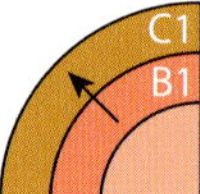

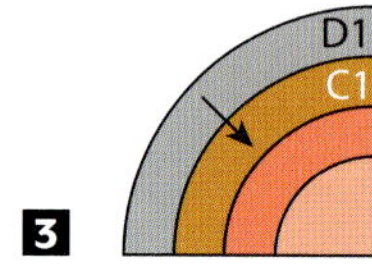

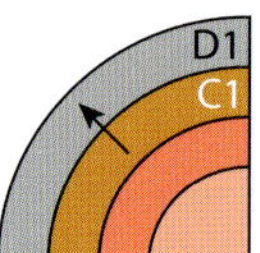

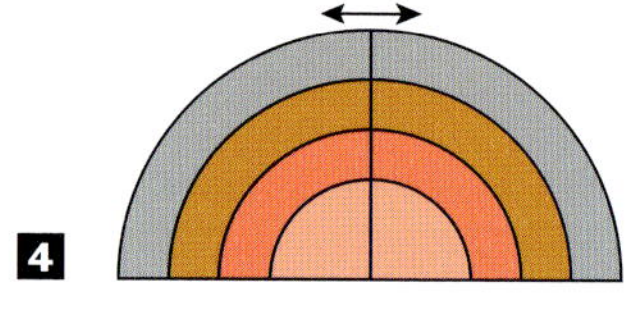

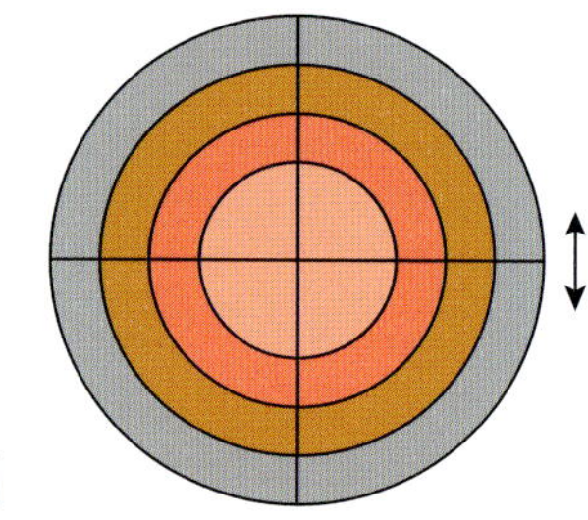

POUCH ASSEMBLY

1. Make a quilt sandwich by layering the lining right side down, then the batting, and finally the Circle block right side up on top. Center the Circle block on the two squares.

POUCH ASSEMBLY

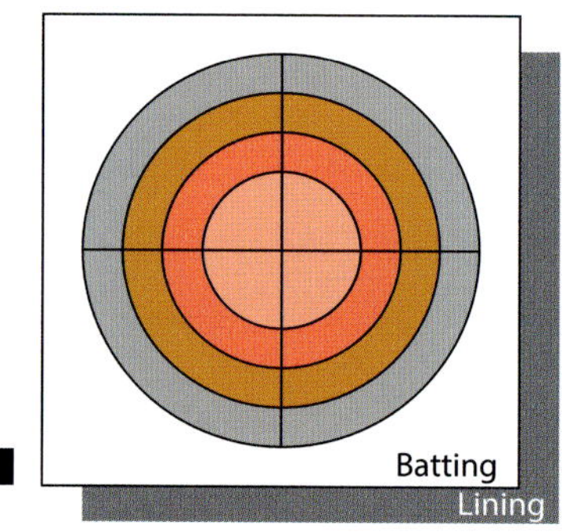

2. Baste the layers together with safety pins or basting spray and quilt as desired. After quilting, sew around the outside edge of the Circle block with a ⅛″ seam allowance to keep the block stable during pouch assembly.

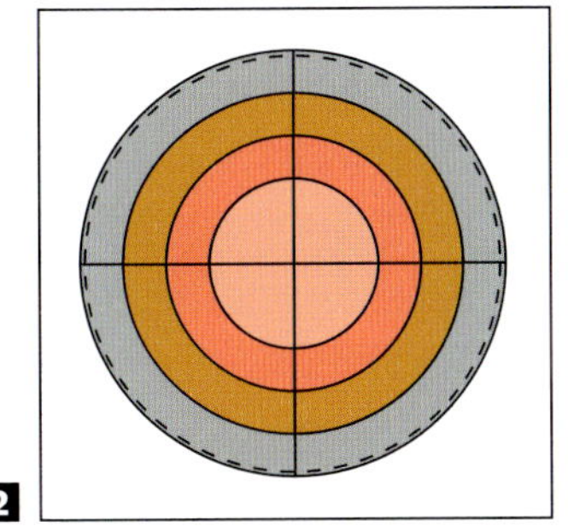

3. Trim the batting and backing even with the edge of the Circle block.

4. Unfold the binding. Fold the short end WST ½″, and press in place.

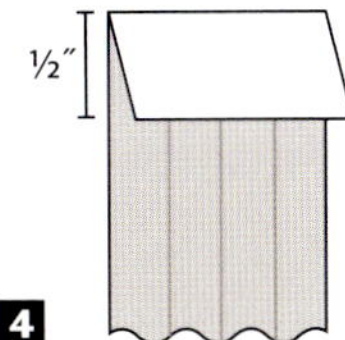

5. Align the raw edge of the binding with the raw edge of the lining side of the Circle block, RST. Pin the binding in place around the perimeter of the lining. Sew with a scant ¼″ seam allowance, just inside the first crease of the binding. Overlap the binding when you reach the starting point and then trim the excess.

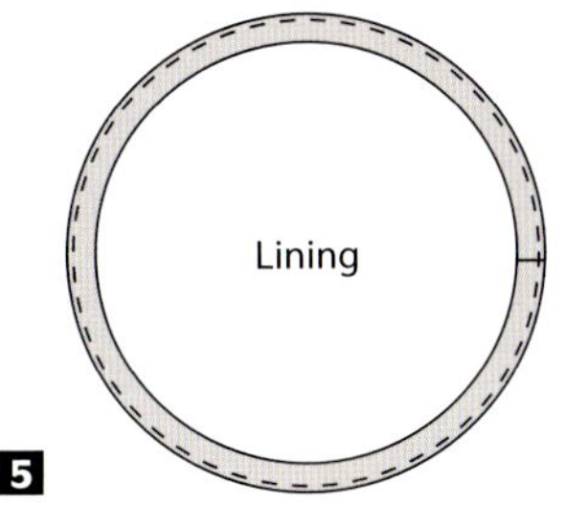

White rectangle outline represents the folded raw end that has been overlapped.

6. Refold the binding over the raw edge of the lining to the front side of the Circle block, so that the binding just covers the stitching from Step 5. Top stitch the binding down ⅛″ from the folded edge.

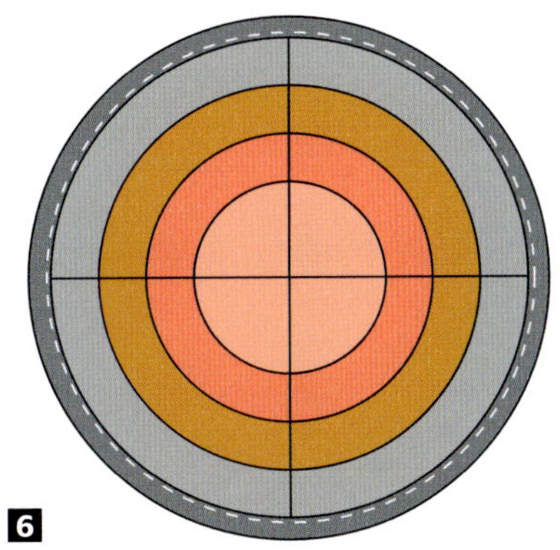

7. Mark the binding as shown in the diagram, ¾″ on either side of 1 center seam. Then mark the binding at the seam on the opposite side of the circle.

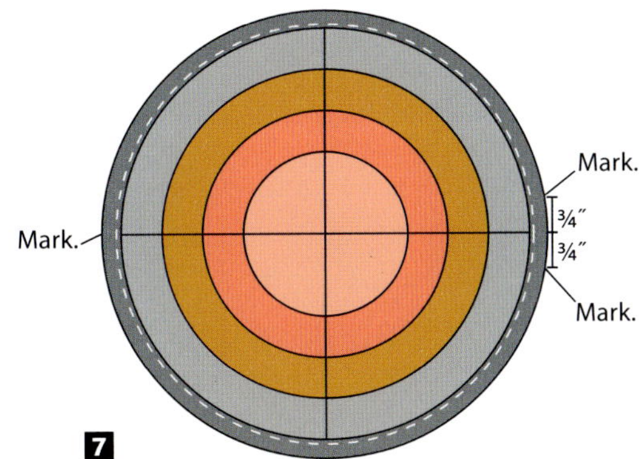

8. Separate the two sides of the zipper. Set one piece aside for a future project or second Rainglow Pouch. Fold the remaining piece of zipper tape in half and mark the middle.

9. Align the middle of the zipper tape with the seam mark on the Circle block, and pin or clip in place with the right side of the zipper tape facing the lining. The edge of the zipper teeth should be flush with the edge of the binding. Continue pinning or clipping the zipper tape all the way around until you reach the ¾˝ marks.

10. Use a zipper foot to sew the zipper ⅛˝ away from zipper teeth and binding edge, starting at the ¾˝ mark on one side of the seam and continuing around the circle to the ¾˝ mark on the opposite side. This should leave a 1½˝ gap with no zipper along the bound edge. Top stitch ⅛˝ away from the inside edge of the binding over the top stitching from Step 6 to further secure the zipper.

11. Align the zipper tape ends and attach the zipper pull. Pull the zipper closed to fold and close the pouch. Then trim the two ends of the zipper tape to be even and approximately 1˝ long.

12. Fold the zipper tab rectangle in half along the 2½˝ side, and press. Open and press all edges in ¼˝. Then, refold along the first crease to create a 1½˝ × 1˝ rectangle with all raw edges pressed to the inside.

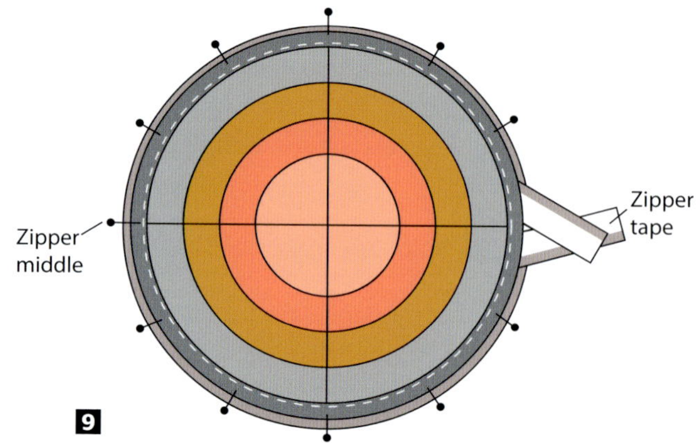

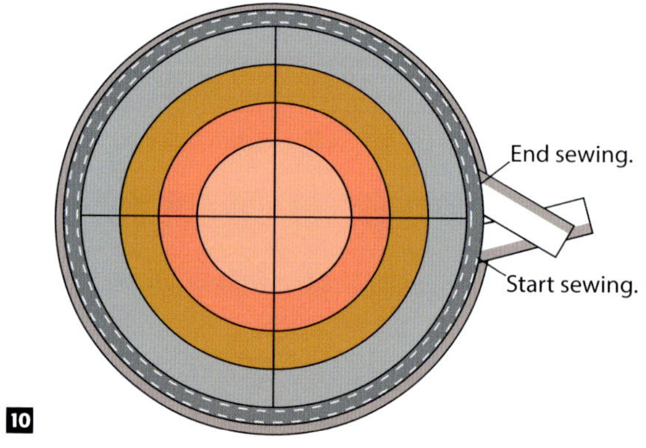

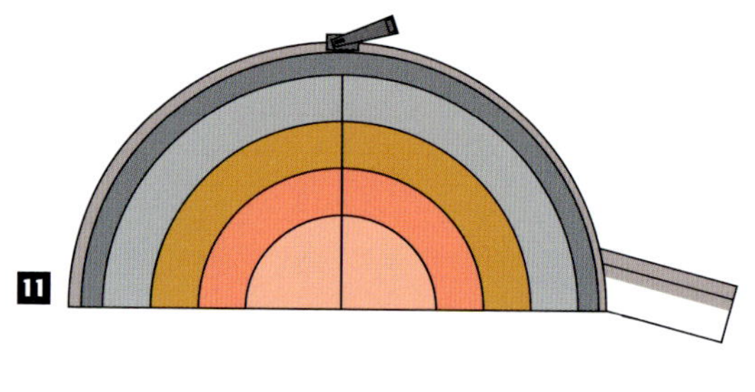

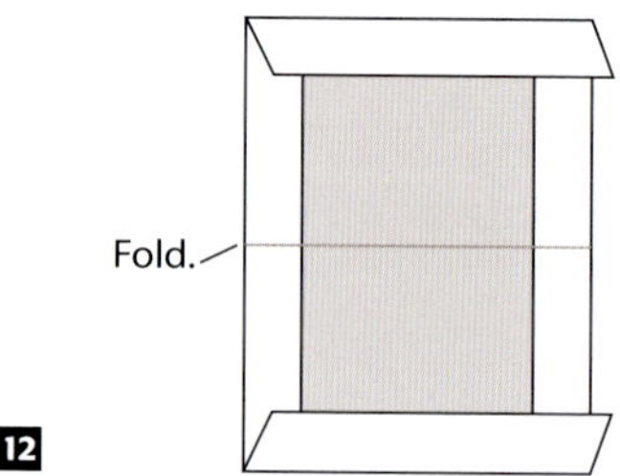

13. Slide the raw zipper end into the folded zipper tab and stitch with a ⅛˝ seam allowance around all four sides of the zipper tab, taking care to stitch carefully over the zipper teeth, to complete the Rainglow Pouch.

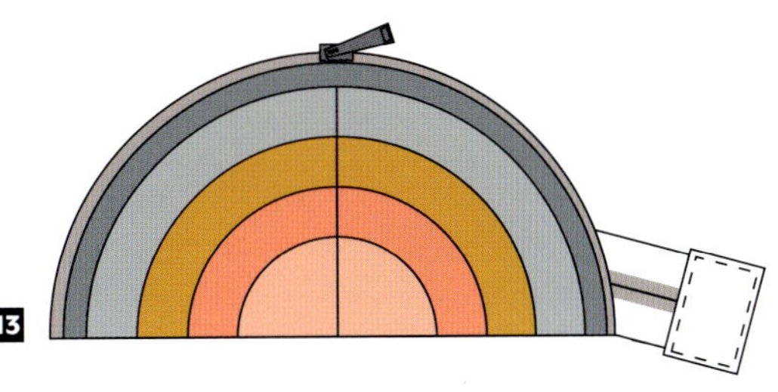

FLEURISTE QUILT

Finished Block Size: 8˝ × 8˝ || **Finished Quilt:** 55˝ × 75˝

The Fleuriste Quilt is inspired by the colorful spring tulips that are ubiquitous with the season. These beautiful blooms found spilling out of gardens and flower boxes in the spring are a celebration of renewal and warmer weather. This design is sure to brighten up any room with spring cheer. Enjoy and share your project online with the hashtag **#fleuristequilt**

FABRICS & SUPPLIES

Yardages are based on 42˝ wide fabric.

Light purple (Fabric A): 1 fat quarter

Light peach (Fabric B): 1 fat quarter

Light pink (Fabric C): 1 fat quarter

Light orange (Fabric D): 1 fat quarter

Medium purple (Fabric E): 1 fat eighth

Medium peach (Fabric F): 1 fat eighth

Medium pink (Fabric G): 1 fat eighth

Medium orange (Fabric H): 1 fat eighth

Gold (Fabric I): ½ yard

Gold or green (Fabric J): ⅜ yard

Cream (Background Fabric K): 3½ yards

Binding: ⅝ yard

Backing: 3¾ yards (using a horizontal seam)

Material Notes

The fabrics used in this quilt are Art Gallery Fabrics Sugar Plum, Grapefruit, Quartz Pink, Apricot Crepe, Bewitched, Miami Sunset, Dried Roses, Dried Carrot, Skipping Stones, Picnic on the Meadow Wide, and Bandana Bound Amber. Fabrics A–H are for the flowers, Fabric I is for the pollen between the tulips, and Fabric J is for the leaves.

CUTTING INSTRUCTIONS

Label each piece as specified in the parenthesis in the cutting lists. For each fat quarter and fat eighth, label the pieces with the fabric color letter and the number in parenthesis. For example, a 4½˝ × 8½˝ rectangle from Fabric B should be labeled B2.

Fabrics A–D

Cut from each FQ:

- 4 rectangles 4½˝ × 8½˝ (2)
- 4 squares 5˝ × 5˝ (1)

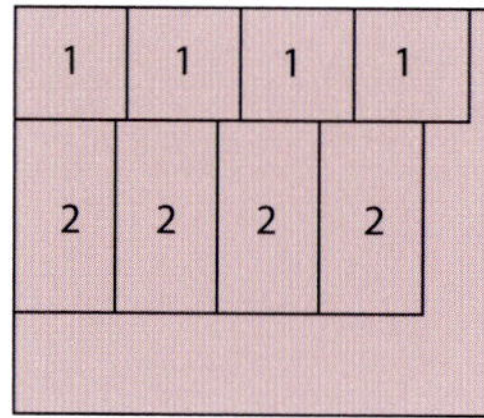

Fabrics E–H

Cut from each FE:

- 2 squares 5½˝ × 5½˝ (1)

Fabric I

Cut 4 strips 3˝ × WOF; subcut into:

- 48 squares 3˝ × 3˝ (I1)

Fabric J

Cut 3 strips 3½˝ × WOF; subcut into:

- 16 rectangles 3½˝ × 5½˝ (J1)

Fabric K

Cut 2 strips 5½˝ × WOF; subcut into:

- 8 squares 5½˝ × 5½˝ (K1)
- 6 rectangles 2½˝ × 10½˝ (K9)

Cut 3 strips 3½˝ × WOF; sew together and subcut into:

- 2 strips 3½˝ × 55½˝ (K12)

Cut 13 strips 3½˝ × WOF; subcut into:

- 10 rectangles 3½˝ × 25½˝ (K10)
- 5 rectangles 3½˝ × 17½˝ (K11)
- 32 rectangles 3˝ × 4¼˝ (K6)
- 16 squares 3˝ × 3˝ (K8)

Cut 5 strips 2½˝ × WOF; subcut into:

- 2 rectangles 2½˝ × 10½˝ (K9)
- 64 squares 2½˝ × 2½˝ (K2)

Cut 11 strips 1¾˝ × WOF; subcut into:

- 32 rectangles 1¾˝ × 3˝ (K7)
- 192 squares 1¾˝ × 1¾˝ (K5)

Cut 13 strips 1½˝ × WOF; subcut into:

- 20 rectangles 1½˝ × 10½˝ (K4)
- 32 rectangles 1½˝ × 8½˝ (K3)

Cut 3 strips 1½˝ × WOF; sew together and subcut into:

- 2 strips 1½˝ × 55½˝ (K13)

Binding Fabric

Cut 7 strips 2½˝ × WOF

Quilted by Tamara Darragh of Remi Vail Studio

Block Assembly

Seam allowances are ¼″ unless otherwise noted. Pressing direction is indicated by the arrows in the diagrams.

TULIP BLOCKS

1. Mark a diagonal line, corner-to-corner, on the wrong side of all K1 squares.

2. Pair each E1, F1, G1, and H1 square with a marked K1 square and follow the instructions in 2-at-a-Time Half-Square Triangles (page 12) to make each pair into 2 HSTs. Trim each unit to a 5″ × 5″ square.

3. Mark a diagonal line, corner-to-corner, on the wrong side of each A1, B1, C1, and D1 square.

4. Pair each A1 square with an E/K half-square triangle, RST. The marked diagonal line on A1 should be perpendicular to the seam on the HST. Repeat, pairing the B1 squares with F/K HSTs, C1 squares with G/K HSTs, and D1 squares with H/K HSTs.

5. Follow the instructions in 2-at-a-Time Half-Square Triangles (page 12) with each pair from Step 4. This creates 2 quarter-square triangles (QSTs) from each pair (8 of each color combination). Trim to 4½″ × 4½″ squares.

6. Arrange two mirrored A/E QSTs as shown with the Fabric E sides matched up. Sew together and press the seam open.

7. Repeat Step 6 with all remaining QSTs pairing mirrored units of the same colors. Make a total of 16 QST units, 4 in each color combination (A/E, B/F, C/G, D/H).

8. Mark a diagonal line, corner-to-corner, on the wrong side of all K2 squares.

9. Pin K2 squares RST on two adjacent corners on the long side of one A2 rectangle as shown.

10. Sew on both marked lines. Cut away excess fabric ¼″ away from the sewn lines. Press the seams toward Fabric K.

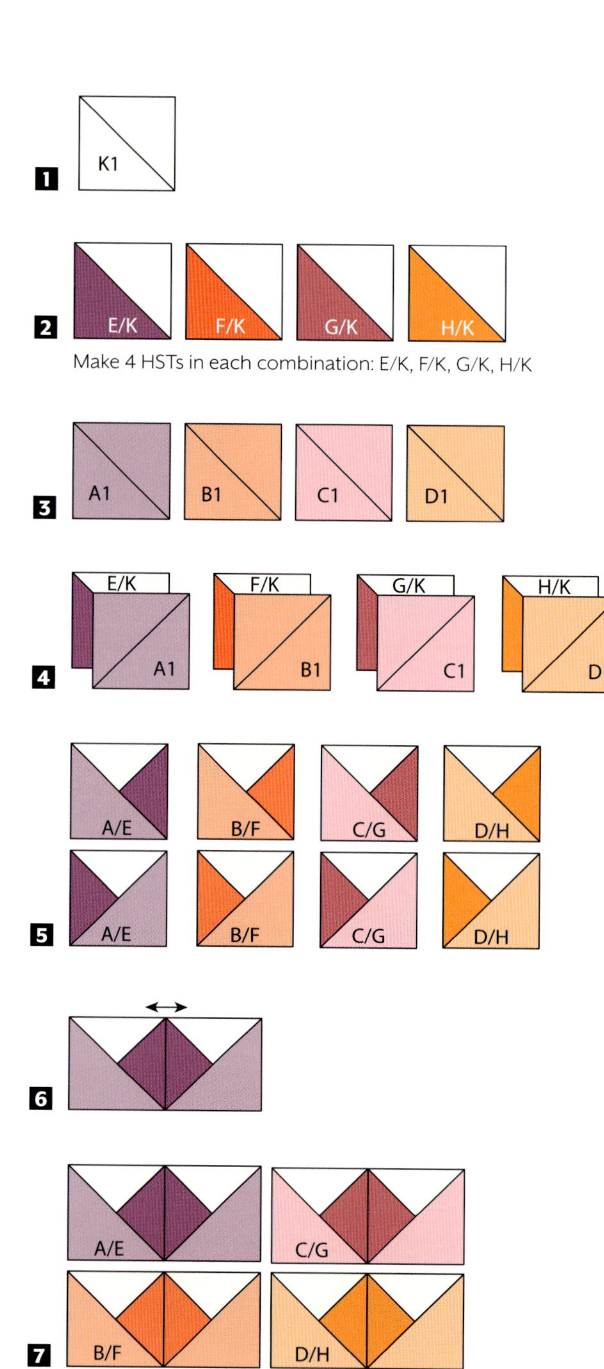

Make 4 HSTs in each combination: E/K, F/K, G/K, H/K

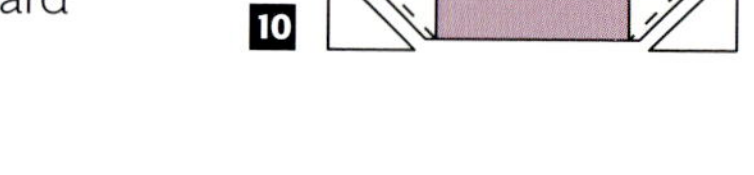

11. Repeat Steps 9–10, pairing K2 squares with all A2, B2, C2, and D2 rectangles, to yield a total of 4 units in each color.

12. Arrange 1 A/E unit from Step 7 with 1 A2 unit from Step 11. Sew together as shown and press the seam toward the A2 unit to complete 1 Tulip block.

13. Repeat Step 12, pairing the remaining A/E units with A2 units, B/F units with B2 units, C/G units with C2 units, and D/H units with D2 units. Make a total of 16 Tulip blocks, 4 in each color combination.

14. Sew 1 K3 rectangle to the left and right of each Tulip block. Press the seams toward the K3 rectangles.

LEAVES

1. Pin 2 K2 squares RST on opposite corners of 1 J1 rectangle as shown. Repeat with 2 more K2 squares on the opposite corners of another J1 rectangle. Mirror the orientation of the squares between the two J1 rectangles.

2. Sew on all marked lines. Cut away excess corner fabric ¼˝ away from the sewn lines. Press the seams toward Fabric K to complete 2 mirrored leaves.

3. Arrange the Step 2 leaves side-by-side, mirrored as shown, and sew together. Press the seam open.

4. Sew a K4 rectangle to the top of the leaves from Step 3. Press the seam toward the K4 rectangle to complete one Leaf unit.

5. Repeat Steps 1–4 to make a total of 8 Leaf units.

POLLEN

1. Mark a diagonal line, corner-to-corner, on the wrong side of all K5 squares.

2. Pin 2 K5 squares on opposite corners of 1 I1 square, as shown.

3. Sew on the marked lines. Cut away excess corner fabric ¼˝ away from the sewn lines. Press the seams toward Fabric K.

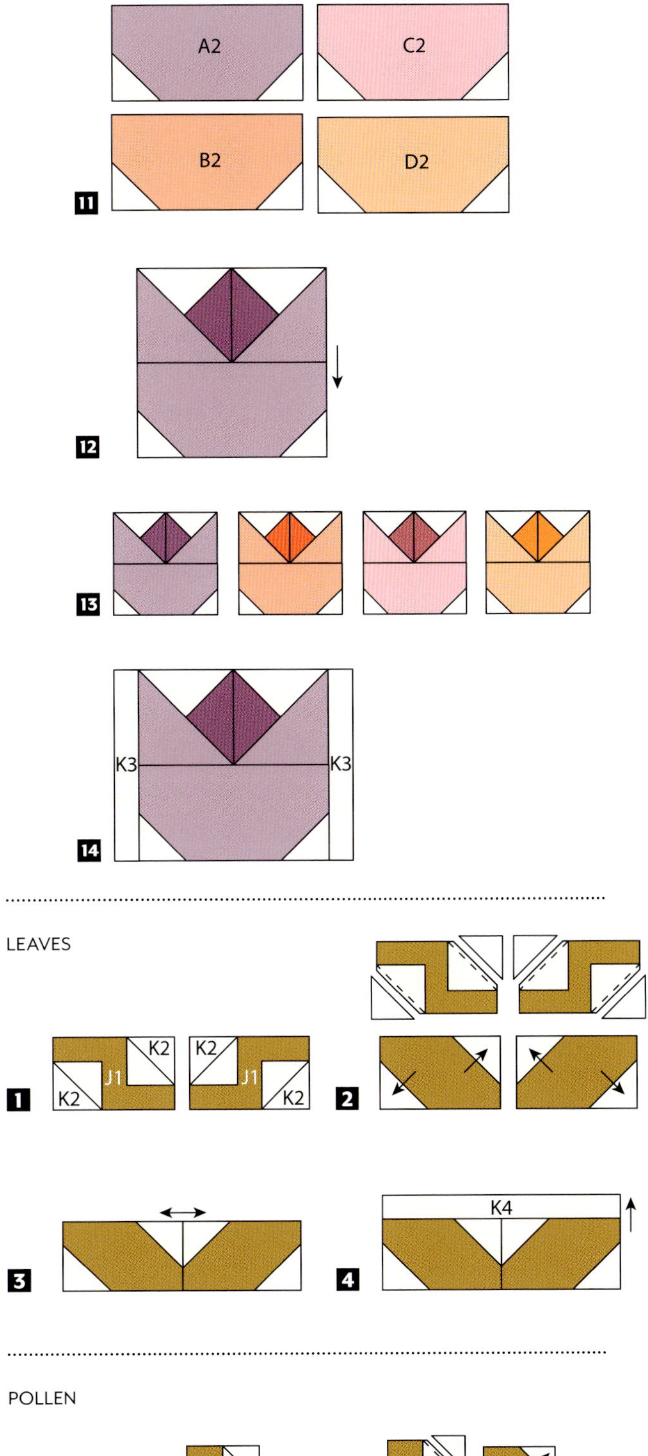

4. Pin 2 K5 squares on the remaining corners of the I1 square.

5. Sew on the marked lines. Cut away excess corner fabric ¼˝ away from the sewn lines. Press the seams toward Fabric K to complete 1 Diamond-in-a-Square unit.

6. Repeat Steps 2–5 to make a total of 48 Diamond-in-a-Square units.

7. Sew a K6 rectangle on the left and right side of a Diamond-in-a-Square unit to make a row. Sew a K8 square between 2 Diamond-in-a-Square units. Sew a K7 rectangle on either side of the same Diamond-in-a-Square unit to create a second row. Press the seams as directed by the arrows.

8. Sew the Step 7 rows together. Press the seam open to complete 1 Pollen unit.

9. Repeat Steps 7–8 to make a total of 16 Pollen units.

10. Arrange 2 Pollen units on either side of a K9 rectangle. Note the orientation of the Pollen units should be mirrored, as shown. Sew together and press the seams toward the K9 rectangle to make a Pollen section.

11. Repeat Step 10 to make a total of 8 Pollen sections.

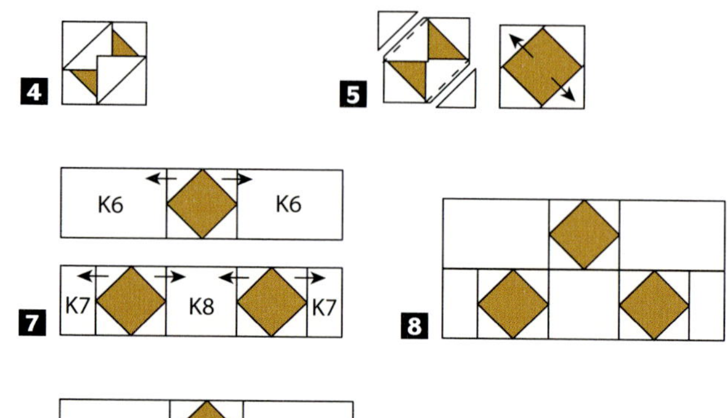

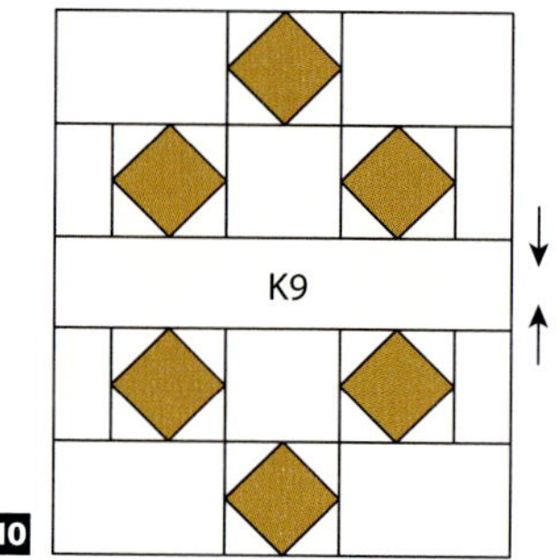

TULIP SECTION A

1. Arrange 1 Pollen section, 1 K4 rectangle, 1 Fabric A/E Tulip block, and 1 Leaf unit as shown.

2. Sew together, and press the seams toward the K4 rectangles to complete 1 Tulip Section A.

3. Repeat Steps 1–2 to make 2 Tulip Section As in each color combination: A/E, B/F, C/G, and D/H.

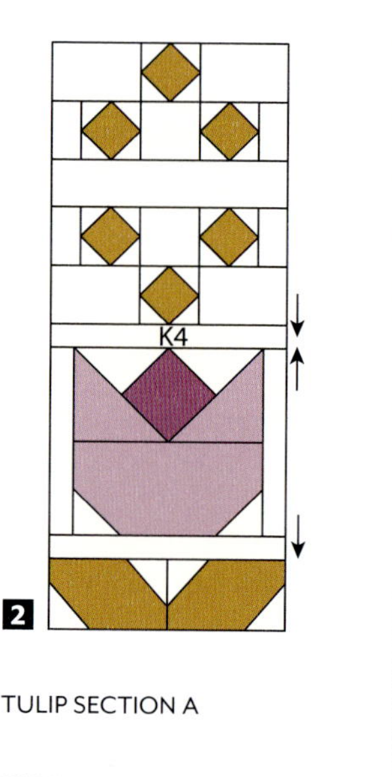

TULIP SECTION B

1. Arrange 1 B/F Tulip block, 1 K4 rectangle, and 1 C/G Tulip block as shown.

2. Sew together, and press the seams toward the K4 rectangle to complete Tulip Section B.

3. Repeat Steps 1–2 to make 1 Tulip Section B in each of the following color combinations: C/G and B/F, D/H and A/E, B/F and D/H, A/E and C/G.

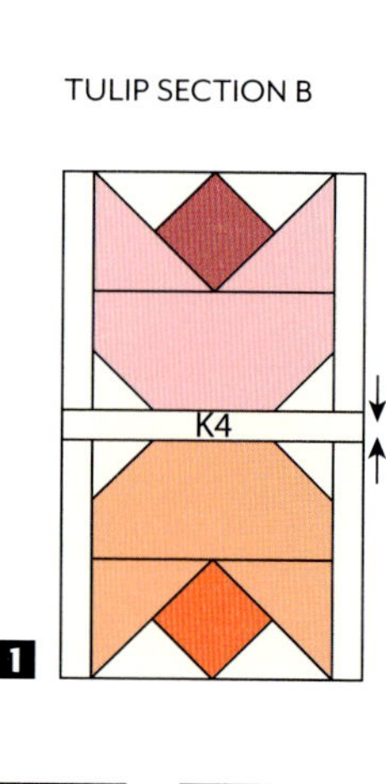

Quilt Assembly

1. Arrange 5 K10 rectangles and 4 upside-down Tulip Section As, 1 in each color combination. The Tulip Section As should be arranged as follows: A/E Tulip A, B/F Tulip A, C/G Tulip A, D/H Tulip A. Sew together, and press the seams toward the K10 rectangles. This is the top row.

2. Arrange 5 K10 rectangles and 4 Tulip Section As, 1 in each color combination. The Tulip Section As should be arranged as follows: D/H Tulip A, C/G Tulip A, A/E Tulip A, B/F Tulip A. Sew together, and press the seams toward the K10 rectangles. This is the bottom row.

3. Arrange 5 K11 rectangles and the 4 Tulip Section Bs. The Tulip Section Bs should be arranged as follows: CG/BF Tulip B, DH/AE Tulip B, BF/DH Tulip B, AE/CG Tulip B. Sew together, and press the seams toward the K11 rectangles. This is the center row.

4. Arrange the 3 rows in order with K13 sashing strips between the rows. Add K12 sashing strips to the top and bottom of the quilt. Sew together and press the seams toward the sashing strips to complete the Fleuriste quilt top.

5. Finish the quilt as desired (see Quilt Finishing, page 17).

1 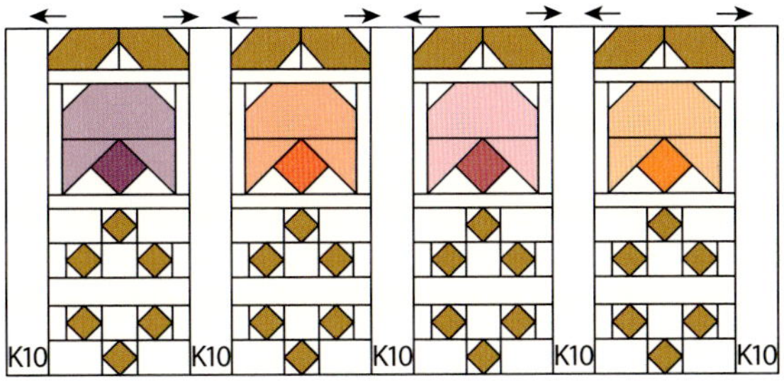 K10 K10 K10 K10 K10

2 K10 K10 K10 K10 K10

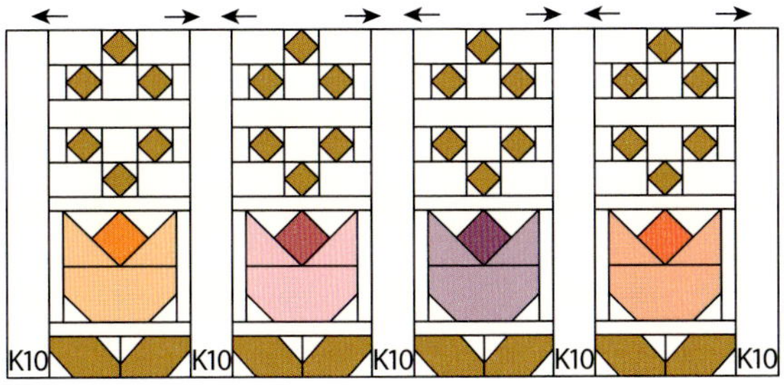

3 K11 K11 K11 K11 K11

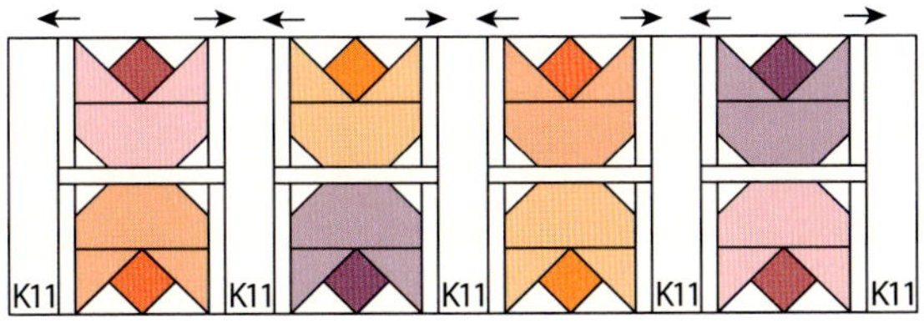

4 K12 K13 K13 K12

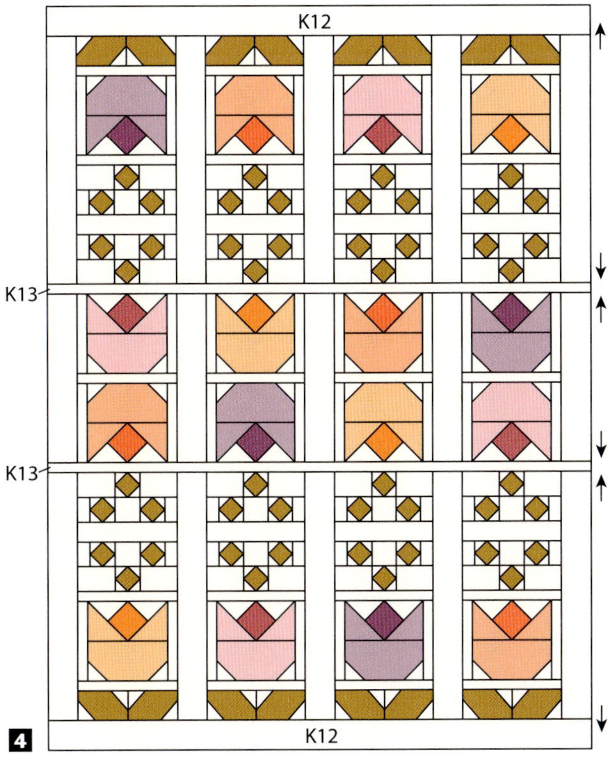

SUMMER

Summer is a time ripe for adventure. It brings sunshine and warm weather and invites swimming at the lake and picnics at the park, campouts in the woods and road trips to new places near and far. The projects in this chapter are ready for summer fun. The Sunprint Plaid Quilt (page 50) is the perfect take-along quilt for playdates, picnics, and potlucks with its cheerful plaid and glowy stars. The Sweetberry Market Tote (page 56) has a sweet strawberry motif and is generously sized to stash all your farmer's market finds, rummage sale treasures, and beach gear. The Rainbright Quilt (page 66) is a colorful celebration of nourishing summer rains, while the Sunglow Quilt (page 72) revels in the beauty of the season's long golden evenings.

SUNPRINT PLAID QUILT

Finished Block Size: 5˝ × 5˝ || **Finished Quilt:** 65˝ × 75˝

The Sunprint Plaid Quilt is inspired by the process of sun printing or cyanotype printing, where sunlight is used to develop a photographic element. The process creates a negative silhouette of an object that seems to glow in stark contrast to the area of the print that was exposed to the sun. In this design, the stars create an eye-catching negative image on a picnic plaid, so you'll feel doused in sunshine whether adventuring on a warm summer day or relaxing outdoors. Share your project online with the hashtag **#sunprintplaidquilt**

FABRICS & SUPPLIES

Yardages are based on 42˝ wide fabric.

Dark peach (Fabric A): 1¼ yards

Medium peach (Fabric B): 2⅛ yards

Light peach (Fabric C): ⅝ yard

Dark orange (Fabric D): ¼ yard

Medium yellow (Fabric E): ⅔ yard

Cream (Fabric F): 1¾ yards

Binding: ⅝ yard

Backing: 4⅛ yards (using a horizontal seam)

Material Notes

The fabrics used in this quilt are Art Gallery Fabrics Snapdragon, Shrimpy, Blushing, Spiced, Queen Bee, Show Time Honey, and Flowery Meadow Sunlit.

CUTTING INSTRUCTIONS

Label each piece as specified in the parenthesis in the cutting lists.

Fabric A

Cut 6 strips 5½˝ × WOF; subcut into:

- 39 squares 5½˝ × 5½˝ (A1)

Cut 3 strips 3˝ × WOF; subcut into:

- 40 squares 3˝ × 3˝ (A2)

Fabric B

Cut 14 strips 3½˝ × WOF (B1)

Cut 14 strips 1½˝ × WOF (B2)

Fabric C

Cut 2 strips 3½˝ × WOF (C2)

Cut 8 strips 1½˝ × WOF (C1)

Fabric D

Cut 2 strips 1½˝ × WOF (D1)

Fabric E

Cut 14 strips 1½˝ × WOF (E1)

Fabric F

Cut 2 strips 5½˝ × WOF; subcut into:

- 10 squares 5½˝ × 5½˝ (F1)

Cut 6 strips 3½˝ × WOF (F2)

Cut 6 strips 3˝ × WOF; subcut into:

- 80 squares 3˝ × 3˝ (F3)

Cut 6 strips 1½˝ × WOF (F4)

Binding Fabric

Cut 8 strips 2½˝ × WOF

Block Assembly

Seam allowances are ¼˝ unless otherwise noted. Pressing direction is indicated by the arrows in the diagrams.

DIAMOND-IN-A-SQUARE BLOCKS

1. Mark a diagonal line, corner-to-corner, on the wrong side of all A2 squares.

2. Pin 2 A2 squares on opposite corners of 1 F1 square RST, as shown.

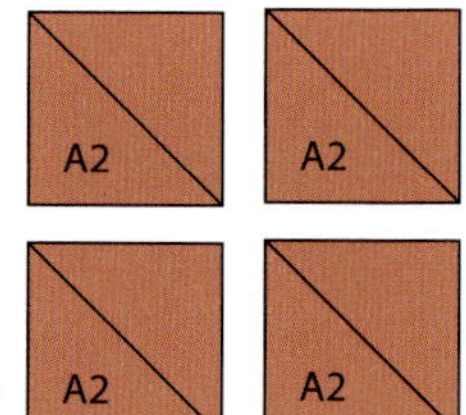

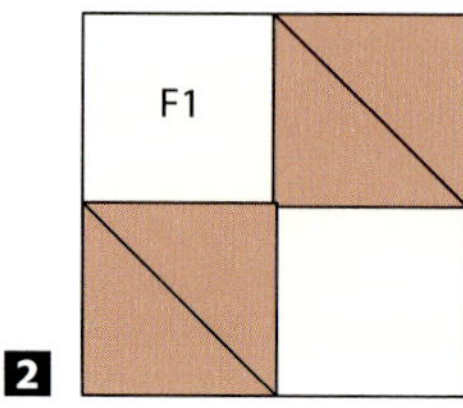

3. Sew on the marked lines. Cut away excess corner fabric ¼″ away from the sewn lines. Press the seams toward the A2 fabric.

4. Pin 2 A2 squares on the remaining corners of the F1 square.

5. Sew on the marked lines. Cut away excess corner fabric ¼″ away from the sewn lines. Press the seams toward the A2 fabric to make 1 Diamond-In-a-Square Block (DB).

6. Repeat Steps 2–5 to make a total of 10 DBs.

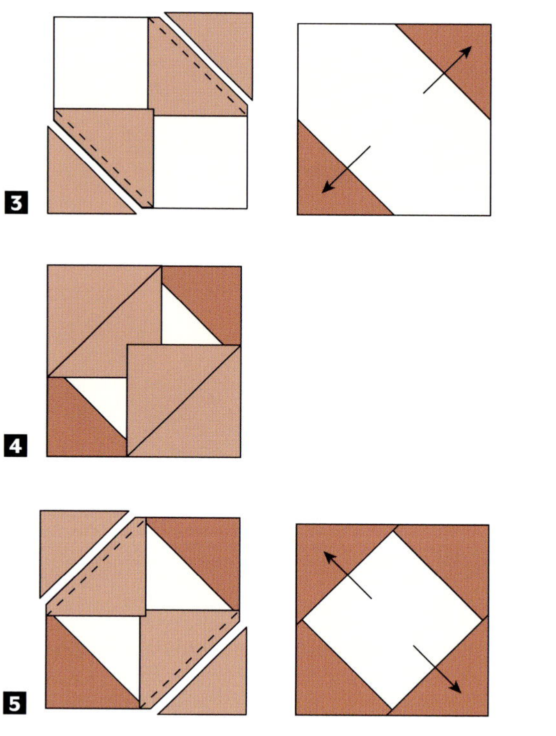

STRIPE BLOCKS

1. Sew a B2 strip to the top of an E1 strip. Sew a B1 strip to the bottom of the E1 strip. Press the seams away from the E1 strip.

2. Cut the B/E strip unit into 7 squares 5½″ × 5½″ to make 7 Stripe Blocks (SB).

3. Repeat Steps 1–2 to make a total of 98 SBs (cut from 14 B/E strip units).

STRIPE BLOCKS

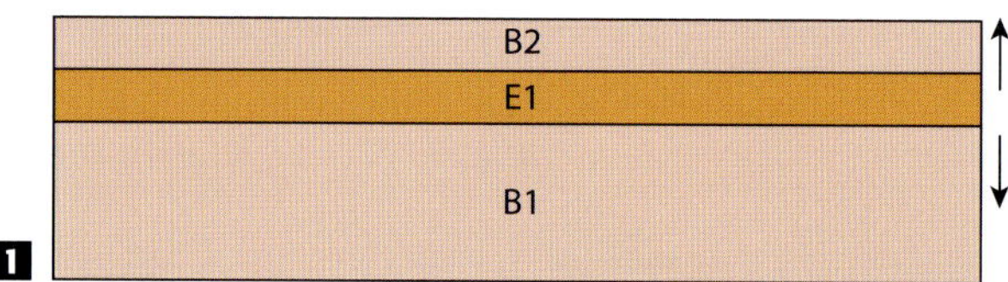

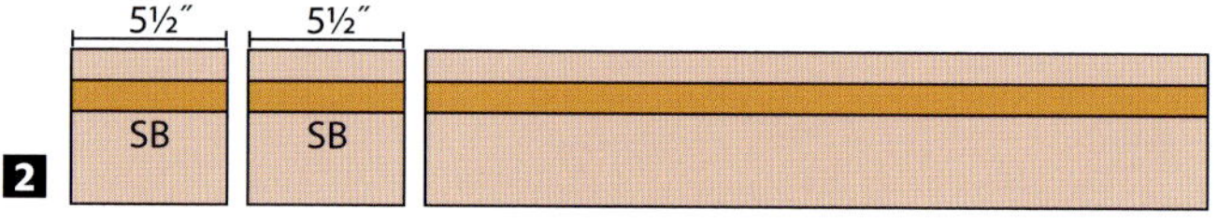

STAR POINT BLOCKS

1. Mark a diagonal line, corner-to-corner, on the wrong side of all F3 squares.

2. Gather 2 Stripe blocks and mirror them. Pin an F3 square to the bottom left corner of each Stripe Block with the marked line as shown.

STAR POINT BLOCKS

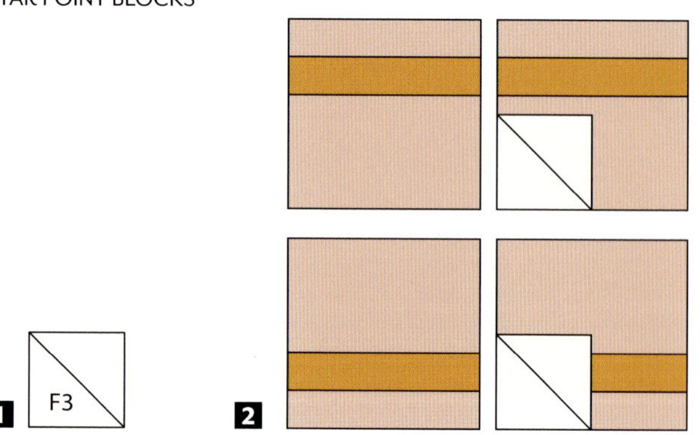

3. Sew on the marked lines and cut away excess corner fabric ¼″ away from the sewn lines. Press the seams toward the F fabric.

4. Pin an F3 square to the bottom right corner of each unit from Step 3 as shown.

5. Sew on the marked lines and cut away excess corner fabric ¼″ away from the sewn lines. Press the seams toward the F fabric to complete one of each Star Point Block A (SP/A) and Star Point Block B (SP/B).

6. Repeat Steps 2–5 to make a total of 20 Star Point Block A and 20 Star Point Block B.

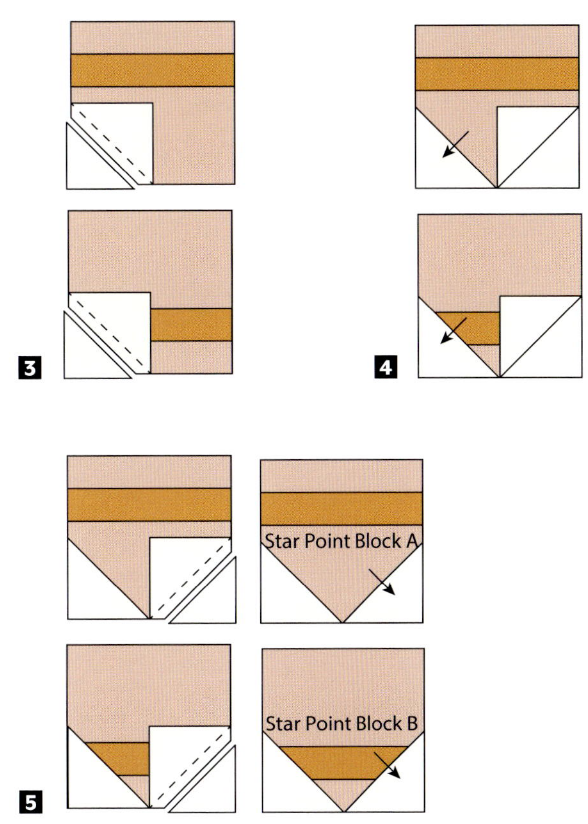

CROSS BLOCKS

1. Sew an F4 strip to the top of a C1 strip. Sew an F2 strip to the bottom of the C1 strip. Press the seams toward the C1 strip.

2. Repeat Step 1 to make a total of 6 C/F strip units.

3. Cut 4 of the C/F strip units into 48 rectangle segments 3½″ × 5½″ (S3 rectangles).

4. Cut the remaining 2 C/F strip units into 48 rectangles 1½″ × 5½″ (S1 rectangles).

CROSS BLOCKS

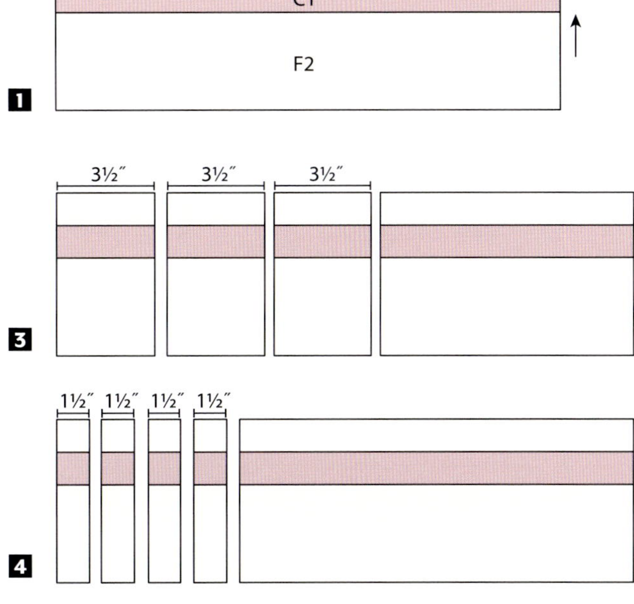

5. Sew a C1 strip to the top of a D1 strip. Sew a C2 strip to the bottom of the D1 strip. Press the seams toward the D1 strip to complete a C/D strip unit.

6. Repeat Step 5 to make a total of 2 C/D strip units.

7. Cut the 2 C/D strip units into 48 rectangles 1½″ × 5½″ (S2 rectangles).

8. Arrange 1 of each S1, S2, and S3 segments as shown. Sew together. Press the seams toward the S2 segment to complete 1 Cross Block (CB).

9. Repeat Step 8 to make a total of 48 CBs.

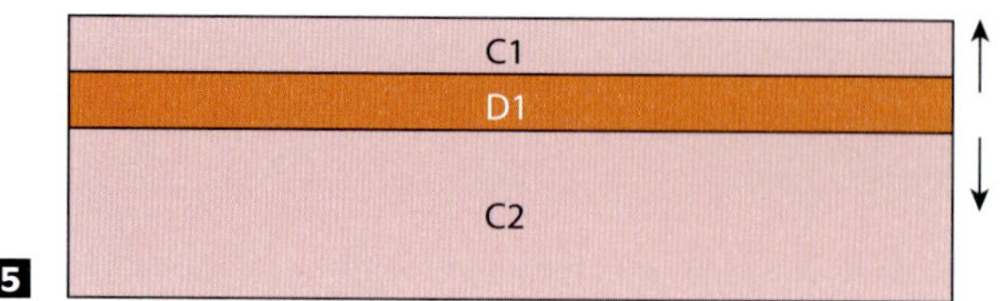

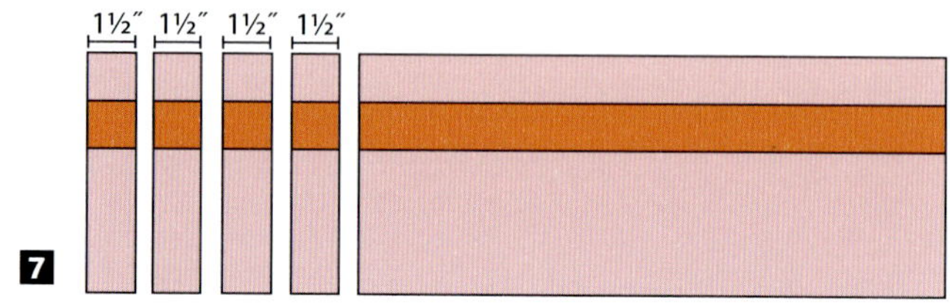

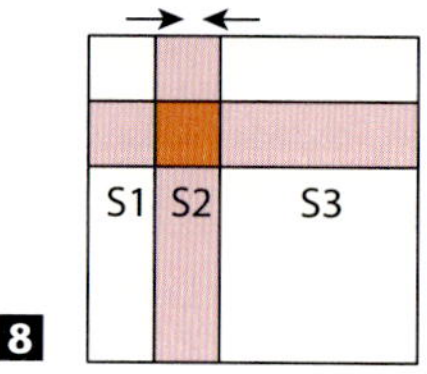

Row Assembly

Be sure to note the orientation of the blocks in each row during row assembly, as they differ between rows.

ROW 1

1. Arrange blocks in the order listed, as shown: SB + CB + SB + CB + SB + CB + SP/A + CB + SB + CB + SB + CB + SB

2. Sew the blocks together and press the seams to the right to complete Row 1 (R1).

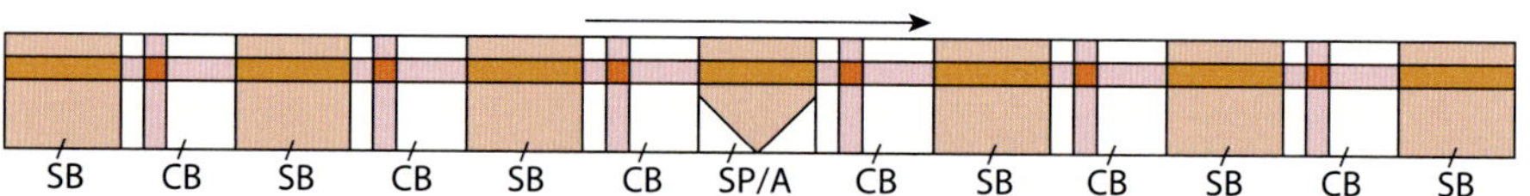

ROW 2

1. Arrange blocks in the order listed, as shown:A1 + SB + A1 + SB + A1 + SP/A + DB + SP/B + A1 + SB + A1 + SB + A1

2. Sew the blocks together and press the seams to the left to complete a Row 2 (R2).

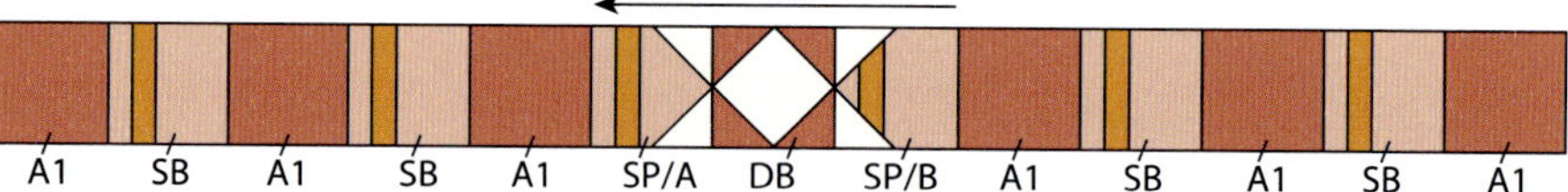

3. Repeat Steps 1–2 to make a total of 4 R2s.

ROW 3

1. Arrange blocks in the order listed, as shown: SB + CB + SP/A + CB + SB + CB + SP/B + CB + SB + CB + SP/A + CB + SB

2. Sew the blocks together and press the seams to the right to complete a Row 3 (R3).

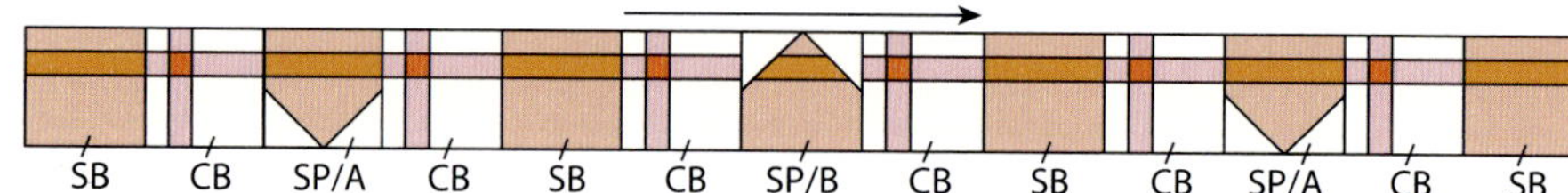

3. Repeat Steps 1–2 to make a total of 3 R3s.

ROW 4

1. Arrange blocks in the order listed, as shown: A1 + SP/A + DB + SP/B + A1 + SB + A1 + SB + A1 + SP/A + DB + SP/B + A1

2. Sew the blocks together and press the seams to the left to complete a Row 4 (R4).

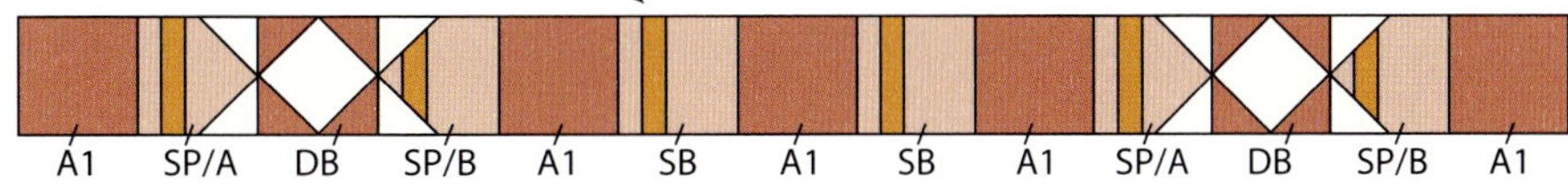

3. Repeat Steps 1–2 to make a total of 3 R4s.

ROW 5

1. Arrange blocks in the order listed, as shown: SB + CB + SP/B + CB + SB + CB + SP/A + CB + SB + CB + SP/B + CB + SB

2. Sew the blocks together and press the seams to the right to complete a Row 5 (R5).

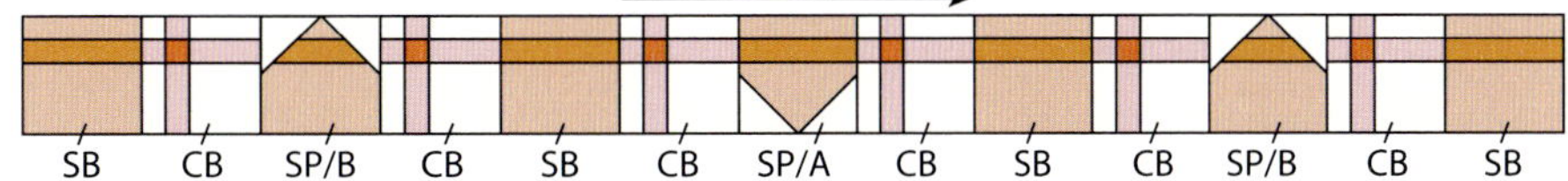

3. Repeat Steps 1–2 to make a total of 3 R5s.

ROW 6

1. Arrange blocks in the order listed, as shown: SB + CB + SB + CB + SB + CB + SP/B + CB + SB + CB + SB + CB + SB

2. Sew the blocks together and press the seams to the right to complete Row 6 (R6).

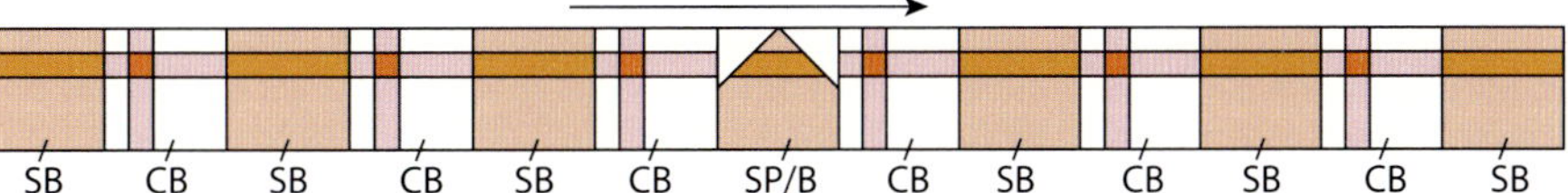

Quilt Assembly

1. Arrange rows in the order listed, as shown. From top to bottom: R1 + R2 + R3 + R4 + R5 + R2 + R3 + R4 + R5 + R2 + R3 + R4 + R5 + R2 + R6

2. Sew the rows together, taking care to nest the seams. Press the seams open or all in one direction to complete the Sunprint Plaid quilt top.

3. Finish the quilt as desired (see Quilt Finishing, page 17).

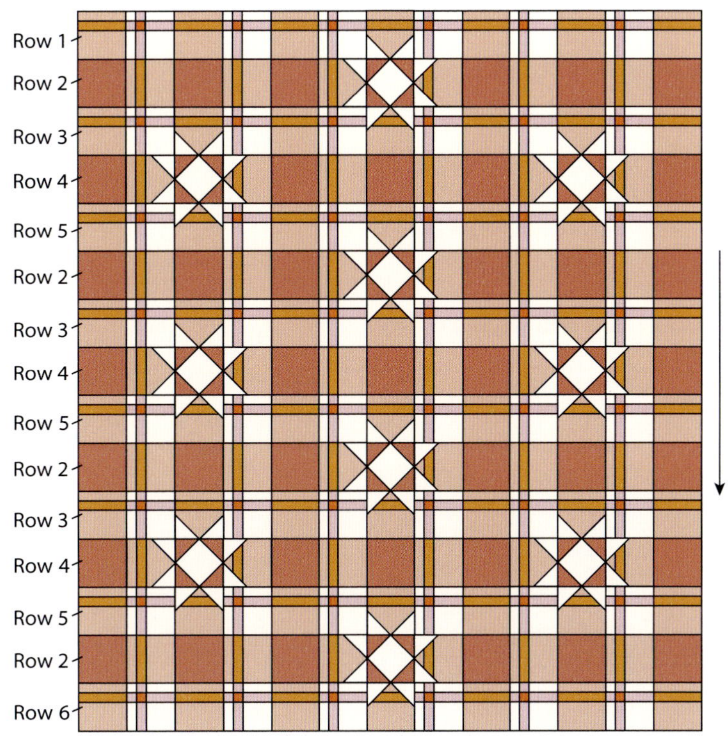

SWEETBERRY MARKET TOTE

Finished Berry Block Size: 8″ × 11″ || **Finished Blossom Block Size:** 5″ × 8″ || **Finished Tote:** 16″ × 18″

The Sweetberry Market Tote captures the sweetness of early summer strawberry picking with a darling motif of berries and blossoms. The tote is sized just right to take along to the local farmer's market or craft fair and fill with goodies. Be sure to share your project online with the hashtag **#sweetberrymarkettote**

FABRICS & SUPPLIES

Yardages are based on 42″ wide fabric.

Dark pink (Fabric A): ¼ yard

Cream (Fabric B): ⅛ yard

Dusty green (Fabric C): ⅛ yard

Gold (Fabric D): ⅛ yard

Peach (Background Fabric E): ⅞ yard

Strawberry print (Lining Fabric F): 1 yard

1″-wide webbing: 1⅝ yards

Pellon Flex Foam Two-Sided Fusible Foam Interfacing: 1⅓ yards

8″ separating zipper

Material Notes

The fabrics used in this quilt are Art Gallery Fabrics Miami Sunset, Snow, Spruce, Raw Gold, Flights of Fancy Peach, and Berry Drizzle.

CUTTING INSTRUCTIONS

Label each piece as specified in the parenthesis in the cutting lists.

Fabric A

Cut 1 strip 3″ × WOF; subcut into:

- 4 squares 3″ × 3″ (A4)
- 4 rectangles 3″ × 2½″ (A6)

From the remainder of the 3″ strip, cut 2 strips 1½″ × 20″; subcut into:

- 4 rectangles 1½″ × 3½″ (A3)
- 4 rectangles 1½″ × 2″ (A9)
- 4 rectangles 1½″ × 1¾″ (A5)
- 2 rectangles 1″ × 3½″ (A2)

Cut 1 strip 2½″ × WOF; subcut into:

- 1 rectangle 2½″ × 13″ (A1)
- 2 rectangles 2½″ × 8½″ (A7)
- 4 squares 2″ × 2″ (A8)

Fabric B

Cut 1 strip 1¾″ × WOF; subcut into:

- 1 rectangle 1¾″ × 8″ (B3)
- 4 squares 1¾″ × 1¾″ (B4)
- 1 rectangle 1″ × 13″ (B1)
- 1 rectangle 1″ × 10″ (B2)

Fabric C

Cut 1 strip 2″ × WOF; subcut into:

- 4 rectangles 2″ × 3½″ (C3)
- 4 rectangles 2″ × 3¼″ (C1)
- 2 rectangles 1″ × 2½″ (C2)

Fabric D

Cut 2 squares 1¾″ × 1¾″ (D1)

Background Fabric E

Cut 1 strip 20½″ × WOF; subcut into:

- 1 rectangle 20½″ × 23½″ (E11)
- 1 rectangle 20½″ × 1½″ (E10)
- 2 rectangles 16½″ × 2½″ (E9)
- 2 rectangles 8½″ × 1¾″ (E8)
- 2 rectangles 8″ × 1¾″ (E6)
- 4 rectangles 4¼″ × 2⅝″ (E7)
- 4 squares 3½″ × 3½″ (E1)
- 4 rectangles 2½″ × 1½″ (E4)

Cut 2 strips 2¾″ × WOF; subcut into:

- 2 strips 2¾″ × 30″ (E12)
- 8 squares 2″ × 2″ (E5)
- 4 squares 1¾″ × 1¾″ (E2)

Cut 1 strip 2½″ × WOF; subcut into:

- 2 strips 2½″ × 21″ (E13)

Cut 1 strip 1″ × WOF; subcut into:

- 4 rectangles 1″ × 3¼″ (E3)

Lining Fabric F

Cut 1 strip 20½″ × WOF; subcut into:

- 1 rectangle 20½″ × 40½″ (F4)

Cut 1 strip 8″ × WOF; subcut into:

- 1 rectangle 8″ × 32″ (F5)

Cut 2 strips 2½″ × WOF; subcut into:

- 2 strips 2½″ × 21½″ (F1)
- 2 rectangles 2½″ × 9″ (F3)
- 2 rectangles 2½″ × 7″ (F2)

Webbing

Cut 2 pieces 29″ long

Foam Interfacing

Cut 1 rectangle 20″ × 40½″

Berry Block

Seam allowances are ¼″ unless otherwise noted. Pressing direction is indicated by the arrows in the diagrams.

BERRY UNIT

1. Sew the B1 strip to the top of the A1 strip, RST. Press the seam toward Fabric A.

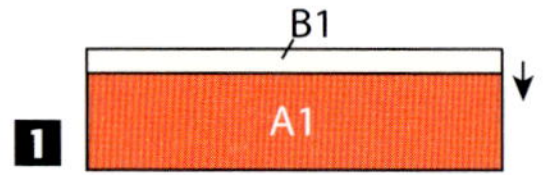

2. Cut 2 rectangles 1½″ wide from the Step 1 unit. These are S1 rectangles. Set 1 aside for the second Berry block.

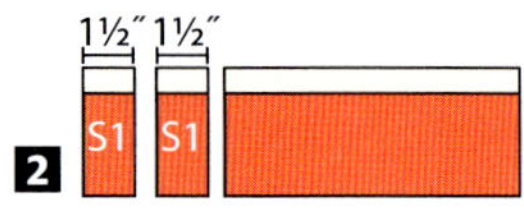

3. Trim the remaining A/B strip unit to 10″ in length. Sew the B2 rectangle to the A fabric of the unit. Press the seam toward Fabric A.

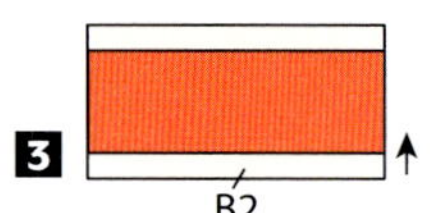

4. Cut 6 rectangles 1½″ wide from the Step 3 strip unit. These are S2 rectangles. Set 3 aside for the second Berry block.

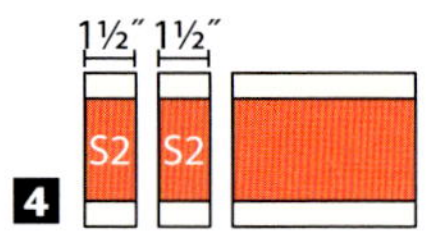

5. Sew an A2 rectangle on top of an S2 rectangle as shown. Sew an A3 rectangle on the bottom. Press seams away from the S2 rectangle.

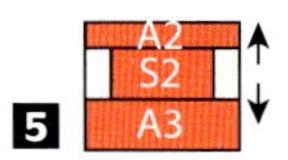

6. Sew an A4 rectangle on either side of the Step 5 unit. Press the seams toward the A4 squares. This is Row 1 (R1).

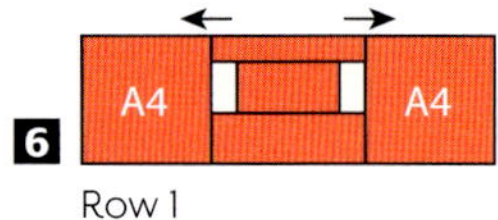

7. Sew 2 A5 rectangles, 1 S1 rectangle, and 1 S2 rectangle together as shown. Press the seams toward Fabric A. This is Row 2 (R2).

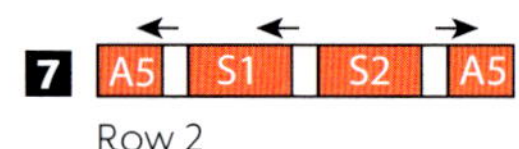

8. Sew an A3 rectangle on top of an S2 rectangle. Press the seam toward A3.

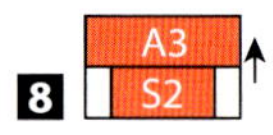

9. Sew an A6 rectangle on either side of the Step 8 unit. Press the seams toward the A6 rectangles. This is Row 3 (R3).

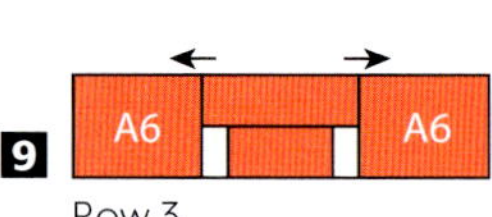

10. Sew Rows 1, 2, and 3 together as shown. Add an A7 rectangle on the bottom of R3. Press the seams as shown.

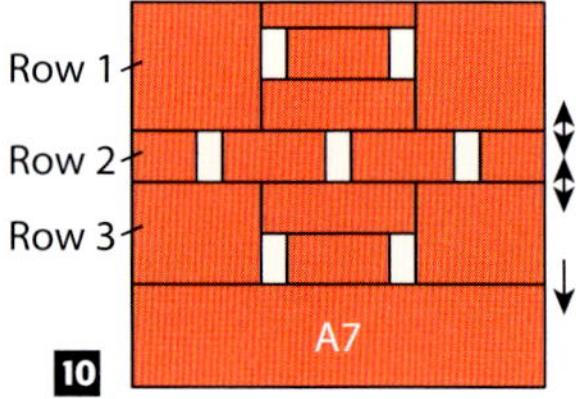

11. Mark a diagonal line, corner-to-corner, on the wrong side of 2 E1 squares.

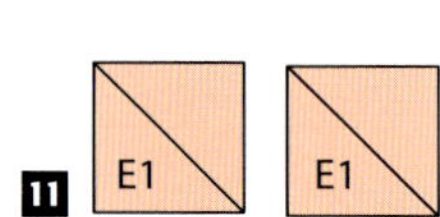

12. Pin the E1 squares RST with the Step 10 unit as shown.

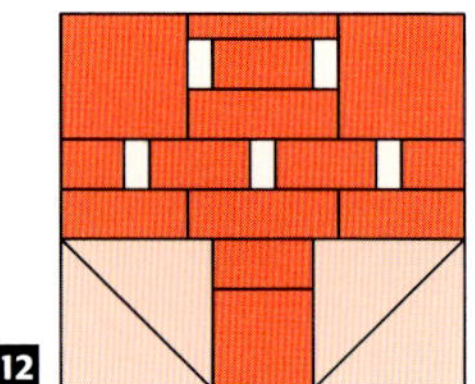

13. Sew on the marked lines, and trim away excess corner fabric ¼″ from the seam. Press the seams toward Fabric E.

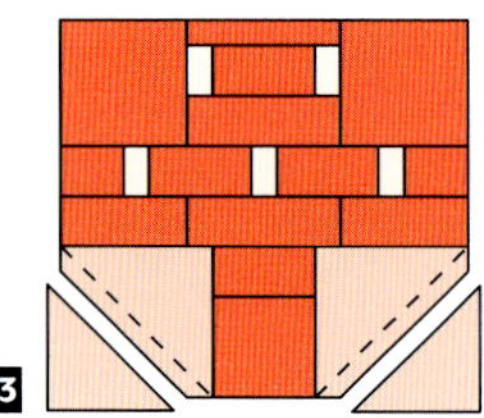

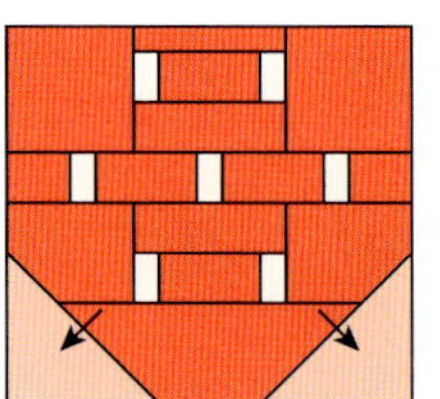

LEAF UNIT

1. Mark a diagonal line, corner-to-corner, across 2 E2 squares.

2. Pin an E2 square on the upper right corner of a C1 rectangle. Pin the other E2 square on the upper left corner of another C1 rectangle. Mirror the orientation of the units.

3. Sew on the marked lines, and trim away the excess corner fabric ¼˝ away from the seams. Press the seams toward Fabric E.

4. Sew an E3 rectangle to the top of each unit. Press the seams toward the E3 rectangles.

5. Sew an E4 rectangle on the side of each unit opposite the E corner (mirrored). Press the seams toward the E4 rectangles.

6. Mark a diagonal line, corner-to-corner, on the wrong side of 2 E5 squares.

7. Pin an E5 square RST on the bottom corner of the E4 side of the Step 5 units, as shown.

8. Sew on the marked lines and trim away the excess corner fabric ¼˝ from the seams. Press the seams toward Fabric E.

9. Sew a C2 rectangle between the mirrored units. Press the seams toward the C2 rectangle.

10. Mark a diagonal line, corner-to-corner, on the wrong side of 2 A8 squares.

11. Pin an A8 square to the right end of a C3 rectangle. Pin the other A8 square on the left end of another C3 rectangle. Mirror the orientation of the marked lines.

12. Sew on the marked lines, and trim away the excess corner fabric ¼˝ from the seams. Press the seams toward Fabric A.

13. Sew an A9 rectangle on the side of each unit opposite the A corner (mirrored). Press the seams toward the A9 rectangles.

14. Mark a diagonal line, corner-to-corner, on the wrong side of 2 E5 squares.

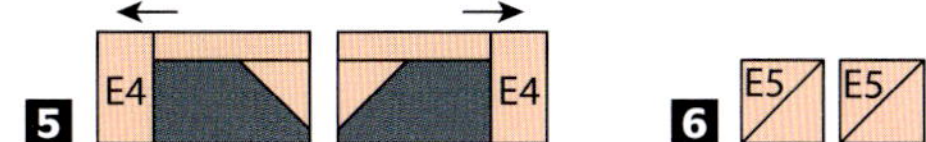

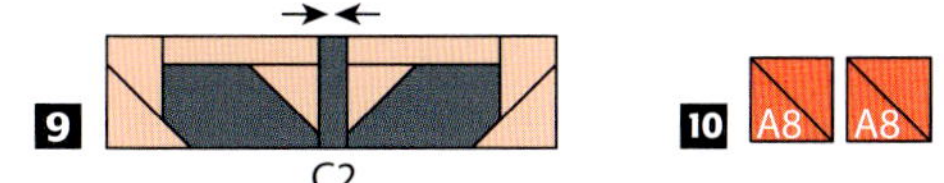

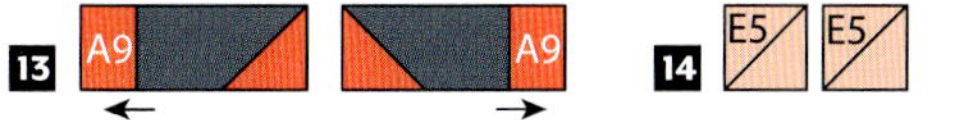

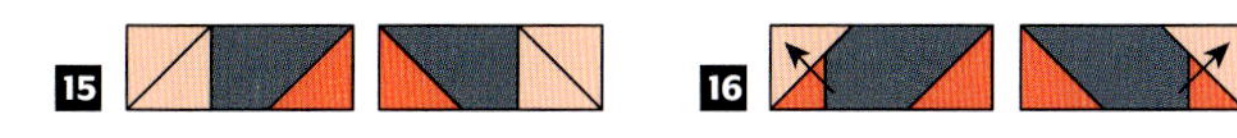

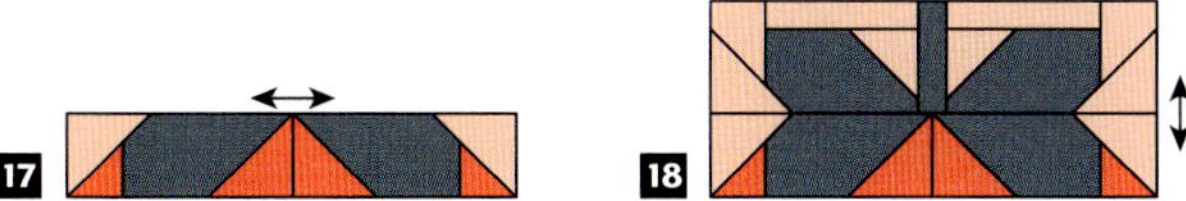

15. Pin an E5 square RST on the A9 rectangle side of each Step 13 unit (mirrored).

16. Sew on the marked lines, and trim away the excess corner fabric ¼˝ from the seams. Press the seams toward Fabric E.

17. Sew the two mirrored units together as shown. Press the seam open.

18. Sew the Step 9 unit on top of the Step 17 unit. Press the seam open to complete the leaf unit.

ASSEMBLY

1. Sew the leaf unit to the top of the berry unit. Press the seam open to complete the Berry block.

2. Repeat all Berry block steps to complete a second Berry block.

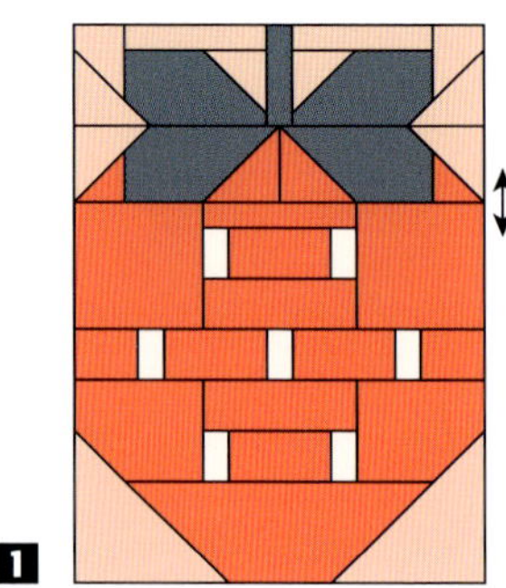

Blossom Block

1. Sew 2 E6 rectangles to a B3 rectangle as shown. Press the seams toward the E6 rectangles.

2. Cut the Step 1 unit into 4 rectangles 1¾″ wide, as shown. Set 2 aside for the second Blossom block.

3. Sew 1 D1 square between 2 B4 squares, as shown. Press the seams toward the D1 square.

4. Sew a rectangle from Step 2 on the left and right sides of the Step 3 unit. Press the seams open.

5. Sew an E7 rectangle on the left and right sides of the Step 4 unit. Press the seams toward the E7 rectangles.

6. Sew an E8 rectangle to the bottom of the Step 5 unit. Press the seam toward the E8 rectangle to complete one Blossom block.

7. Repeat Steps 3–6 to make a second Blossom block.

BLOSSOM BLOCK

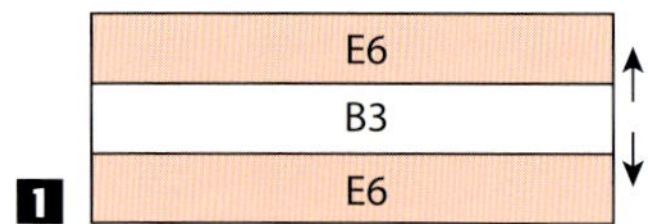

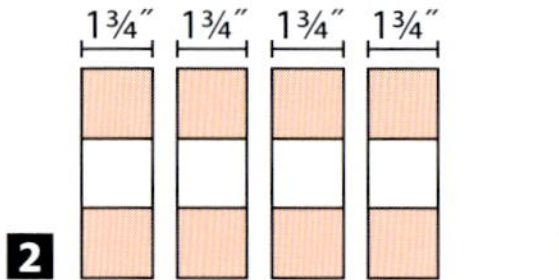

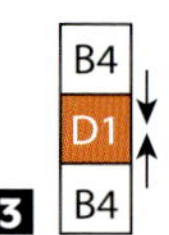

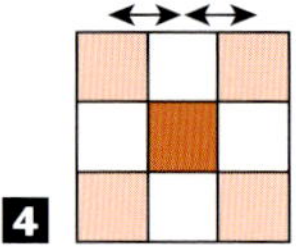

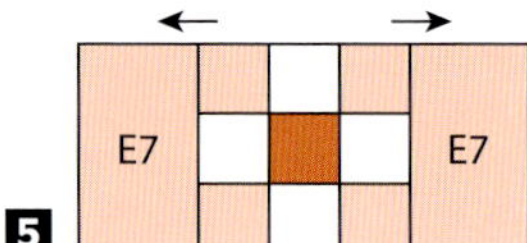

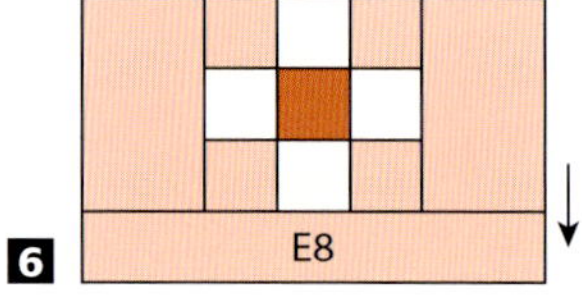

Tote Exterior Assembly

1. Arrange 2 Berry blocks and 2 Blossom blocks into 2 columns, as shown. Note that the order of the blocks is reversed between the 2 columns. Sew the units into columns, pairing each berry with a blossom. Press the seams toward the Blossom blocks. Then, sew the columns together. Press the seam open.

TOTE EXTERIOR ASSEMBLY

2. Sew an E9 rectangle on the left and right sides of the Step 1 unit. Press the seams toward the E9 rectangles.

3. Sew the E10 rectangle on the top of the Step 2 unit. Sew the E11 rectangle on the bottom of the unit. Press the seams toward the E10 and E11 rectangles. This is the finished tote exterior.

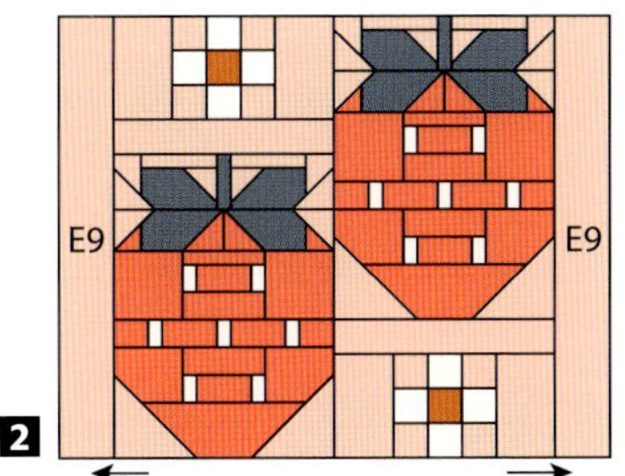

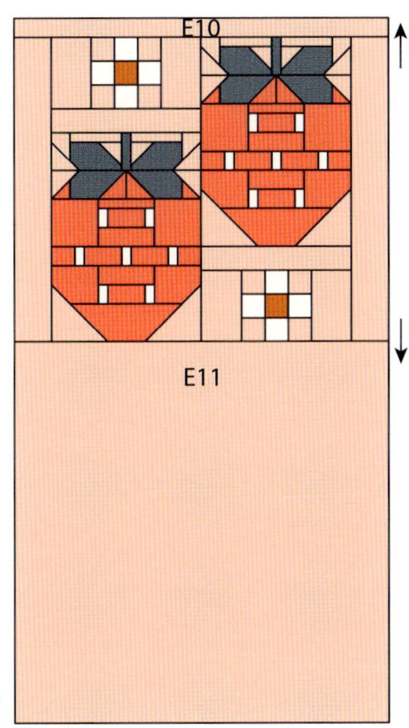

Tote Assembly

QUILTING AND STRAP ASSEMBLY

1. Make a quilt sandwich with the F4 lining rectangle (wrong side up), the fusible foam interfacing, and the tote exterior (right side up). Follow the interfacing manufacturer's instructions to iron and fuse the interfacing to both the lining and the exterior.

2. Quilt the panel as desired. This is the tote body.

3. Press both E12 strips in half lengthwise, RST. Sew the long raw edges together on each strip, creating 2 tubes. Back stitch at the beginning and end of each seam and press the seams open.

4. Turn the tubes made in Step 3 right side out. Press flat with the seam centered on one side.

TOTE ASSEMBLY

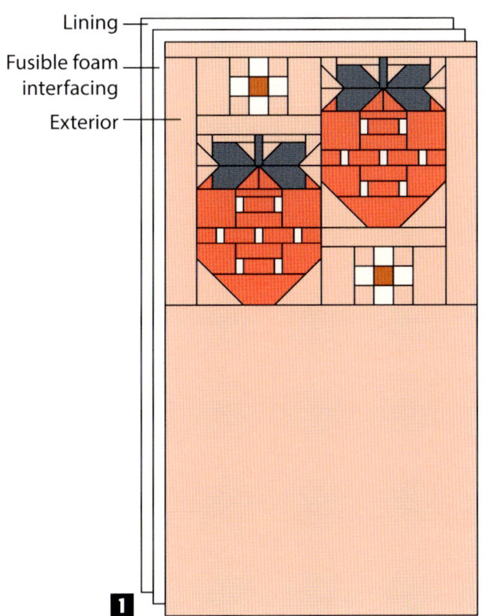

TIP To easily turn tubes, pin a safety pin to one layer of fabric on one end of the tube. Guide and pull the safety pin through the tube to turn it right side out. You can also use a safety pin to guide the webbing through the tubes in Step 5.

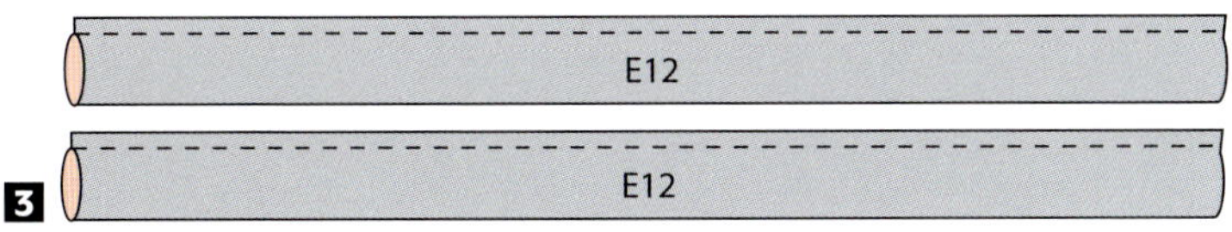

5. Pull 1 piece of webbing through each tube. Center the webbing inside the tubes, leaving approximately ½˝ of fabric on both ends of the webbing.

6. Tuck the raw end of the fabric tube in by ¼˝ at both ends. Pin in place, and press.

7. Sew around the perimeter of the Step 6 units using a ⅛˝ seam allowance and a 3mm stitch length. Back stitch at the beginning and end. These are the straps.

8. Measure and mark 1˝ from both ends of each strap.

9. On the exterior of the tote body, in the top left corner of the bag front (the end of the panel with the berries), measure 3¾˝ from the left side and 2½˝ down from the top. Mark that point. Mark the same point in the top right corner. Then, mark the same 2 points on the opposite side of the tote body.

10. Align the ends of the straps with the marked points on the tote body, and pin. The outer bottom corner of the strap should align with the marks.

11. Sew a square 1˝ × 1˝ with an *X* through the center on each strap end. Be sure the straps aren't twisted before sewing in place.

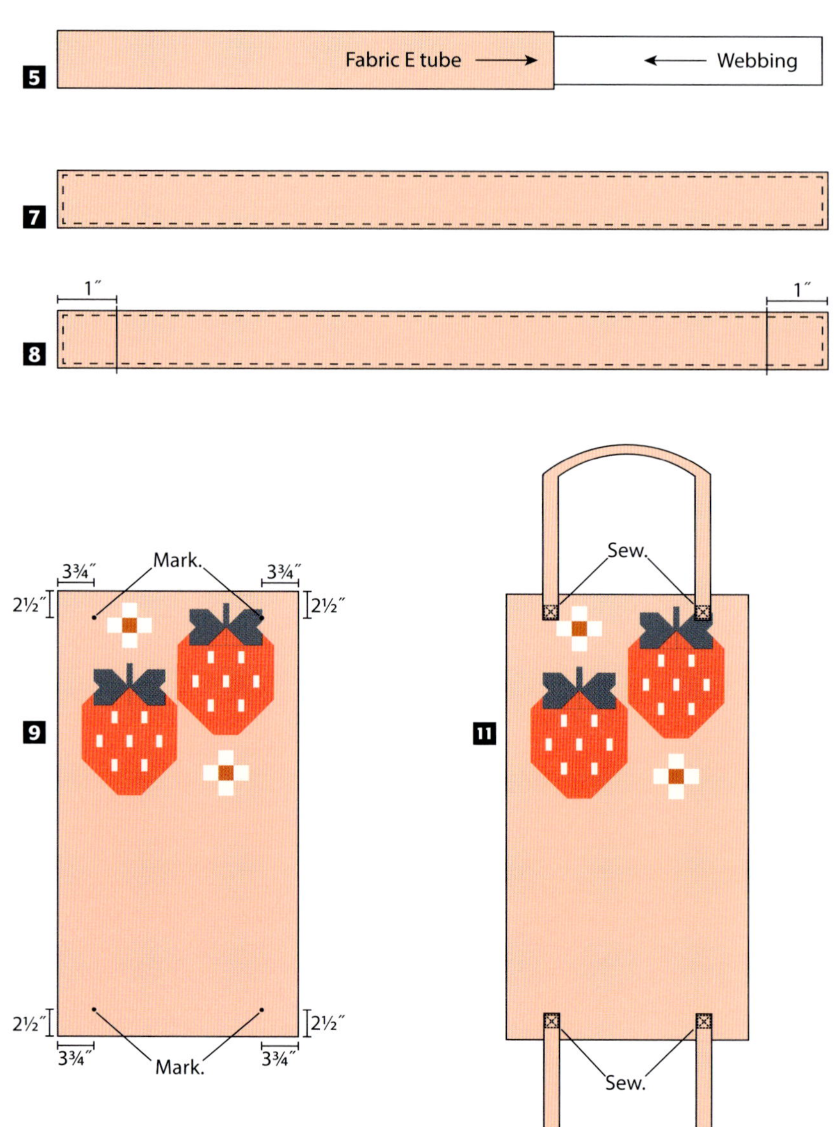

POCKET ASSEMBLY

1. Fold the F5 rectangle in half widthwise WST to make an 8″ × 16″ rectangle. Sew around the 3 raw edges with a ⅛″ seam allowance.

2. Separate the 2 sides of the 8″ zipper and set aside the zipper pull. Align one edge of the zipper tape with an 8″ edge of the Step 1 unit, right side of the zipper facing the fabric. Sew together.

3. Repeat Step 2 with the remaining side of the zipper tape on the other 8″ edge.

4. Press the fabric away from the right side of the zippers on both sides. Top stitch the zippers in place with a ⅛″ seam allowance.

5. Bring the two sides of the zipper together and attach the zipper pull. Pull it halfway across the zipper from left to right and then turn the pocket inside out.

6. Press the pocket flat with the zipper positioned so that it is centered, approximately 2″ from both of the folds, and the open end of the zipper is on the right. Carefully arrange the open zipper tape ends flush against each other and sew both sides of the pocket closed using a ⅛″ seam allowance.

7. Fold each F3 rectangle in half lengthwise, WST, and press.

8. Align the raw edge of an F3 strip with one of the raw edges of the pocket, making sure to leave approximately 1″ of overhang on both ends. Pin or clip in place and sew. Repeat on the other side with the second F3 strip.

9. Fold the binding over the raw edge and clip in place, concealing the raw edges. Fold the overhanging ends of the binding toward the pocket, and then under the folded binding edge to secure. Sew in place using a ⅛″ seam allowance.

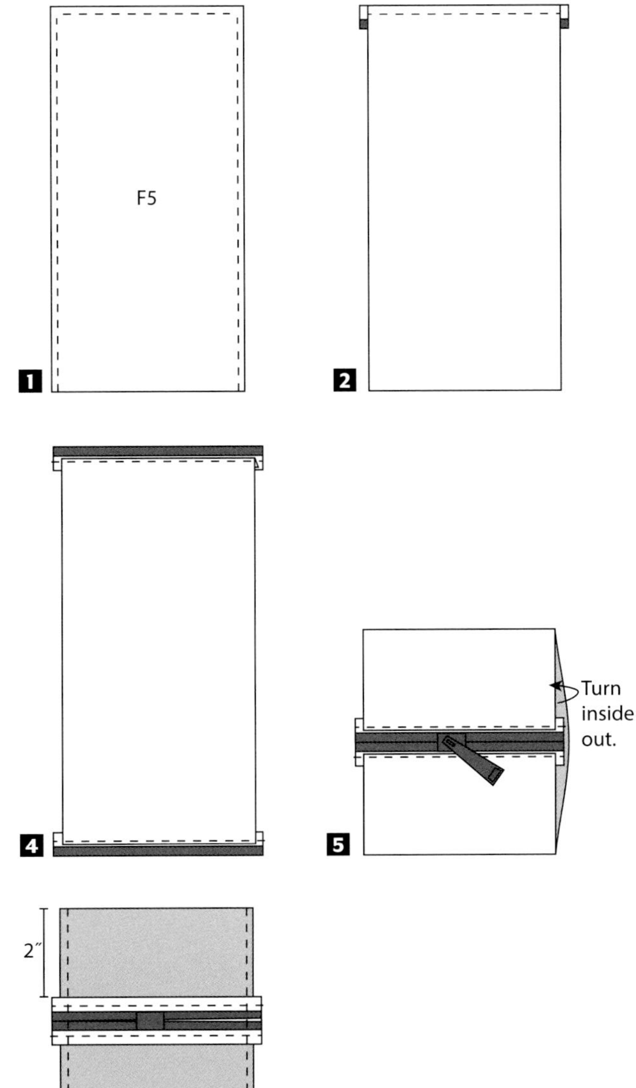

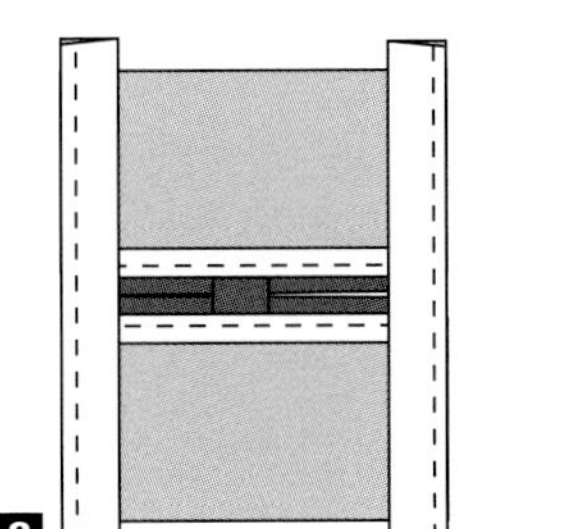

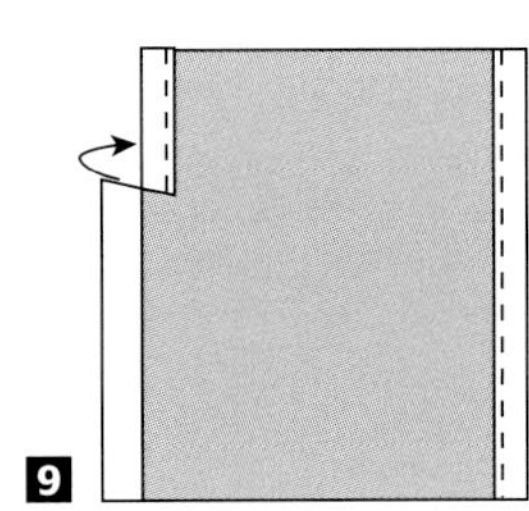

10. Turn the pocket right side out through the zipper opening and then close the zipper. Press.

11. Center the top edge of the pocket (closest to the zipper) along the top edge of the back of the tote body. The wrong side of the pocket should face the lining of the tote body. Center on the backside of the body (opposite the berry design). Pin or clip in place.

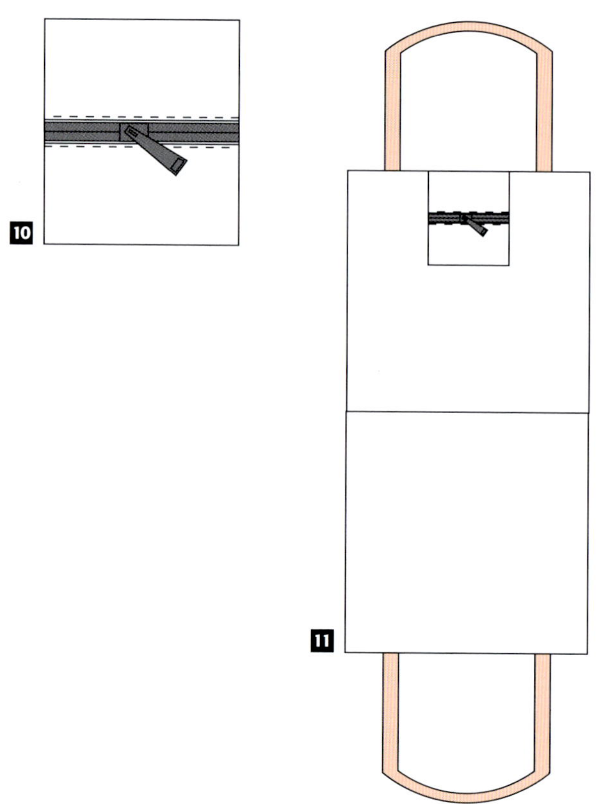

FINAL ASSEMBLY

1. Bind the 2 short ends of the tote body with the E13 strips using the method described in Steps 7–9 in the Pocket Assembly (page 63). Attach the binding to the lining side of the tote body first and then fold over and secure to the exterior side. Trim the ends of the binding flush with the edge of the tote body instead of folding them under the binding edge.

2. Fold the tote in half, RST, and clip or pin the sides together. Sew both sides of the tote.

3. Bind the side seams with F1 strips by following Steps 7–9 in Pocket Assembly (page 63). Extend the binding 1˝ past the tote body at the top of the tote only.

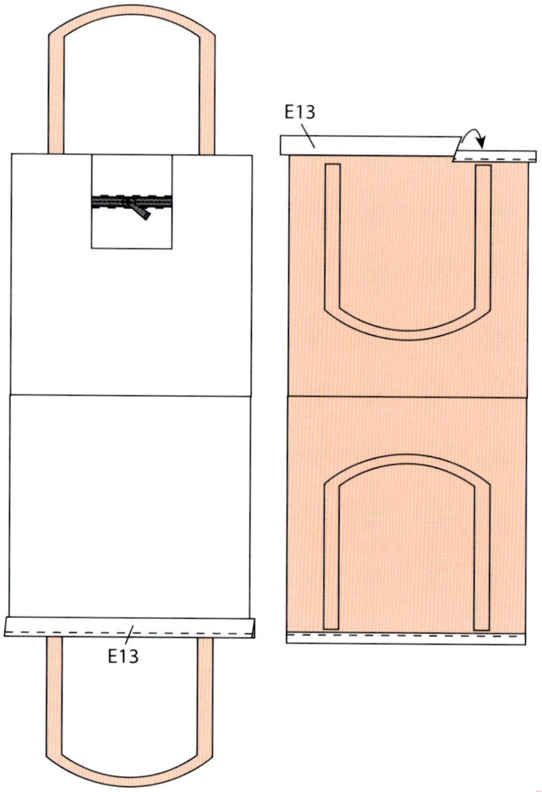

FINAL ASSEMBLY

1
E13
E13
2 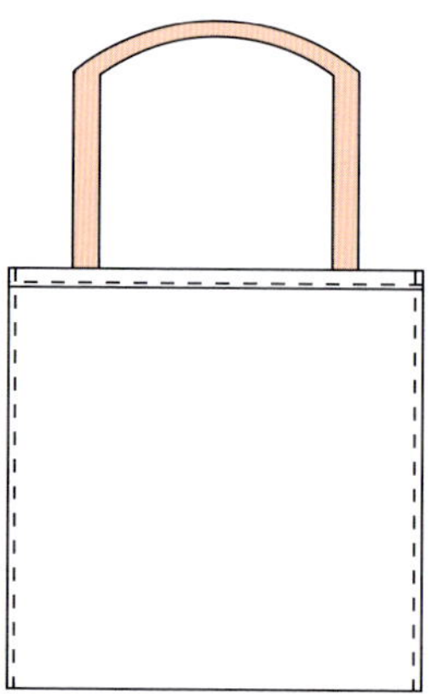
3
F1
F1

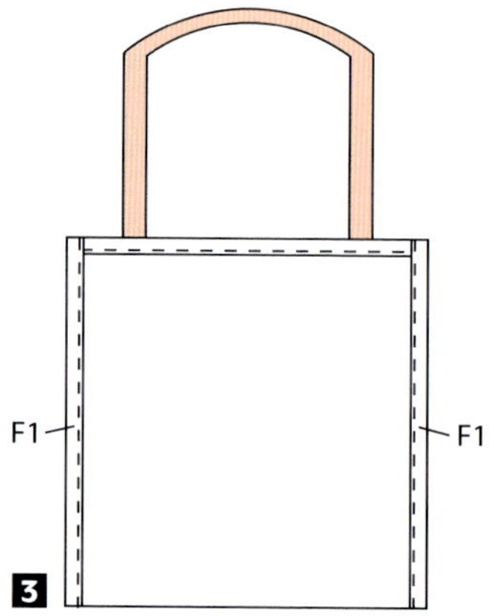

4. Use a ruler to mark a 2½″ × 2½″ square in each bottom corner of the tote. Cut both squares out.

5. Bring the edges of the cut corners together, centering the side seams. Pin in place. Sew each corner closed along the diagonal, backstitching at the beginning and end.

6. Bind each corner with the F2 strips by following Steps 7–9 in Pocket Assembly (page 63). Extend the binding 1″ on both ends of the corners.

7. Turn the tote right side out to complete the Sweetberry Market Tote.

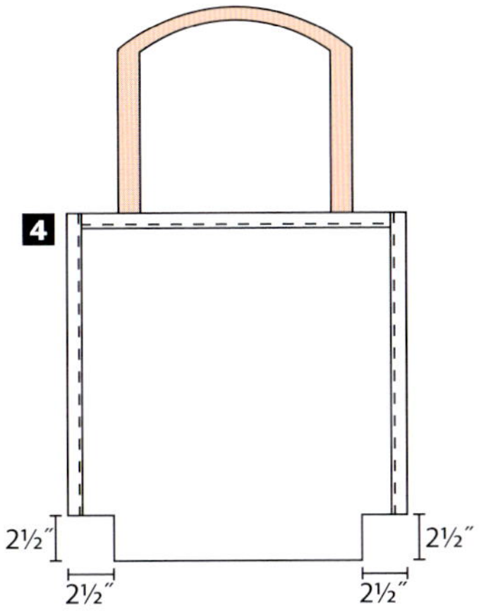

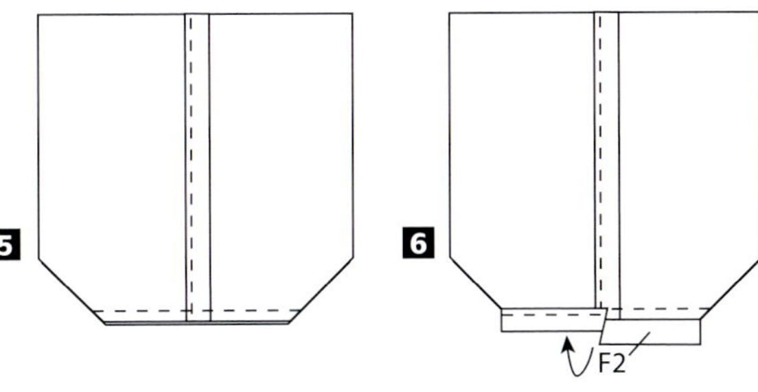

RAINBRIGHT QUILT

Finished Block Size: 15″ × 30″ || **Finished Quilt:** 60″ × 60½″

The Rainbright Quilt is inspired by prisms of color painted across the sky that show us the beauty that comes after a storm. This sweet rainbow and raindrop motif comes together quickly and would be a darling addition to a nursery or child's bedroom. Be sure to share your project online with the hashtag **#rainbrightquilt**

FABRICS & SUPPLIES

Yardages are based on 42″ wide fabric.

Dusty blue (Fabric A): ¾ yard

Peach (Fabric B): ¾ yard

Light peach (Fabric C): ¾ yard

Yellow (Fabric D): ¾ yard

Cream (Background Fabric E): 2⅝ yards

Binding: ⅝ yard

Backing: 3⅞ yards (using a horizontal seam)

Rainbright Quilt Templates (see Templates, page 127)

Material Notes

The fabrics used in this quilt are Art Gallery Fabrics Ocean Fog, Apricot Crepe, Peach Sherbet, Honey, Evermore Bliss, and Small and Sweet.

CUTTING INSTRUCTIONS

Prepare Rainbright Quilt Templates 1–6 for this project (see Templates, page 127). Label each piece as specified in the parenthesis in the cutting lists. When cutting the same pieces from different fabrics, update the labels for each color. For example, label Fabric A Template 5 as A5, Fabric B Template 5 as B5, and so on.

Fabrics A, B, C, and D

Cut 1 strip 6½″ × WOF; subcut into:

- 2 Template 5 (5)

Cut 2 strips 5½″ × WOF; subcut into:

- 2 Template 4 (4)
- 2 Template 3 (3)
- 6 rectangles 5½″ × 4½″ (1)

Cut 1 strip 4½″ × WOF; subcut into:

- 2 Template 2 (2)

Background Fabric E

Cut 2 strips 15½″ × WOF; subcut into:

- 8 Template 6 (E9)
- 8 Template 1 (E8)

Cut 3 strips 5½″ × WOF; subcut into:

- 24 rectangles 5½″ × 4½″ (E3)

Cut 2 strips 5″ × WOF; sew together end-to-end, and cut:

- 1 strip 5″ × 60½″ (E7)

Cut 2 strips 3½″ × WOF; subcut into:

- 6 rectangles 3½″ × 10½″ (E4)

Cut 5 strips 2½″ × WOF; sew together end-to-end, and cut:

- 3 strips 2½″ × 60½″ (E6)

Cut 3 strips 2½″ × WOF; subcut into:

- 48 squares 2½″ × 2½″ (E1)

Cut 1 strip 2″ × WOF; subcut into:

- 4 rectangles 2″ × 10½″ (E5)

Cut 2 strips 1¾″ × WOF; subcut into:

- 48 squares 1¾″ × 1¾″ (E2)

Binding Fabric

Cut 7 strips 2½″ × WOF

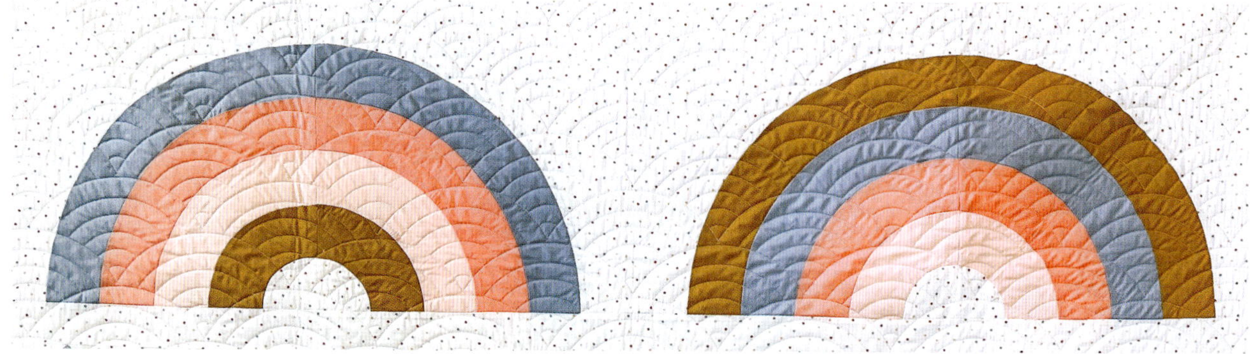

Quilted by Sandy Saengsuk
of Thai Charm LLC

Assembly

Seam allowances are ¼″ unless otherwise noted. Pressing direction is indicated by the arrows in the diagrams.

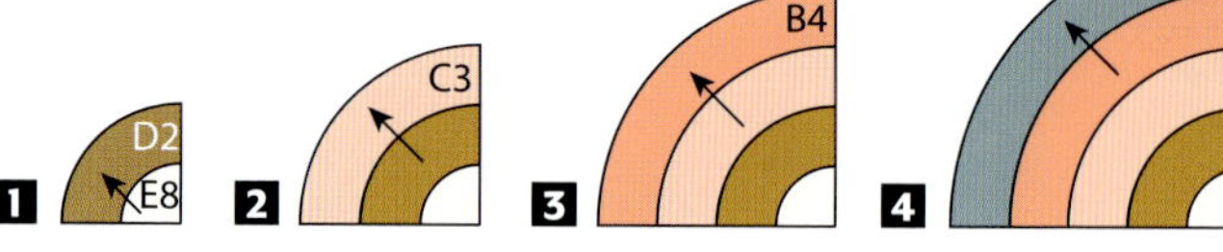

RAINBOW BLOCKS

1. Sew the convex edge of 1 E8 piece to the concave edge of 1 D2 piece (see Curves, page 14). Press the seam toward D2.

2. Sew the convex edge of the Step 1 unit to the concave edge of 1 C3 piece. Press the seam toward C3.

3. Sew the convex edge of the same unit to the concave edge of 1 B4 piece. Press the seam toward B4.

4. Sew the convex edge of the same unit to the concave edge of 1 A5 piece. Press the seam toward A5.

5. Sew the convex edge of the same unit to the concave edge of 1 E9 piece. Press the seam toward E9 to make 1 half-rainbow unit.

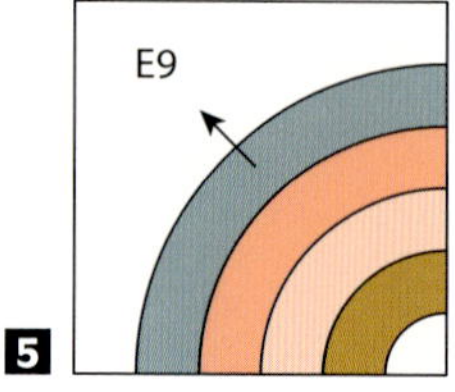

6. Repeat Steps 1–5, pressing all seams toward E8 (opposite the first half-rainbow unit).

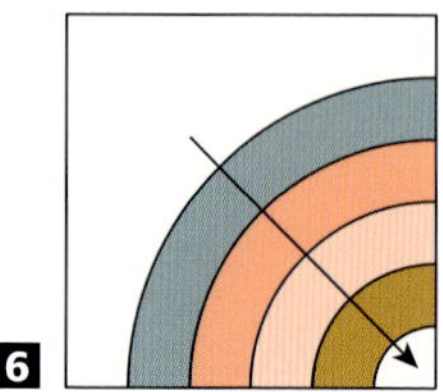

7. Sew the two half-rainbow units together as shown and press the seam open to make Rainbow block 1 (RB1).

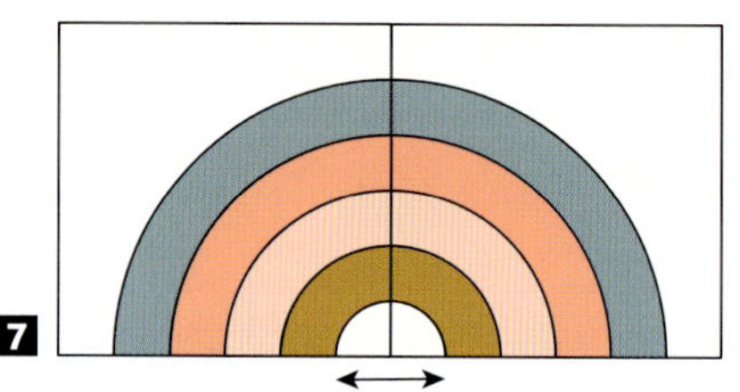

8. Repeat Steps 1–7 to make 3 more Rainbow blocks in the following combinations:

- **RB2:** E8 + C2 + B3 + A4 + D5 + E9
- **RB3:** E8 + B2 + A3 + D4 + C5 + E9
- **RB4:** E8 + A2 + D3 + C4 + B5 + E9

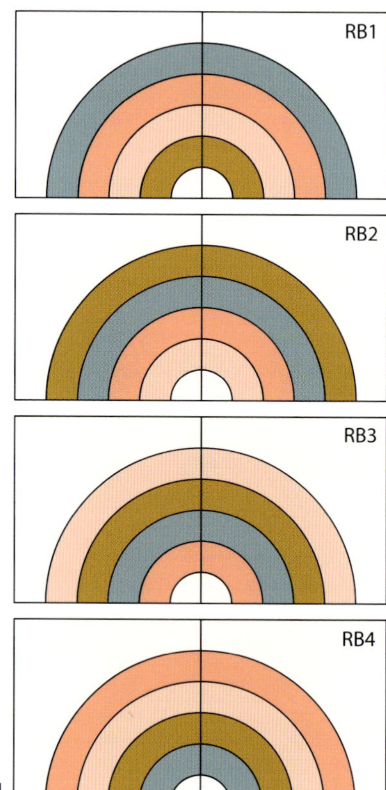

RAINDROP UNIT

1. Mark a diagonal line, corner-to-corner, on the wrong side of all E1 and E2 squares.

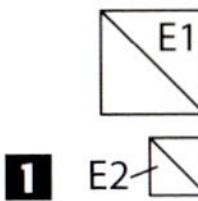

2. Pin 1 E1 square RST on the top right corner of 1 A1 rectangle. Pin 2 E2 squares RST on the bottom right and left corners of the A1 rectangle, as shown.

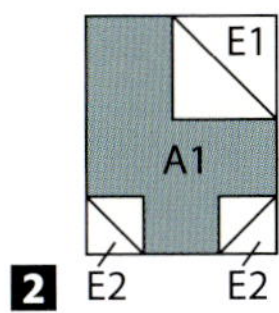

3. Sew on the marked lines, and trim away the excess corner fabric ¼˝ from the seams. Press the seams toward Fabric E.

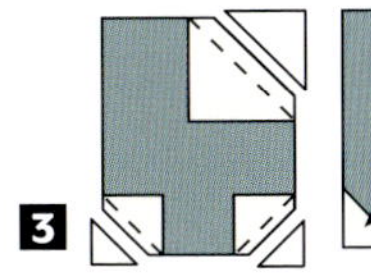

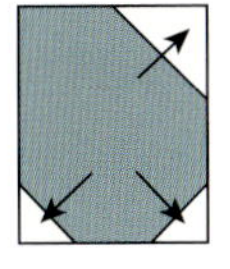

4. Pin another E1 square RST on the top left corner of the A1 rectangle, as shown.

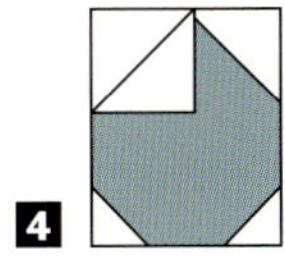

5. Sew on the marked line, and trim away the excess corner fabric ¼˝ from the seam. Press the seam toward Fabric E to complete 1 raindrop A (RA).

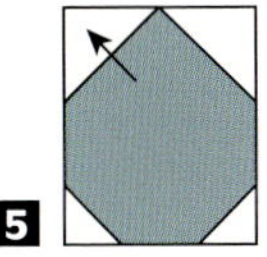

6. Repeat Steps 1–5 with all A1, B1, C1, and D1 rectangles (paired with E1 and E2 squares) to make a total of 6 raindrops in each fabric color (RA, RB, RC, and RD).

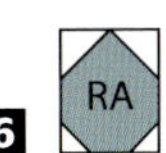

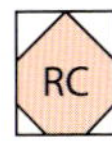

7. Arrange 1 RA, 1 RB, and 1 RC with 3 E3 rectangles as shown. Sew the pieces together into 2 rows and press the seams toward the E3 rectangles.

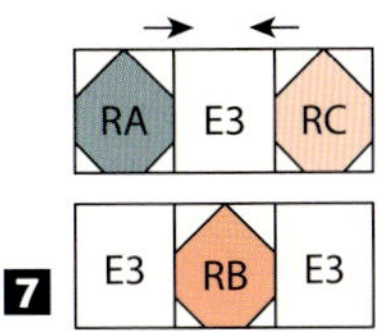

8. Sew the rows together and press the seam open to make raindrop unit 1 (RD1).

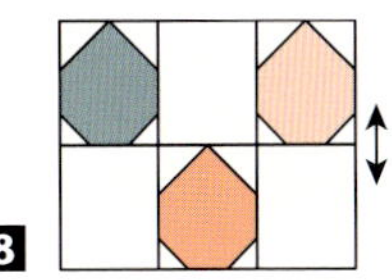

9. Repeat Steps 7–8 combining the following units as shown, to make a total of 8 raindrop units:

- **RD1:** RA + RB + RC
- **RD2**: RD + RC + RA
- **RD3:** RD + RA + RB
- **RD4:** RC + RB + RD
- **RD5:** RC + RD + RA
- **RD6:** RB + RA + RC
- **RD7:** RB + RC + RD
- **RD8:** RA + RD + RB

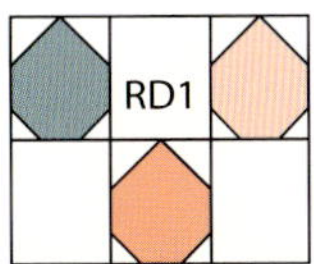

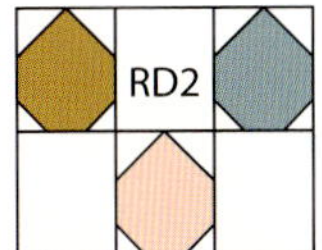

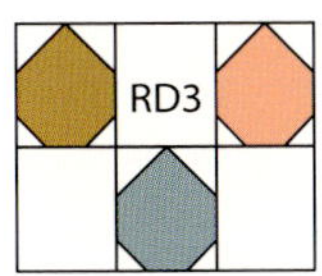

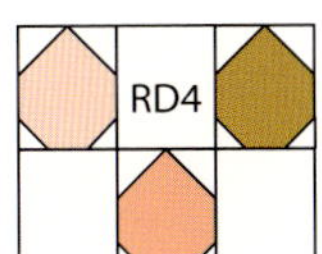

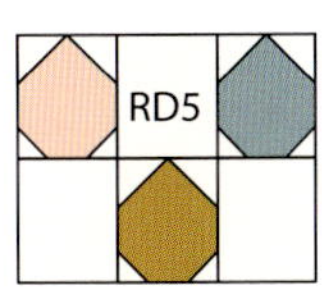

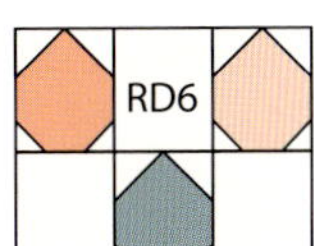

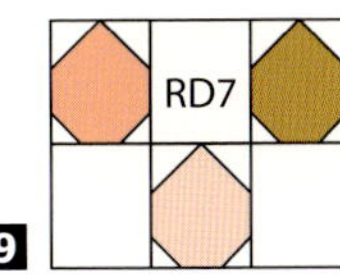

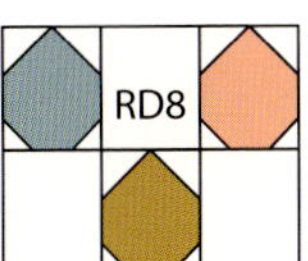

QUILT ASSEMBLY

1. Sew RB1 and RB2 together and press the seam open to make Row 1.

2. Sew RB3 and RB4 together and press the seam open to make Row 3.

3. Arrange RD1, RD2, RD3, and RD4 with E4 rectangles between each unit. Add E5 rectangles on the left side of RD1 and the right side of RD4, as shown. Sew together and press the seams toward the Fabric E rectangles to make Row 2.

4. Arrange RD5, RD6, RD7, and RD8 with E4 rectangles between each unit. Add E5 rectangles on the left side of RD5 and the right side of RD8, as shown. Sew together and press the seams toward the Fabric E rectangles to make Row 4.

5. Sew the rows and sashing together in the following order from top to bottom, and press the seams toward the E6 sashing to complete the Rainbright Quilt top:

E6 + Row 1 + E6 + Row 2 + Row 3 + E6 + Row 4 + E7

6. Finish the quilt as desired (see Quilt Finishing, page 17).

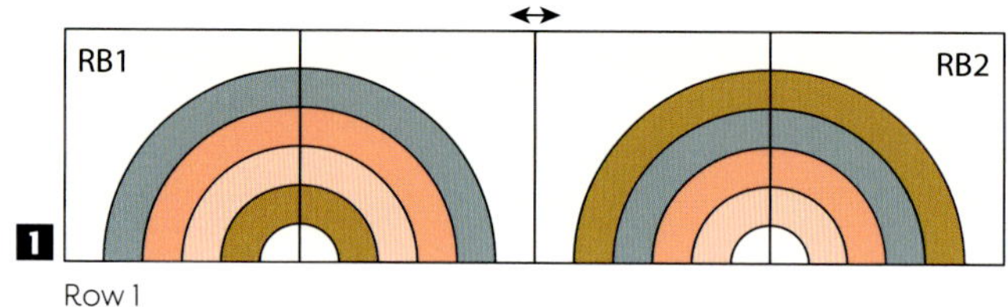

Row 1

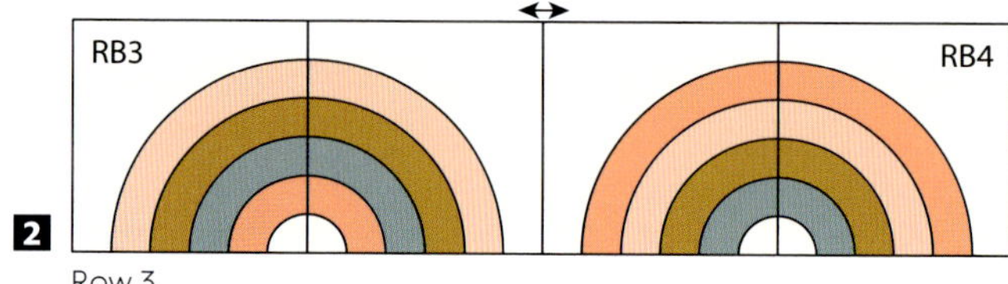

Row 3

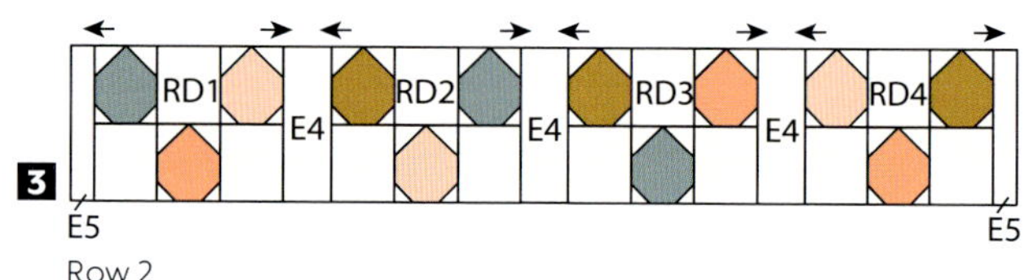

Row 2

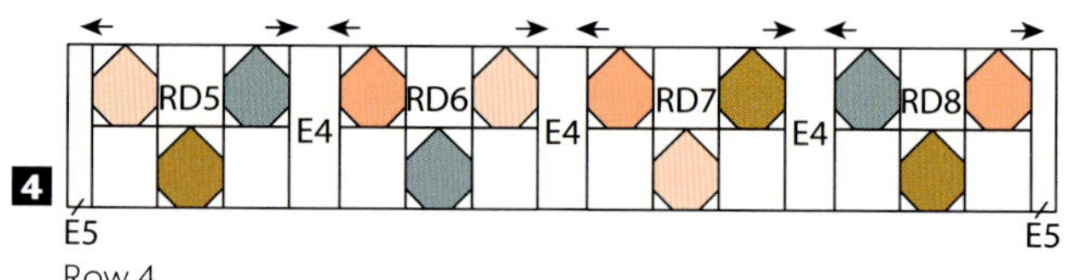

Row 4

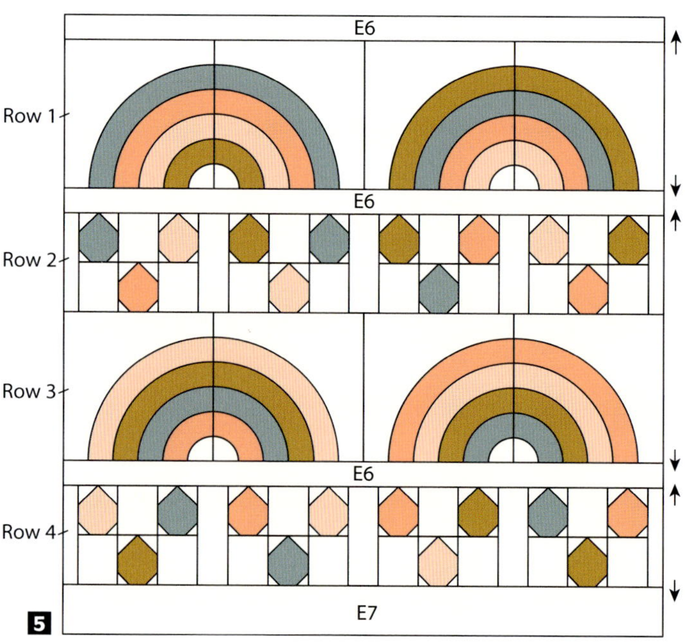

SUNGLOW QUILT

Finished Block Size: 10″ × 10″ || **Finished Quilt:** 60″ × 60″

The Sunglow Quilt is inspired by the glow of the dusky sun. As it slowly sinks to the horizon on summer evenings, it bathes the world in rosy warmth, even as the shadows start to edge toward night. Summer sunsets are a time of wonder and reflection when the world seems to slow for a few minutes and beckons you to bask in the beauty of moments that bridge day and night. Be sure to share your project online with the hashtag **#sunglowquilt**

FABRICS & SUPPLIES

Yardages are based on 42″ wide fabric.

Brown (Fabric A): ⅝ yard

Dark pink (Fabric B): ½ yard

Medium pink (Fabric C): ½ yard

Light pink (Fabric D): ½ yard

Cream (Background Fabric E): 3½ yards

Binding: ⅝ yard

Backing: 3⅞ yards

Sunglow Quilt Templates (see Templates, page 127)

Material Notes

The fabrics used in this quilt are Art Gallery Fabrics Sienna Brick, Cinnamon, Blossomed, Blushing, and Natural Bouquet.

CUTTING INSTRUCTIONS

Prepare Sunglow Quilt Templates 1 and 2 for this project (see Templates, page 127). Label each piece as specified in the parenthesis in the cutting lists. Label each cut with the fabric color letter. For example, a 1½″ × WOF strip from Fabric C should be labeled C1.

Fabric A

Cut 8 strips 2″ × WOF (A1)

Fabrics B, C, and D

Cut 8 strips 1½″ × WOF (1)

Fabric E

Cut 5 strips 11″ × WOF; subcut into:

- 14 squares 11″ × 11″ (E3)

Cut 2 strips 10½″ × WOF; subcut into:

- 8 squares 10½″ × 10½″ (E4)

Cut 4 strips 2½″ × WOF (E2)

Cut 24 strips 1½″ × WOF (E1)

Binding Fabric

Cut 7 strips 2½″ × WOF

Block Assembly

Seam allowances are ¼″ unless otherwise noted. Pressing direction is indicated by the arrows in the diagrams.

1. Sew together 2 each of the A1, B1, C1 and D1 strips, 6 E1 strips, and 1 E2 strip in the following order: A1+ E1 + B1 + E1 + C1 + E1 + D1 + E2 + D1 + E1 + C1 + E1 + B1 + E1 + A1

2. Repeat Step 1 to make 4 total strip sets.

3. Cut 4 Template 1 (T1) and 5 Template 2 (T2) triangles from each strip set, as shown. Take care to align the seams for Fabrics A and E with the lines on the templates to ensure that the stripes will align across the quilt. You will need 16 T1 and 12 T2 triangles for this quilt. Set aside the extra T2 triangles for a future project.

TIP Take care to handle the T1, T2, and E3 triangles gently, as some of the triangle edges are cut on the bias and can easily become distorted.

4. Mark a diagonal line, corner-to-corner, on the wrong side of all E3 squares. Cut on the marked lines to make each E3 square into 2 E3 triangles.

5. Place 1 T1 triangle and 1 E3 triangle RST and sew along the long edge. Press the seam open, and trim minimally as needed to make 1 HST1 block measuring 10½″ × 10½″. Repeat to make a total of 16 HST1 blocks.

6. Repeat Step 5 with 1 T2 triangle and 1 E3 triangle RST to make a total of 12 HST2 blocks measuring 10½″ × 10½″.

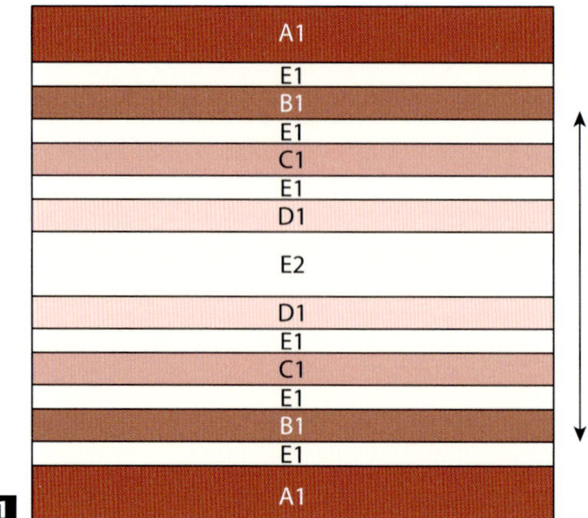

Press the seams open.

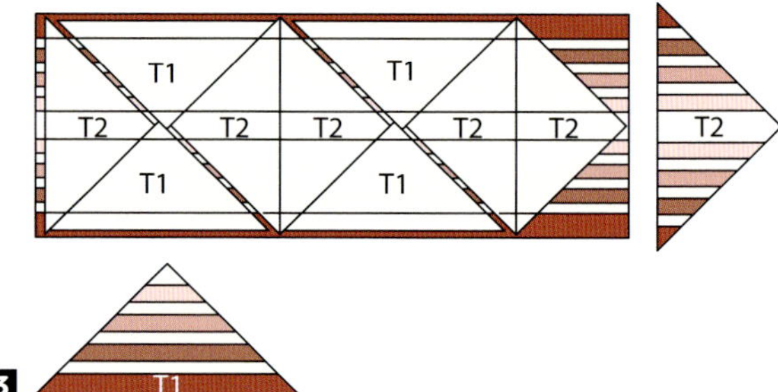

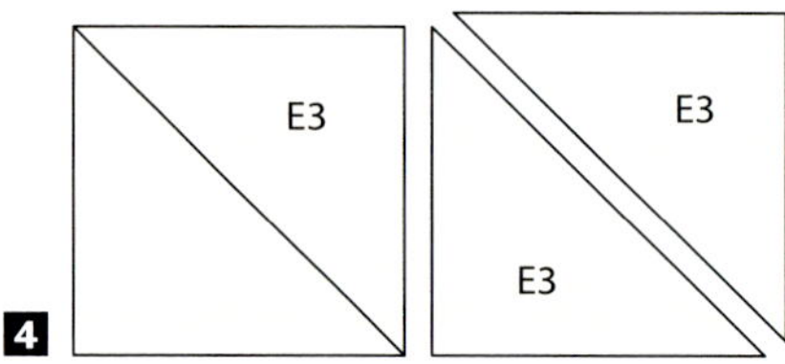

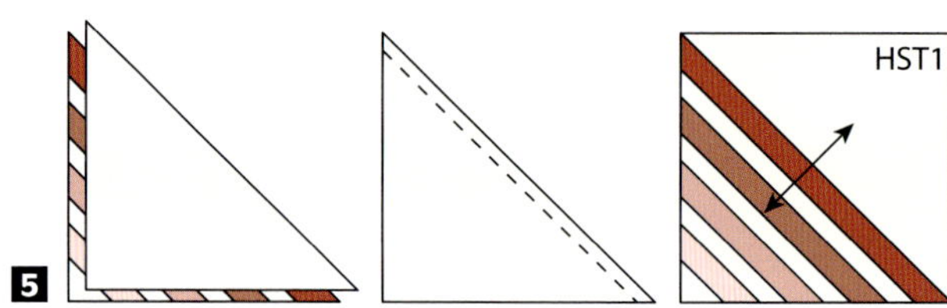

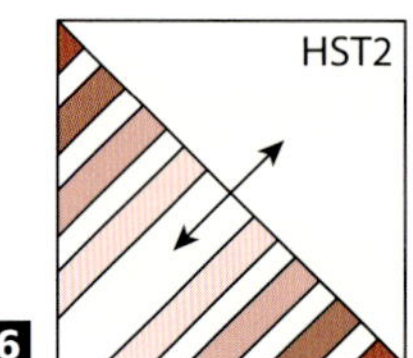

Quilt Assembly

1. Sew the HST1 blocks, HST2 blocks, and E4 squares together in the following order, as shown, to make Rows 1–6. Be sure to note the orientation of the HSTs and press in the direction indicated by the arrow in each row's diagram.

- **Rows 1 and 6:** HST2 + E4 + HST1 + HST1 + E4 + HST2 (press seams toward the right)
- **Rows 2 and 5:** E4 + HST2 + HST1 + HST1 + HST2 + E4 (press seams toward the left)
- **Rows 3 and 4:** HST1 + HST1 + HST2 + HST2 + HST1 + HST1 (press seams toward the right)

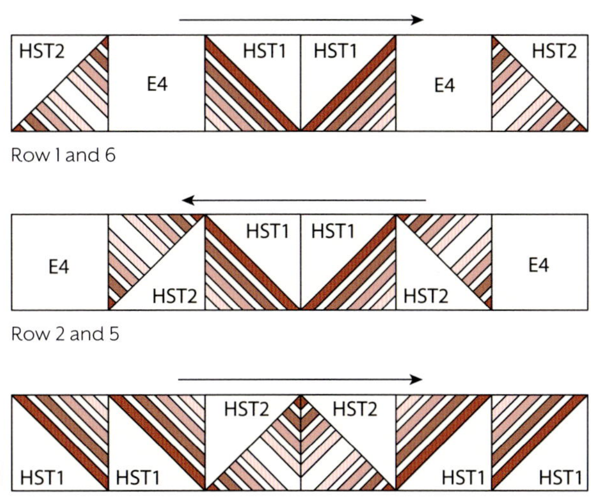

2. Arrange the rows in order 1–6 from top to bottom and sew together. Press the seams open to complete the Sunglow Quilt top.

3. Finish the quilt as desired (see Quilt Finishing, page 17).

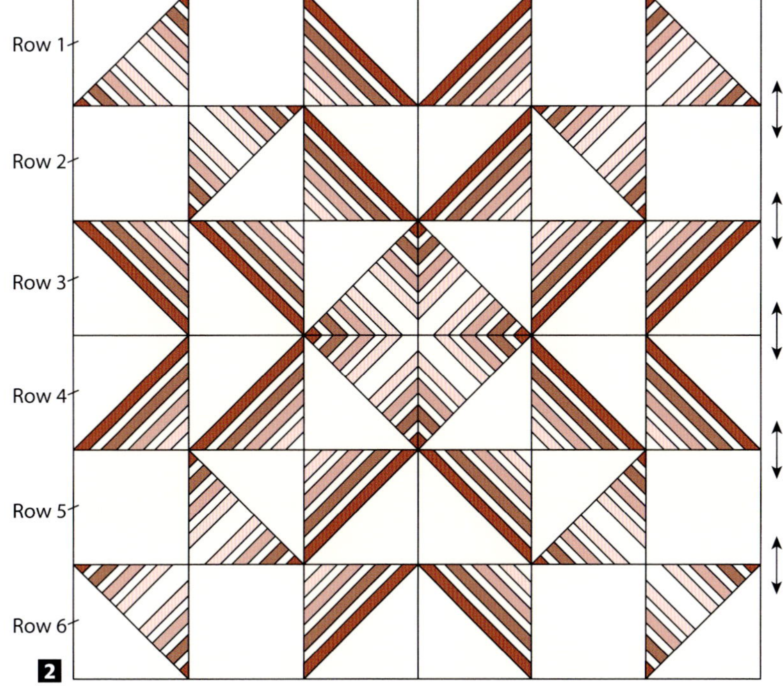

AUTUMN

Autumn is a season of change and the projects in this chapter celebrate the beauty found in the transition. The September Stargazer Quilt (page 78) twinkles in a constellation of stars in the autumn night sky as the days grow shorter and the nights longer. The Last Leaves Table Runner (page 84) shows off the rich colors of the changing maple leaves before they are swept from the branches and fall to blanket the ground. As the leaves take flight, so do Canadian geese heading south before winter. The Migration Quilt (page 90) is a modern take on their ancient rhythm of relocating to a temperate climate each fall and spring. And the Cabin Game Board (page 94) is the perfect companion for gathering together with loved ones around a cozy game of checkers or chess as the temperatures start to fall outside.

SEPTEMBER STARGAZER QUILT

Finished Block Size: 19″ × 19″ || **Finished Quilt:** 62″ × 62″

The September Stargazer Quilt is inspired by warm autumn nights spent outdoors. As the sun sinks past the horizon, the twinkling stars start to appear in the sky offering a beautiful backdrop to friends swapping jokes and stories around bonfires, children laughing and chasing each other across neighborhood backyards, fans cheering their team from the sidelines of hometown sports games, and fireflies blinking as they dance through the air. Be sure to share your project online with the hashtag **#septemberstargazerquilt**

FABRICS & SUPPLIES

Yardages are based on 42″ wide fabric.

Brown (Fabric A): ⅛ yard or 1 FE

Dark orange (Fabric B): ⅛ yard or 1 FE

Dark gold (Fabric C): ⅛ yard or 1 FE

Light brown (Fabric D): ⅛ yard or 1 FE

Peach (Fabric E): ⅛ yard or 1 FE

Light pink (Fabric F): ⅛ yard or 1 FE

Dusty pink (Fabric G): ⅛ yard or 1 FE

Light blue (Fabric H): ⅛ yard or 1 FE

Medium blue (Fabric I): ⅛ yard or 1 FE

Cream (Background Fabric J): 3¾ yards

Binding: ⅝ yard

Backing: 4 yards

Material Notes

The fabrics used in this quilt are Art Gallery Fabrics Chocolate, Sienna Brick, Raw Gold, Toasty Walnut, Shrimpy, Blushing, Cinnamon, Northern Waters, Ocean Fog, and Southern Stars.

CUTTING INSTRUCTIONS

Label each piece as specified in the parenthesis in the cutting lists. For each color, label the pieces with the fabric color letter and the number in parenthesis. For example, a 2½″ × 2½″ square from Fabric B should be labeled B1.

Fabrics A–I

Use the diagrams to cut the following pieces from each ⅛ yard or FE:

- 1 square 3¼″ × 3¼″ (4)
- 4 squares 3″ × 3″ (2)
- 4 squares 2½″ × 2½″ (1)
- 2 rectangles 2″ × 13″ (3)

Fabric J

Cut 2 strips 5½″ × WOF; subcut into:

- 9 squares 5½″ × 5½″ (J2)
- 5 squares 4½″ × 4½″ (J1)

Cut 6 strips 4½″ × WOF; subcut into:

- 36 rectangles 4½″ × 6″ (J3)
- 4 squares 4½″ × 4½″ (J1)

Cut 8 strips 3½″ × WOF; subcut into:

- 36 rectangles 3½″ × 5″ (J10)
- 36 squares 3½″ × 3½″ (J8)

Cut 1 strip 3¼″ × WOF; subcut into:

- 9 squares 3¼″ × 3¼″ (J5)

Cut 6 strips 3″ × WOF; sew together end-to-end, and cut into:

- 2 strips 3″ × 62½″ (J12)
- 2 strips 3″ × 57½″ (J11)

Cut 19 strips 2″ × WOF; subcut into:

- 18 rectangles 2″ × 13″ (J4)
- 36 rectangles 2″ × 8″ (J7)
- 36 rectangles 2″ × 3½″ (J9)
- 36 squares 2″ × 2″ (J6)

Binding Fabric

Cut 7 strips 2½″ × WOF

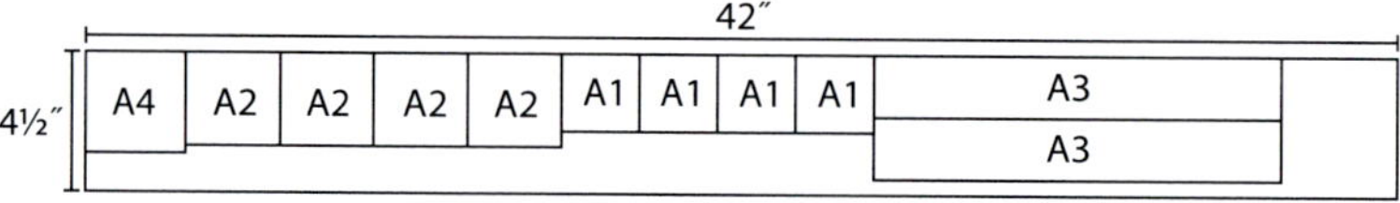

Eighth yard

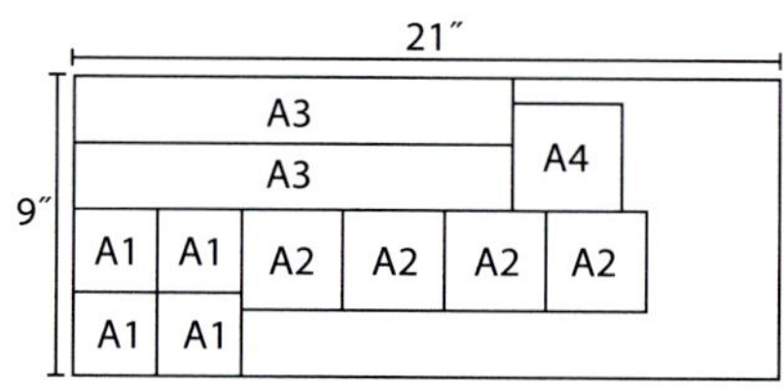

Fat eighth

Diamond-In-a-Square Units

Seam allowances are ¼″ unless otherwise noted. Pressing direction is indicated by the arrows in the diagrams.

1. Mark a diagonal line, corner-to-corner, on the wrong side of 4 A1 squares.

2. Place 2 A1 squares RST on the diagonal corners of a J1 square, as shown.

3. Sew on both marked lines. Cut away the excess corner fabric ¼″ away from the sewn line. Press the seams toward Fabric A.

4. Repeat Steps 1–3 with the remaining 2 A1 squares on the remaining corners of the same J1 square to complete 1 diamond-in-a-square unit.

5. Trim the diamond-in-a-square unit to 4½″ × 4½″ if needed, making sure to leave ¼″ seam allowance at the points of the diamond.

6. Repeat Steps 1–5 with the 4 B1, C1, D1, E1, F1, G1, H1, and I1 squares paired with the remaining J1 squares to make a total of 9 diamond-in-a-square units, one per fabric color.

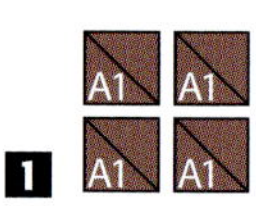

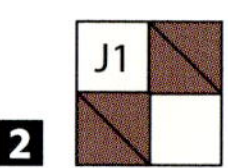

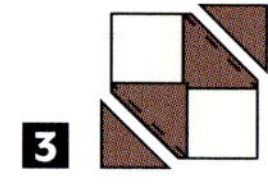

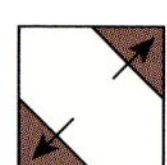

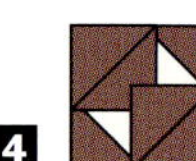

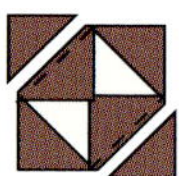

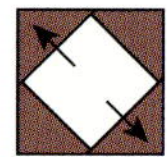

Flying Geese Units

1. Mark a diagonal line, corner-to-corner, on the wrong side of 4 A2 squares.

2. Pair A2 squares with a J2 square and follow the instructions for 4-at-a-Time Flying Geese (page 14) to make 4 A/J flying geese. Trim each flying geese to 2½″ × 4½″, making sure to leave a ¼″ seam allowance at the center point.

3. Repeat Steps 1–2 with 4 B2, C2, D2, E2, F2, G2, H2, and I2 squares paired with the remaining J2 squares to make a total of 36 flying geese, 4 in each fabric color.

4. Sew 1 J3 rectangle on the bottom of 1 A/J flying geese. Press the seam toward J3 to make 1 flying geese unit measuring 4½″ × 8″.

5. Repeat Step 4 with all remaining flying geese paired with J3 rectangles to make a total of 36 flying geese units, 4 in each fabric color.

FLYING GEESE UNITS

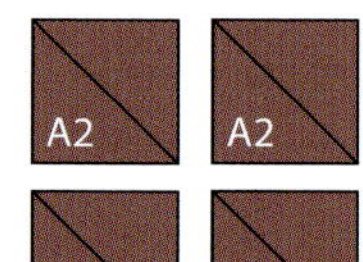

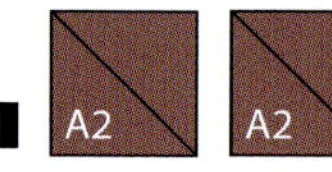

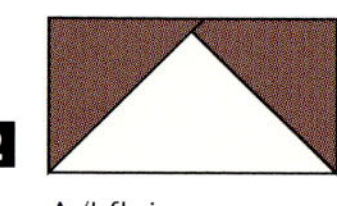

A/J flying geese

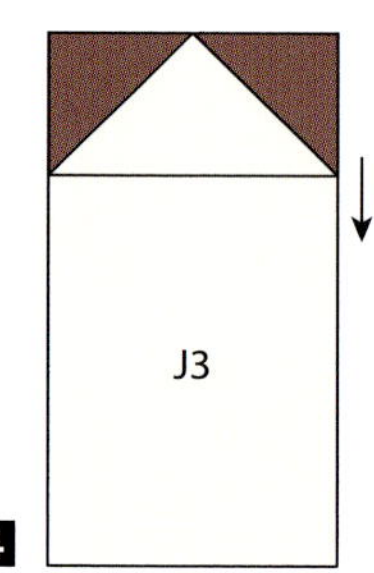

Flying geese unit

4-Patch Units

1. Sew 1 A3 rectangle and 1 J4 rectangle together lengthwise with a ¼″ seam. Press the seam toward Fabric A.

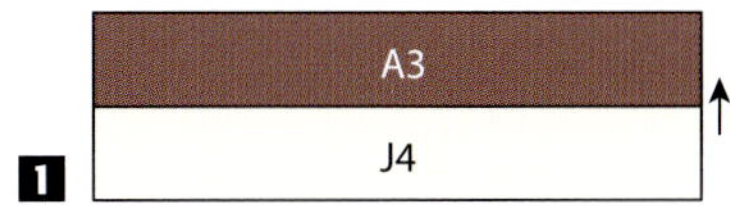

2. Cut the strip set into 6 units 2″ × 3½″.

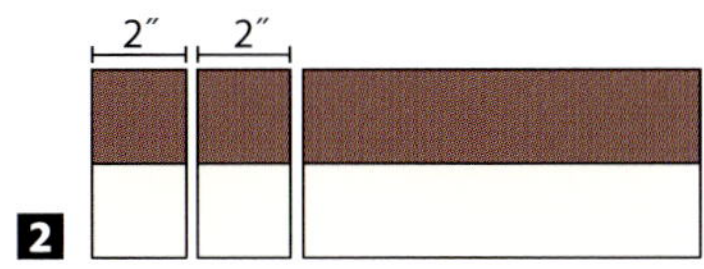

3. Repeat Steps 1–2 with all A3, B3, C3, D3, E3, F3, G3, H3, and I3 rectangles paired with the remaining J4 rectangles to make a total of 12 units in each fabric color.

4. Sew 2 units of the same color together, seams nesting, and press the seam open to make a 4-patch unit measuring 3½″ × 3½″.

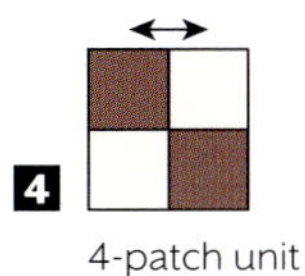

4-patch unit

5. Repeat Step 4 with a total of 8 units from each fabric color to make a total of four 4-patch units in each color. Set aside the remaining 4 units from each color.

Half-Square Triangle Units

HALF-SQUARE TRIANGLE UNITS

1. Mark 2 diagonal lines, corner-to-corner in both directions, on the wrong side of all J5 squares.

2. Pair 1 J5 square with 1 A4 square and follow the instructions for 4-at-a-Time Half-Square Triangles (page 12) to make 4 A/J HSTs. Trim each to 2″ × 2″ square.

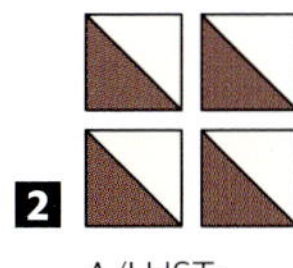

A/J HSTs

3. Repeat Step 2 with B4, C4, D4, E4, F4, G4, H4, and I4 squares paired with the remaining J5 squares to make a total of 36 HSTs, 4 in each fabric color.

4. Sew 1 J6 square to the bottom of 1 HST. Press the seam toward J6.

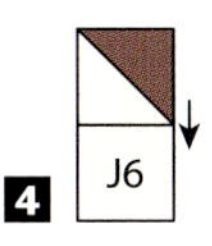

5. Arrange 1 unit from Step 4 with 1 unit set aside from the 4-patch unit construction in Step 5 of 4-Patch Units (above). Sew together and press the seam open to make 1 HST unit.

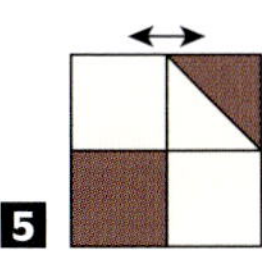

HST unit

6. Repeat Steps 4–5 with all HSTs, J6 squares, and remaining units from the 4-patch unit construction to make a total of 36 HST units, 4 in each fabric color.

Block Assembly

1. Arrange 1 J7 rectangle, 1 J8 square, 1 J9 rectangle, 1 J10 rectangle, 1 4-patch unit, and 1 HST unit of the same fabric color as the 4-patch unit into 3 rows, as shown. Sew the pieces into rows, and press the seams toward Fabric J.

2. Sew the rows together and press the seams away from the center row to complete 1 corner unit measuring 8˝ × 8˝.

3. Repeat Steps 1–2 to make a total of 36 corner units, 4 in each fabric color.

4. Arrange 4 corner units of the same fabric color with 4 flying geese units of a second color into rows. Place 1 diamond-in-a-square unit of the second fabric color in the center of the middle row, as shown. Pair whichever 2 colors you prefer.

5. Sew the units into rows and press the seams open.

6. Sew the rows together. Press the seams open to make 1 Stargazer block measuring 19½˝ × 19½˝ from raw edge to raw edge.

7. Repeat Steps 4–6 with the remaining corner units, flying geese units, and diamond-in-a-square units to make a total of 9 Stargazer blocks. Make sure to use different colors for the flying geese/diamond-in-a-square units and the corner units.

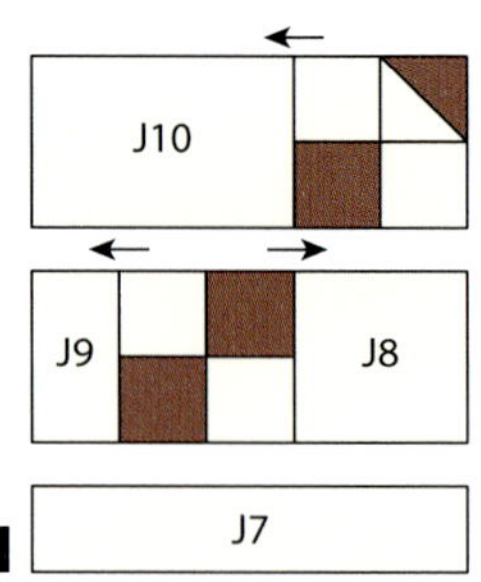

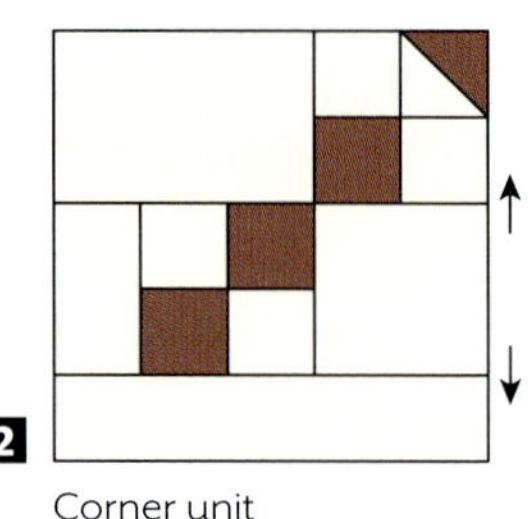

Corner unit

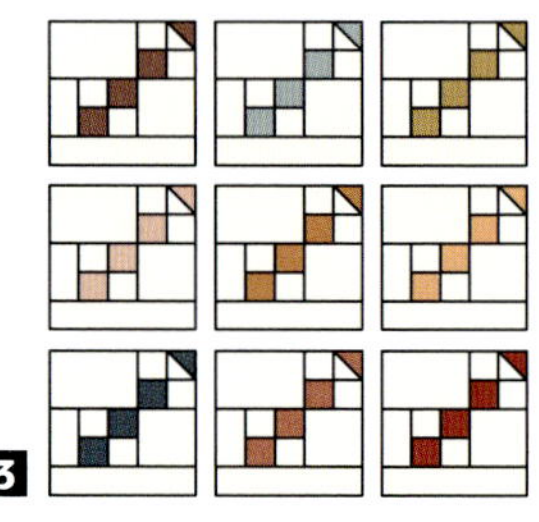

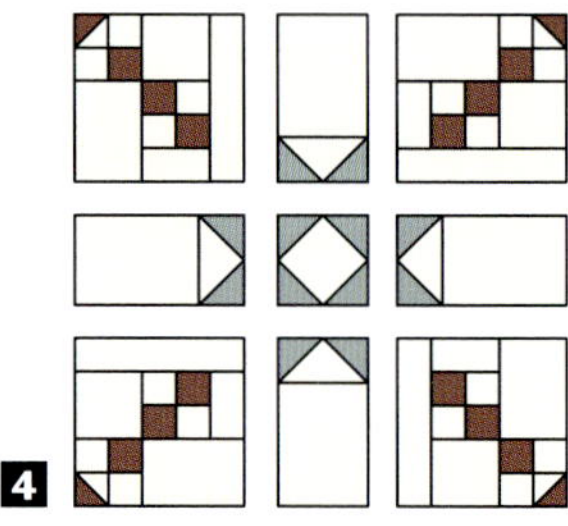

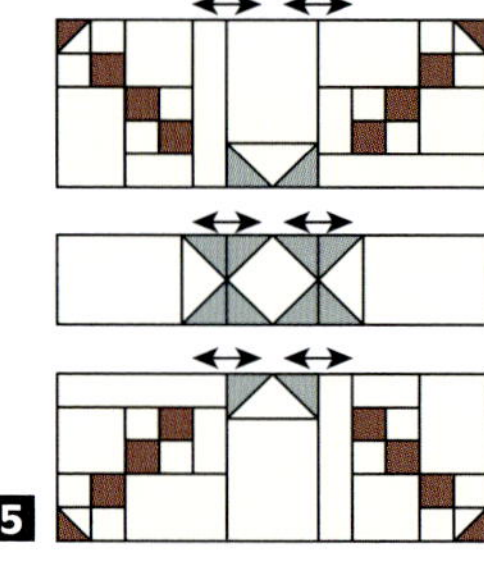

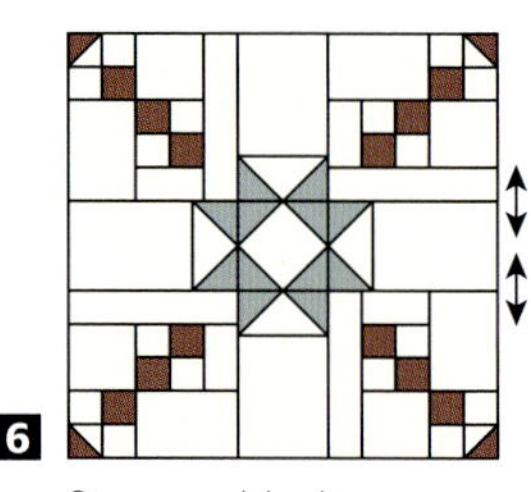

Stargazer block

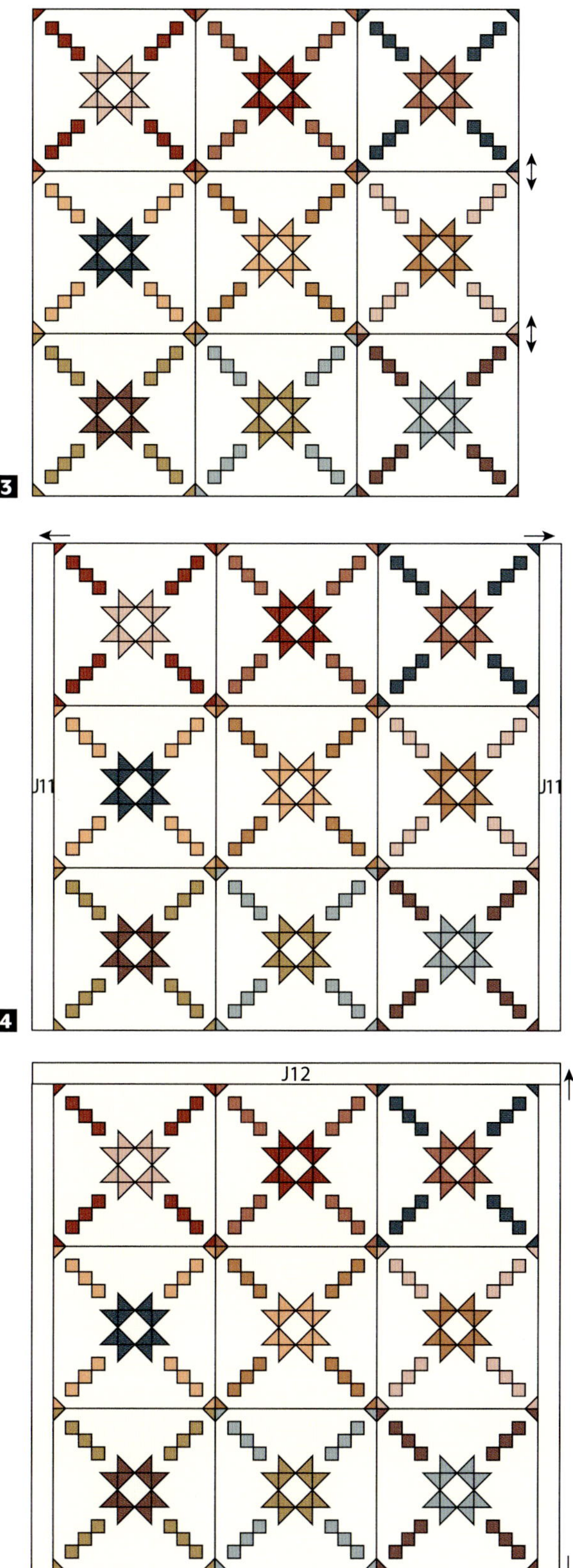

Final Assembly

1. Arrange the Stargazer blocks into 3 rows of 3 each. You can arrange the colors however you would like.

2. Sew the blocks into rows and press the seams open.

3. Sew the rows together and press the seams open.

4. Sew the J11 border strips to the left and right sides of the quilt top. Press the seams toward the J11 strips.

5. Sew the J12 border strips to the top and bottom of the quilt top. Press the seams toward the J12 strips to complete the September Stargazer quilt top.

6. Finish the quilt as desired (see Quilt Finishing, page 17).

LAST LEAVES TABLE RUNNER

Finished Leaf Block Size: 7½˝ × 7½˝ || **Finished Quilt:** 20˝ × 64˝

The Last Leaves Table Runner is inspired by swirling maple leaves turning vibrant shades of red, orange, and yellow before being swept by the blustery fall winds to carpet the ground in a final blaze of autumn colors. This table runner is the perfect way to enjoy those brilliant fall colors a little longer. Whether adding the finishing touch to your fall holiday table or warmth to your wall or dresser top, this cozy design celebrates autumn's beauty long after the last leaves have fallen. Be sure to share your project online with the hashtag **#lastleavestablerunner**

FABRICS & SUPPLIES

Yardages are based on 42˝ wide fabric.

Burgundy (Fabric A): ¼ yard

Dusty purple (Fabric B): ⅛ yard

Red (Fabric C): ¼ yard

Pink (Fabric D): ⅛ yard

Orange (Fabric E): ¼ yard

Yellow (Fabric F): ⅛ yard

Cream (Background Fabric G): 1⅛ yards

Binding: ½ yard

Backing: 2 yards

Material Notes

The fabrics used in this quilt are Art Gallery Fabrics Velvet, Thistle, Desert Dunes, Cinnamon, Sienna Brick, Queen Bee, Soft Sand, and Prairie House.

CUTTING INSTRUCTIONS

Label each piece as specified in the parenthesis in the cutting lists. For each color, label the pieces with the fabric color letter and the number in parenthesis. For example, a 3½˝ × 3½˝ square from Fabric C should be labeled C3.

Fabrics A, C, and E

Cut 1 strip 3½˝ × WOF; subcut into:

- 4 squares 3½˝ × 3½˝ (3)
- 2 squares 3¼˝ × 3¼˝ (1)

Cut 1 strip 2½˝ × WOF; subcut into:

- 8 squares 2½˝ × 2½˝ (2)
- 4 squares 2˝ × 2˝ (4)

Fabrics B, D, and F

Cut 1 strip 3¼˝ × WOF; subcut into:

- 2 squares 3¼˝ × 3¼˝ (1)
- 4 rectangles 2˝ × 5˝ (3)
- 4 squares 2½˝ × 2½˝ (2)

Background Fabric G

Cut 1 strip 8˝ × WOF; subcut into:

- 8 rectangles 8˝ × 4¼˝ (G8)

Cut 1 strip 4½˝ × WOF; subcut into:

- 6 squares 4½˝ × 4½˝ (G2)

Cut 1 strip 3¼˝ × WOF; subcut into:

- 12 squares 3¼˝ × 3¼˝ (G1)

Cut 3 strips 3˝ × WOF; sew together end-to-end, and cut:

- 2 strips 3˝ × 60½˝ (G9)

Cut 1 strip 2½˝ × WOF; subcut into:

- 2 strips 2½˝ × 20½˝ (G10)

Cut 2 strips 2¼˝ × WOF; subcut into:

- 24 squares 2¼˝ × 2¼˝ (G3)
- 12 squares 2˝ × 2˝ (G4)

Cut 2 strips 2˝ × WOF; subcut into:

- 24 rectangles 2˝ × 3½˝ (G5)

Cut 2 strips 1½˝ × WOF; subcut into:

- 12 rectangles 1½˝ × 3½˝ (G7)
- 12 rectangles 1½˝ × 2½˝ (G6)

Binding Fabric

Cut 5 strips 2½˝ × WOF

Basic Assembly

Seam allowances are ¼″ unless otherwise noted. Pressing direction is indicated by the arrows in the diagrams.

HALF-SQUARE TRIANGLES

1. Mark 2 diagonal lines on the wrong side of each G1 square.

2. Pair 1 G1 square and 1 A1 square and follow the directions for 4-at-a-Time Half-Square Triangles (page 12) to make 4 A/G HSTs. Press the seams toward Fabric A. Trim each HST to 2″ × 2″ square.

3. Repeat Step 2 with all A1, B1, C1, D1, E1, and F1 squares paired with G1 squares to make a total of 48 HSTs, 8 in each fabric color.

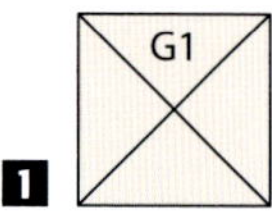

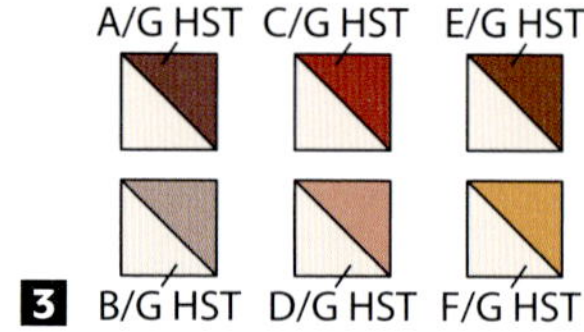

FLYING GEESE

1. Mark a diagonal line on the wrong side of 4 each of the A2, B2, C2, D2, E2, and F2 squares.

2. Pair each set of 4 squares from Step 1 with a G2 square and follow the directions for 4-at-a-Time Flying Geese (page 14) to make a total of 24 flying geese, 4 in each fabric color. Trim each flying geese unit to 2″ × 3½″ making sure to leave a ¼″ seam allowance at the center point.

FLYING GEESE

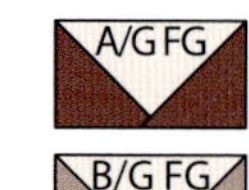

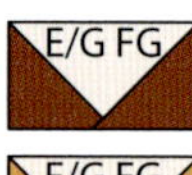

Light Leaf Units

1. Arrange 1 Fabric B flying geese, 2 Fabric B HSTs, 1 B3 rectangle, and 1 G4 square into 2 rows as shown. Sew the pieces into rows. Press the seams in the top row to the right and the seam in the bottom row to the left.

2. Sew the rows together and press the seam toward the bottom row.

3. Sew a G5 rectangle to the left side of the unit. Press the seam toward G5 to complete 1 light leaf B unit measuring 3½″ × 8″.

4. Repeat Steps 1–3 to make a total of 12 light leaf units, 4 each in the colors B, D, and F.

LIGHT LEAF UNITS

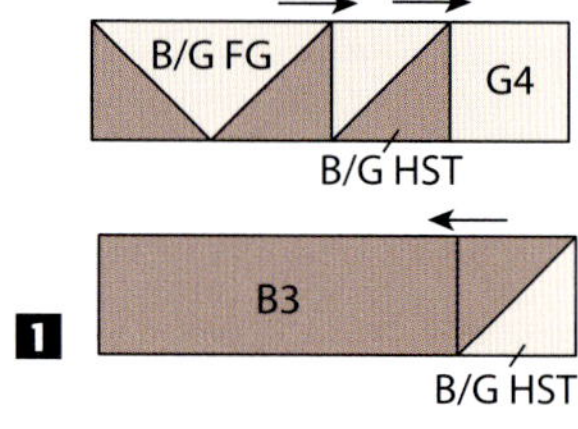

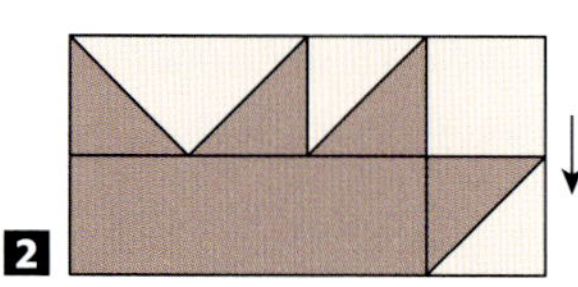

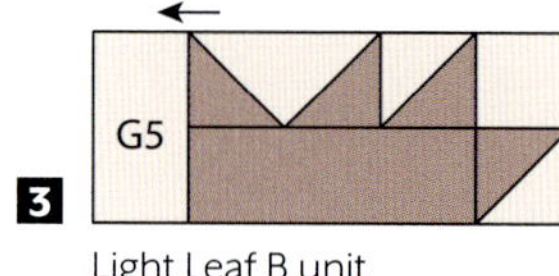

Light Leaf B unit

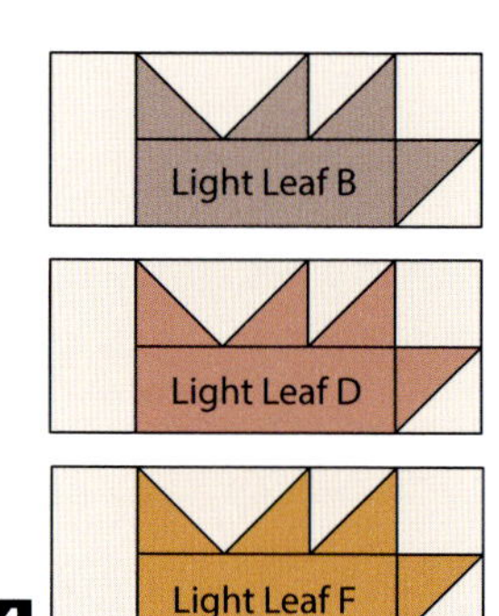

Dark Leaf Units

1. Arrange 1 Fabric A flying geese, 1 Fabric A HST, 1 A3 square, and 1 G5 rectangle into 2 rows as shown. Sew the pieces into rows. Press the seam toward A3 in the top row and toward G5 in the bottom row.

2. Sew the rows together and press the seam toward the top row to complete 1 dark leaf A unit measuring 5″ × 5″. Repeat Steps 1 and 2 to make a total of 12 dark leaf units, 4 each in the colors A, C, and E.

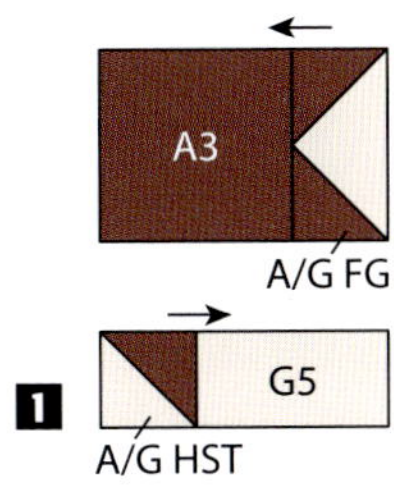

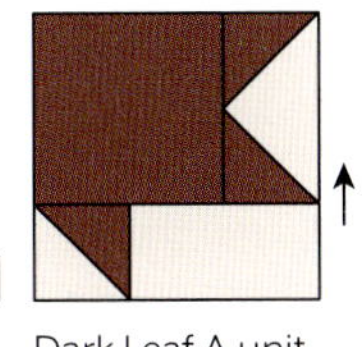

Dark Leaf A unit

Stem Units

1. Mark a diagonal line on the wrong side of each G3 square.

2. Place 1 G3 square RST on the bottom right corner of 1 A2 square as shown.

3. Sew on the marked line. Cut away the excess corner fabric ¼″ from the sewn line, and press the seam toward Fabric G.

4. Repeat Steps 2–3 with a second G3 square on the top left corner of the A2 square to make 1 stem unit measuring 2½″ × 2½″.

5. Repeat Steps 1–4 with 4 each of the A2, C2, and E2 squares paired with the remaining G3 squares to make a total of 12 stems, 4 in each fabric color.

6. Sew 1 G6 rectangle to the bottom of each stem. Press the seams toward G6.

7. Sew 1 G7 rectangle to the left side of each stem. Press the seams toward G7.

8. Sew each remaining A/G HST to an A4 square, each C/G HST to a C4 square, and each E/G HST to an E4 square, as shown. Press the seams toward the squares to make a total of 4 units in each color.

9. Sew 1 Fabric A unit from Step 8 to the top of 1 Fabric A unit from Step 7. Press the seam up to make 1 Stem A unit measuring 3½″ × 5″.

10. Repeat Step 9 to make a total of 12 stem units, 4 each in Fabrics A, C, and E.

STEM UNITS

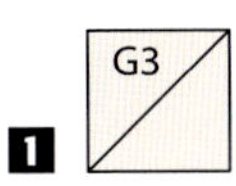

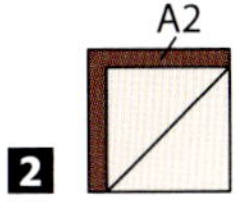

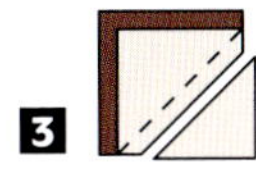

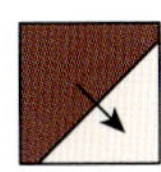

Stem

5

Stem A

Stem C

Stem E

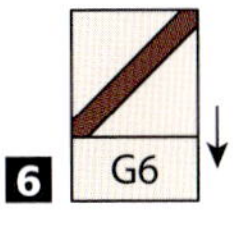

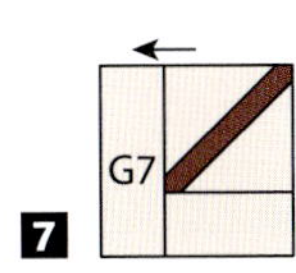

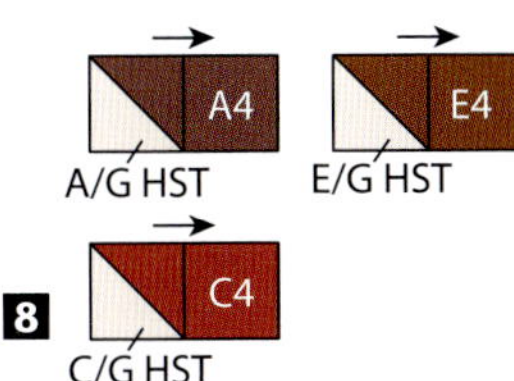

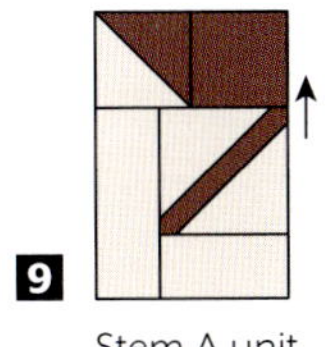

Stem A unit

10

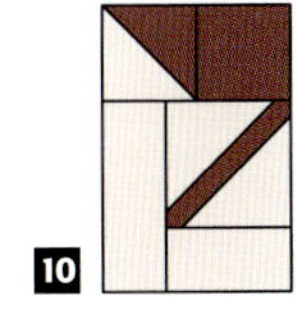
Stem A unit

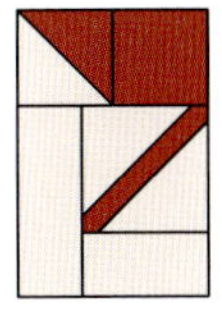
Stem C unit

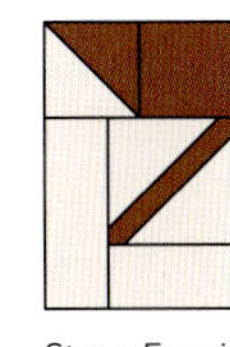
Stem E unit

Leaf Block Assembly

1. Sew 1 Dark Leaf A unit to the right of 1 Fabric A stem unit. Press the seam toward the dark leaf unit.

2. Sew 1 Light Leaf B unit to the top of the unit from Step 1. Press the seam toward the light leaf unit to make 1 A/B Leaf block measuring 8˝ × 8˝.

3. Repeat Steps 1–2 to make a total of 12 Leaf blocks, 4 in each of the following combinations: A/B, C/D, and E/F.

1

Stem A unit Dark leaf A unit

2

A/B Leaf block

Table Runner Assembly

1. Sew 1 G8 rectangle to the top and bottom of each A/B leaf to make 4 A/B leaf sections. Press the seams toward the G8 rectangles.

2. Sew 1 C/D leaf to the top of 1 E/F leaf with the stems meeting on the left side. Press the seam open to make leaf set A. Make 2.

3. Sew 1 C/D leaf to the top of 1 E/F leaf mirroring the unit from Step 2. Press the seam open to make leaf set B. Make 2.

4. Sew 1 A/B leaf section to the left side of each leaf set A as shown. Press the seams open to make 2 block As. Each should measure 15½˝ × 15½˝.

5. Sew 1 A/B leaf section to the right side of each leaf set B as shown, mirroring the Step 5 block. Press the seams open to make 2 block Bs. Each should measure 15½˝ × 15½˝.

6. Arrange the 4 blocks in an A + B + A + B column. Sew together. Press the seams open.

TABLE RUNNER ASSEMBLY

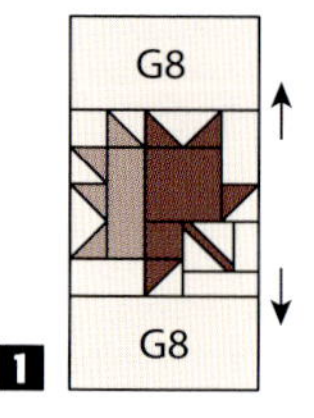

1

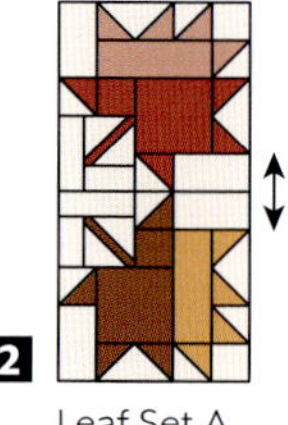

2

Leaf Set A

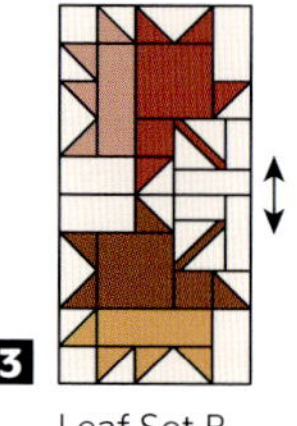

3

Leaf Set B

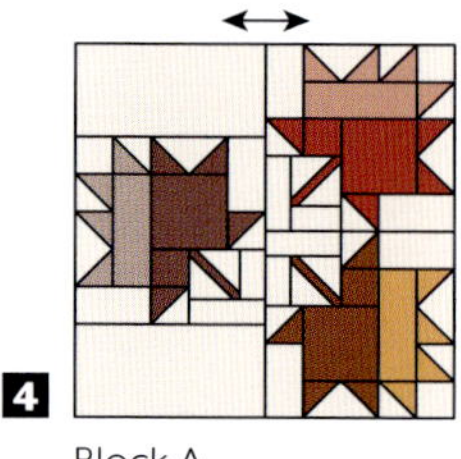

4

Block A

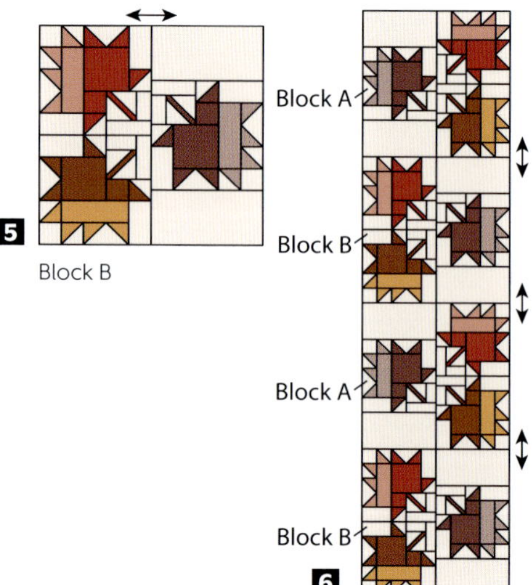

5

Block B

6

7. Sew a G9 strip to the right and left sides of the table runner. Press the seams toward G9.

8. Sew a G10 strip to the top and bottom of the table runner. Press the seams toward G10 to complete the Last Leaves Table Runner quilt top.

9. Finish the quilted table runner as desired (see Quilt Finishing, page 17).

MIGRATION QUILT

Finished Block Size: 24˝ × 66˝ || **Finished Quilt:** 60˝ × 74˝

The Migration Quilt is inspired by the annual migrations of wild geese. Their distinctive triangular shape in the sky is ubiquitous with fall and signals the coming of cold weather. Then, their return in the spring serves as a reminder that warmer days will soon arrive. This modern interpretation of nature's rhythm is striking in its simplicity and a cozy seasonal addition to the contemporary home. Be sure to share your project online with the hashtag **#migrationquilt**

FABRICS & SUPPLIES

Yardages are based on 42˝ wide fabric.

Dusty purple (Fabric A): ½ yard

Burgundy (Fabric B): ½ yard

Orange (Fabric C): ½ yard

Yellow (Fabric D): ¼ yard

Tan (Fabric E): ½ yard

Cream (Background Fabric F): 2½ yards

Binding: ⅝ yard

Backing: 3⅞ yards (using a horizontal seam)

Material Notes

The fabrics used in this quilt are Art Gallery Fabrics Thistle, Candied Cherry, Sienna Brick, Queen Bee, Toasty Walnut, Coming Home Ballerina, and Great Plains Red Rock.

CUTTING INSTRUCTIONS

Label each piece as specified in the parenthesis in the cutting lists.

Fabric A

Cut 2 strips 7˝ × WOF; subcut into:

- 8 squares 7˝ × 7˝ (A1)
- 2 rectangles 6½˝ × 12½˝ (A2)

Fabric B

Cut 2 strips 7˝ × WOF; subcut into:

- 8 squares 7˝ × 7˝ (B1)
- 2 rectangles 6½˝ × 12½˝ (B2)

Fabric C

Cut 2 strips 7˝ × WOF; subcut into:

- 8 squares 7˝ × 7˝ (C1)
- 2 rectangles 6½˝ × 12½˝ (C2)

Fabric D

Cut 1 strip 7˝ × WOF; subcut into:

- 6 squares 7˝ × 7˝ (D1)

Fabric E

Cut 1 strip 7˝ × WOF; subcut into:

- 4 squares 7˝ × 7˝ (E1)

Cut 1 strip 6½˝ × WOF; subcut into:

- 2 rectangles 6½˝ × 12½˝ (E2)

Fabric F

Cut 2 strips 12½˝ × WOF; subcut into:

- 2 rectangles 12½˝ × 24½˝ (F3)
- 4 squares 6½˝ × 6½˝ (F2)

Cut 3 strips 7˝ × WOF; subcut into:

- 18 squares 7˝ × 7˝ (F1)

Cut 8 strips 4½˝ × WOF; sew together end-to-end, and subcut into:

- 3 strips 4½˝ × 66½˝ (F4)
- 2 strips 4½˝ × 60½˝ (F5)

Binding Fabric

Cut 8 strips 2½˝ × WOF

Quilted by Sandy Saengsuk of Thai Charm LLC

Half-Square Triangles

Seam allowances are ¼″ unless otherwise noted. Pressing direction is indicated by the arrows in the diagrams.

1. Mark a diagonal line, corner-to-corner, on the wrong side of all A1, B1, C1, D1, and E1 squares.

2. Pair 1 A1 and 1 F1 square and follow the directions for 2-at-a-Time Half-Square Triangles (page 12) to make 2 A/F HSTs. Trim both HSTs to 6½″ × 6½″.

3. Repeat Step 2 to make the following total numbers of HSTs per fabric combination:

A/F: 12 HSTs (6 sets)

A/B: 4 HSTs (2 sets)

B/F: 8 HSTs (4 sets)

B/C: 4 HSTs (2 sets)

C/F: 8 HSTs (4 sets)

C/D: 4 HSTs (2 sets)

D/F: 4 HSTs (2 sets)

D/E: 4 HSTs (2 sets)

E/F: 4 HSTs (2 sets)

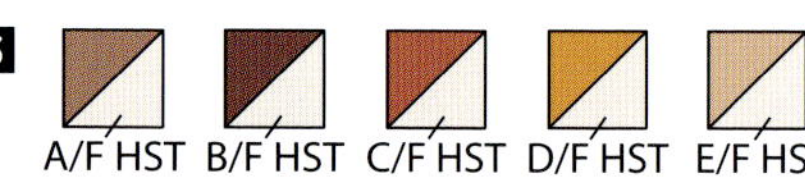

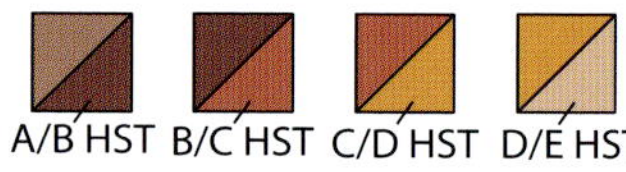

MIGRATION BLOCK ASSEMBLY

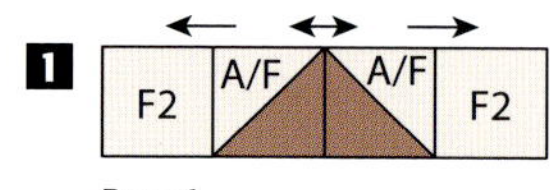

Row 1

Row 2

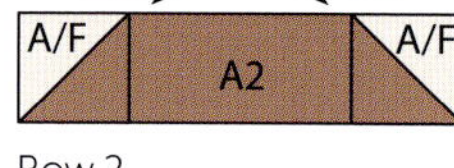

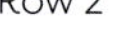

Row 3

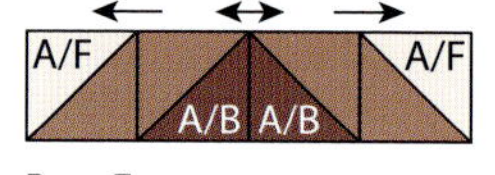

Row 4

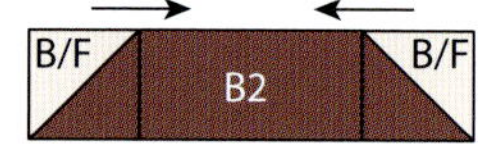

Row 5

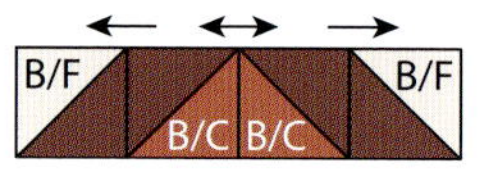

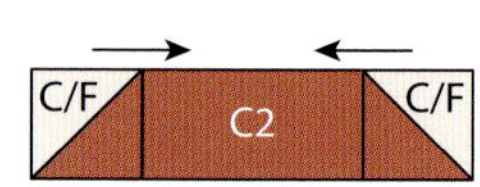

Row 6

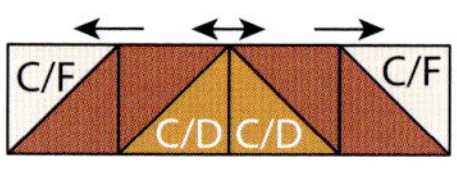

Row 7

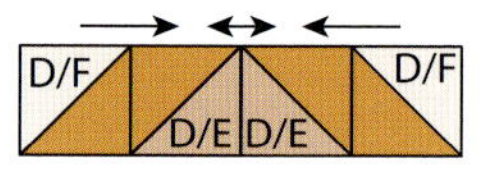

Row 8

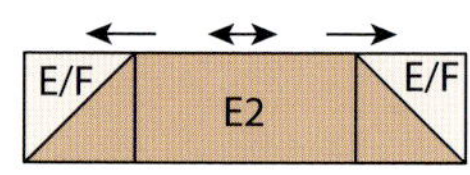

Row 9

Migration Block Assembly

1. Arrange the following pieces in order shown. Sew together into Rows 1–9. Press all seams as shown so the seams will nest.

Row 1: F2 + A/F + A/F + F2

Row 2: A/F + A2 + A/F

Row 3: A/F + A/B + A/B + A/F

Row 4: B/F + B2 + B/F

Row 5: B/F + B/C + B/C + B/F

Row 6: C/F + C2 + C/F

Row 7: C/F + C/D + C/D + C/F

Row 8: D/F + D/E + D/E + D/F

Row 9: E/F + E2 + E/F

2. Sew the rows together and press the seams all in one direction.

3. Sew 1 F3 rectangle to the bottom of the Step 2 unit. Press the seam toward F3 to complete 1 Migration block.

4. Repeat Steps 1–3 to make a second Migration block.

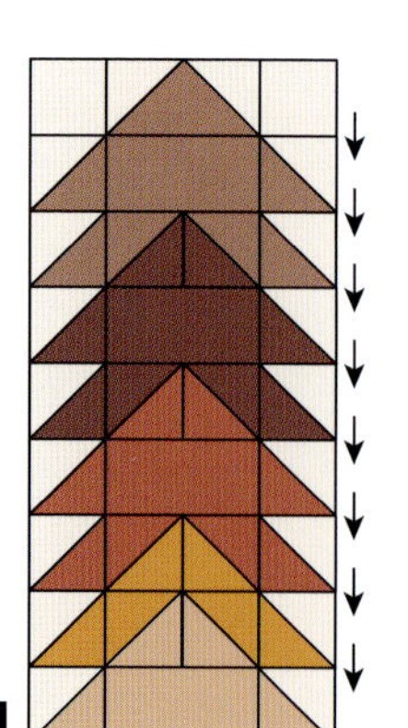

Quilt Assembly

1. Arrange the Migration blocks in opposite directions with an F4 sashing strip between them. Sew together and press the seams toward the F4 strip.

2. Sew F4 strips to the left and right sides of the quilt top. Press the seams toward the F4 strips.

3. Sew F5 strips to the top and bottom of the quilt top. Press the seams toward the F5 strips to complete the Migration Quilt top.

4. Finish the quilt as desired (see Quilt Finishing, page 17).

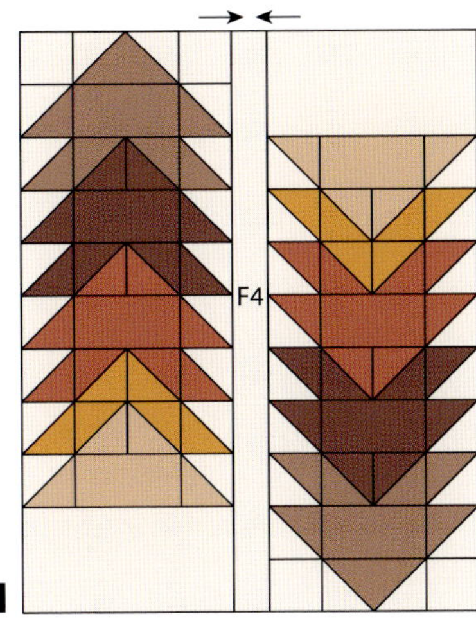

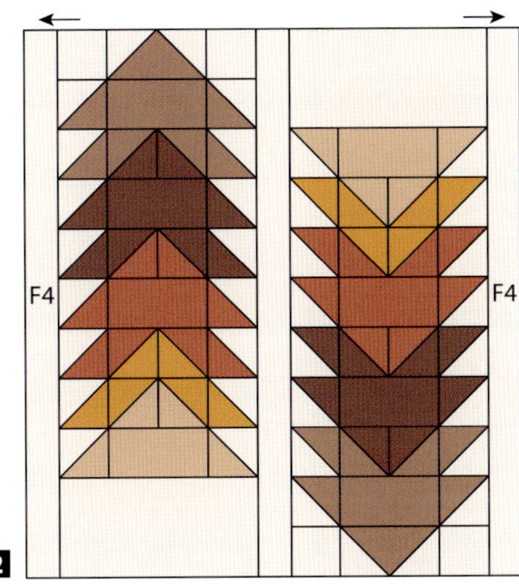

CABIN GAME BOARD

Finished Board: 10″ × 16″ (unfolded)

The Cabin Game Board is an interchangeable checkers and chess board with a handy zippered pocket to store the game pieces. Whether playing in the car on the way to visit family over the holidays or stashed in a backpack to pull out while camping or for a cabin weekend, this game board is the perfect activity for all ages to enjoy together on the go. Be sure to share your project online with the hashtag **#cabingameboard**

FABRICS & SUPPLIES

Yardages are based on 42″ wide fabric.

Tan (Fabric A): ⅛ yard

Light brown (Fabric B): ⅛ yard

Medium brown (Fabric C): ⅛ yard

Dark brown (Fabric D): ⅛ yard

Dark green (Fabric E): ⅛ yard

Dark teal (Fabric F): ⅛ yard

Medium teal (Fabric G): ⅛ yard

Light teal (Fabric H): ⅛ yard

Cream (Background Fabric I): ⅓ yard

Accent (Fabric J): ⅓ yard

Exterior (Fabric K): ⅓ yard

Pellon 987F Fusible Fleece (or similar): ⅓ yard

Metal prong snap fastener (can substitute a plastic snap or 1″ square hook-and-loop tape)

#5 nylon coil handbag zipper: 7″ (or a 7″ #5 separating zipper)

Game Pieces

The board is suited to hold 1″ round game pieces. Checkers requires 12 pieces in 2 different colors. Chess requires 16 pieces in 2 different colors with rank indicated on each piece. Consider simple 1″ round wood slices, small felt circles, or buttons in two colors instead of formal game pieces.

Material Notes

The fabrics used in this quilt are Art Gallery Fabrics Vanilla Custard, Toasty Walnut, Sienna Brick, Chocolate, Evergreen, Zambia Stone, Swimming Pool, Ocean Fog, White Linen, Trouvaille Routes Sparkler, and Timberline Dusk.

CUTTING INSTRUCTIONS

Label each piece as specified in the parenthesis in the cutting lists. For each color, label the pieces with the fabric color letter and the number in parenthesis. For example, a 1½″ × 8½″ strip from Fabric B should be labeled B1.

Fabrics A–H

Cut 1 strip 1½″ × 8½″ (1)

Fabric I

Cut 3 strips 1½″ × WOF; subcut into:

- 10 strips 1½″ × 8½″ (I1)

Cut 1 strip 4½″ × WOF; subcut into:

- 2 rectangles 4½″ × 10½″ (I2)
- 1 rectangle 2½″ × 10½″ (I3) for pocket lining

Fabric J

Cut 1 strip 2½″ × WOF; subcut into:

- 1 rectangle 2½″ × 16½″ (J1)
- 1 rectangle 2½″ × 10½″ (J2) for pocket front

Cut 1 strip 2″ × WOF; subcut into:

- 2 rectangles 2″ × 10½″ (J3) for pocket binding
- 2 rectangles 1½″ × 5″ (J4) for zipper tabs

Cut 2 strips 2″ × WOF (J5) and sew together for binding

Fabric K

Cut 1 rectangle 8½″ × 16½″ (K1)

Fusible Fleece

Cut 1 rectangle 10½″ × 16½″ (FF1)

Cut 1 rectangle 2½″ × 10½″ (FF2)

Unit Assembly

Seam allowances are ¼″ unless otherwise noted. Pressing direction is indicated by the arrows in the diagrams.

INTERIOR PANEL

1. Arrange 4 I1 strips between the A1, C1, E1, and G1 strips in the following order: A1 + I1 + C1 + I1 + E1 + I1 + G1 + I1. Sew together. Press the seams away from Fabric I.

2. Cut the strip set into 4 segments each measuring 1½″ × 8½″ (segment A).

3. Arrange 4 I1 strips between the B1, D1, F1, and H1 strips in the following order: I1 + B1 + I1 + D1 + I1 + F1 + I1 + H1. Sew together. Press the seams away from Fabric I.

4. Cut the strip set into 4 segments each measuring 1½″ × 8½″ (segment B).

5. Alternate the B and A segments, as shown, starting with segment B. Sew together, and press the seams open.

6. Sew I1 strips to the top and bottom. Press the seams toward the I1 strips.

7. Sew I2 rectangles to the left and right sides. Press the seams toward the I2 rectangles to complete the interior panel.

EXTERIOR PANEL

1. Sew the J1 rectangle to the top long edge of the K1 rectangle. Press the seam toward the K1 rectangle.

2. Follow the fusible fleece manufacturer's instructions to fuse the FF1 rectangle to the wrong side of the Step 1 unit.

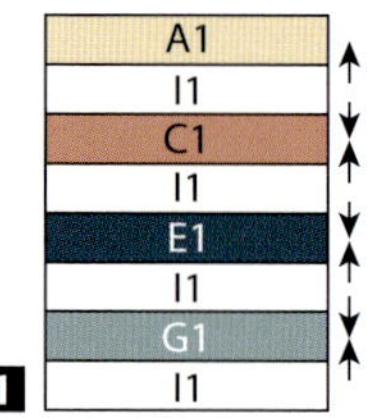

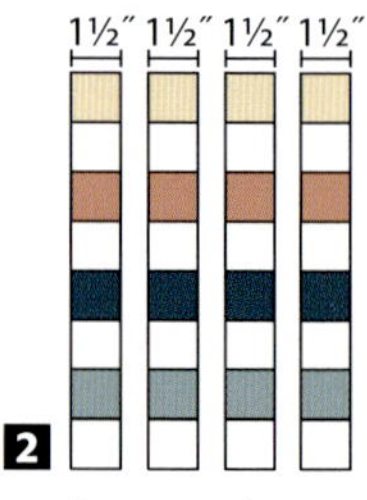

Segment A

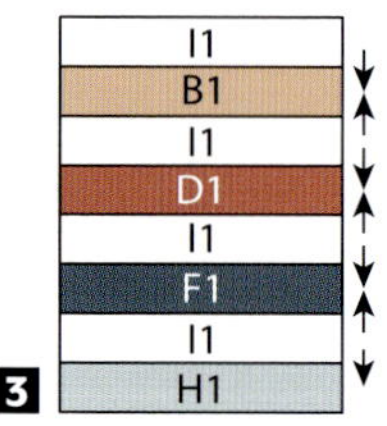

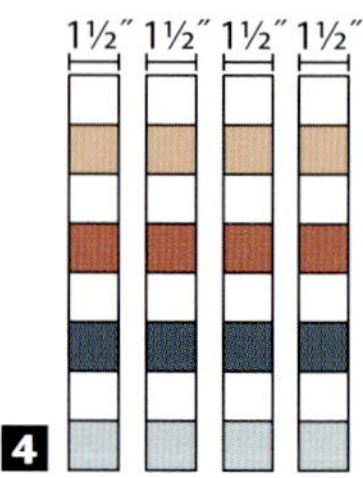

Segment B

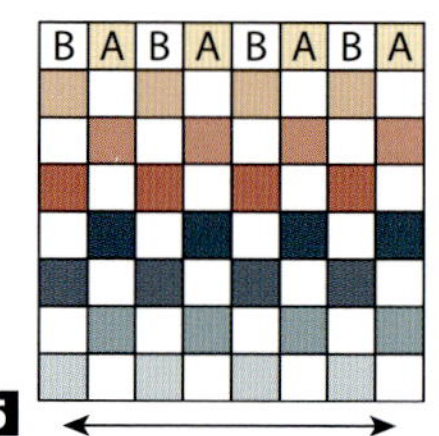

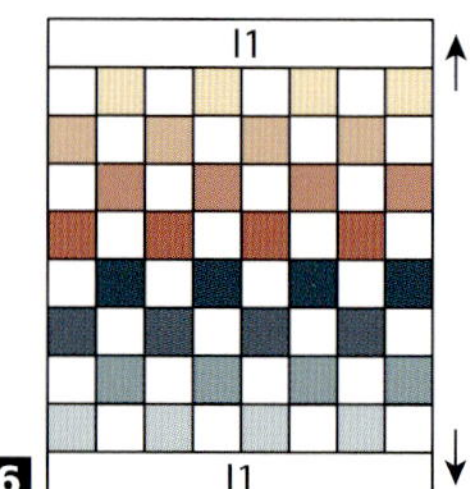

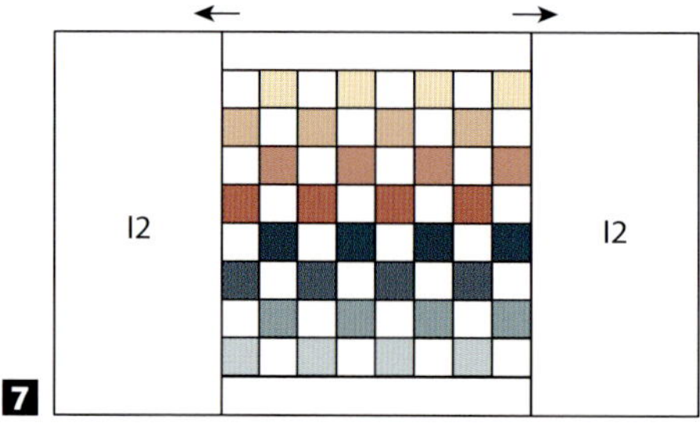

EXTERIOR PANEL

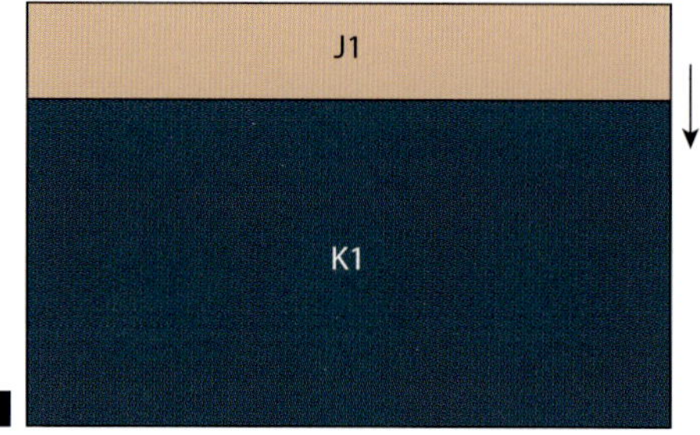

3. Measure 9½″ from the left side and 5¼″ from the top of the unit, and mark that point.

4. Follow manufacturer's instructions included with the metal prong snap fastener to install the socket side of the fastener on the marked point. The socket should be on the right side of the fabric, and the open prong should be on the fleece side. This completes the exterior panel.

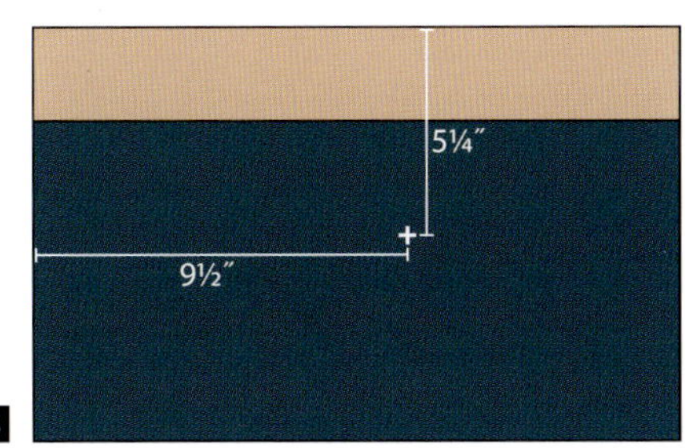

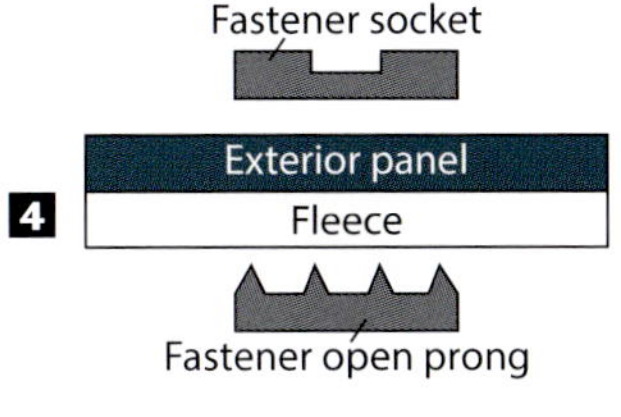

Side view

POCKET

1. Follow the fusible fleece manufacturer's instructions to fuse the FF2 rectangle to the wrong side of the J2 rectangle to make the pocket front.

2. Fold both J3 rectangles in half lengthwise WST and press to make the pocket binding.

3. Pin the pocket front from Step 1 to the I3 pocket lining rectangle WST. Align the raw edges of 1 pocket binding rectangle from Step 2 with the top edge of the I3 side of the unit. Sew the raw edges together through all layers.

4. Fold the binding over to the front side of the pocket, concealing the top raw edges. Sew ⅛″ from the folded edge of the binding to secure in place.

5. Fold both J4 zipper tabs in half widthwise RST so that they measure 1½″ × 2½″.

6. Close the zipper with the pull to the left. Sandwich the end of the zipper tape inside 1 zipper tab with the fold aligned with the bottom edge of the zipper tape, wrong side facing out. Sew along the raw edge of the zipper tab and zipper tape edge.

7. Repeat Step 6 to add the second zipper tab to the opposite end of the zipper tape. Pull the zipper tabs outward (so the right side of the fabric shows) and press the seams.

POCKET

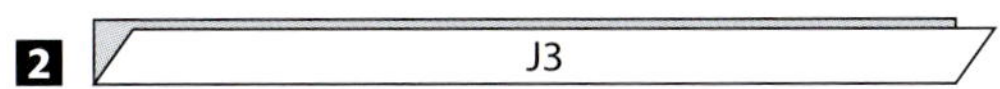

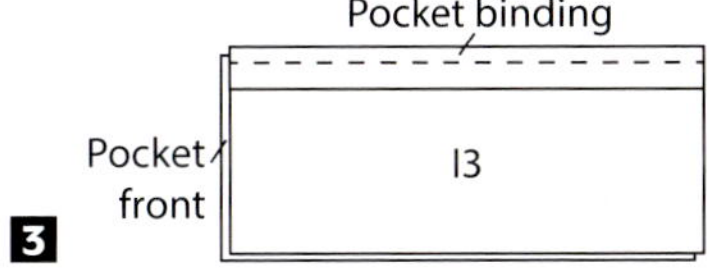

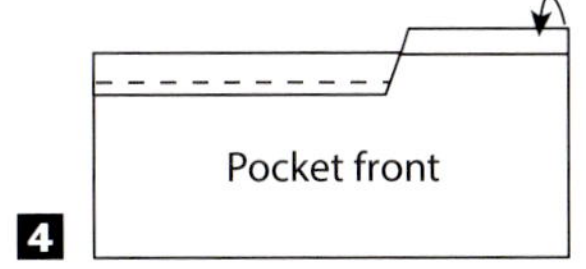

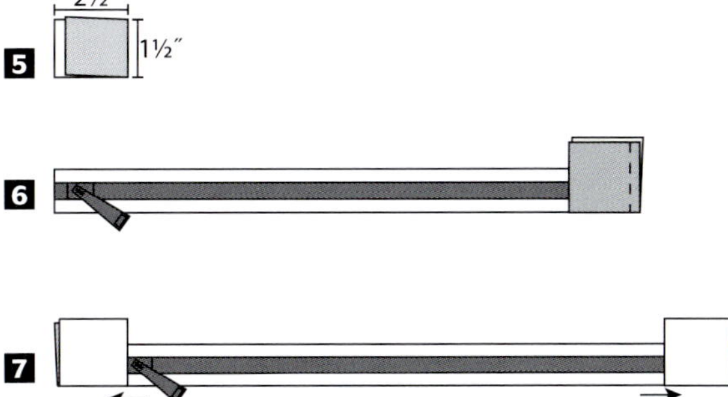

8. Center the zipper, with the pull on the left, on the top bound edge of the pocket front, zipper facing up with the pocket on top. With the pocket ⅛˝ away from the zipper teeth, sew in place ⅛˝ away from the bound edge. Then, resew along the previous binding seam through the front of the pocket.

9. Center the remaining pocket binding from Step 2 on the wrong side of the zipper, with the raw edges aligned to the top edge of the zipper tape. Sew in place using ¼˝ seam.

10. Fold the binding over to the right side of the zipper tape and sew in place ⅛˝ from the folded edge of the binding.

11. Trim the zipper tabs flush with the binding and pocket to complete the pocket.

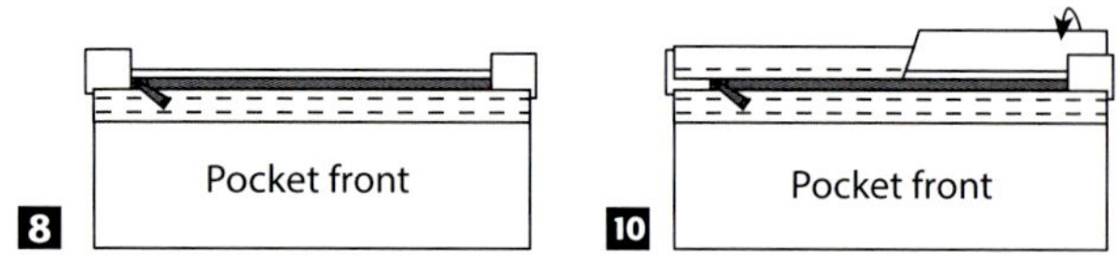

FINAL ASSEMBLY

Final Assembly

1. Align the bottom of the pocket with the left edge of the interior panel, and pin in place. Using ⅛˝ seam, sew around all 4 sides of the pocket, through the interior panel.

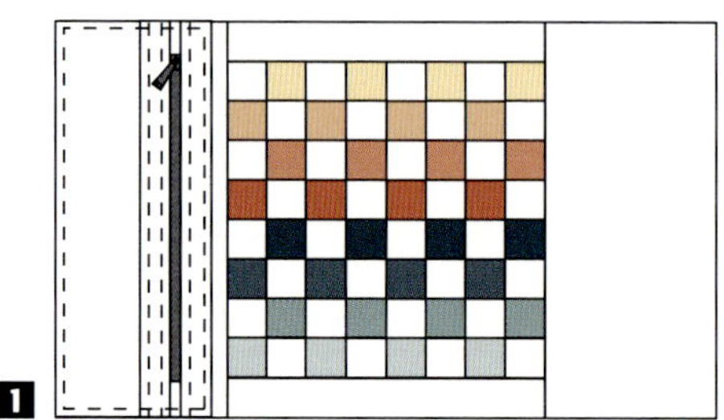

2. Arrange the interior panel and the exterior panel WST and baste in place with pins. Use a temporary fabric marker to mark on the interior panel where the metal prong snap fastener is located on the exterior panel.

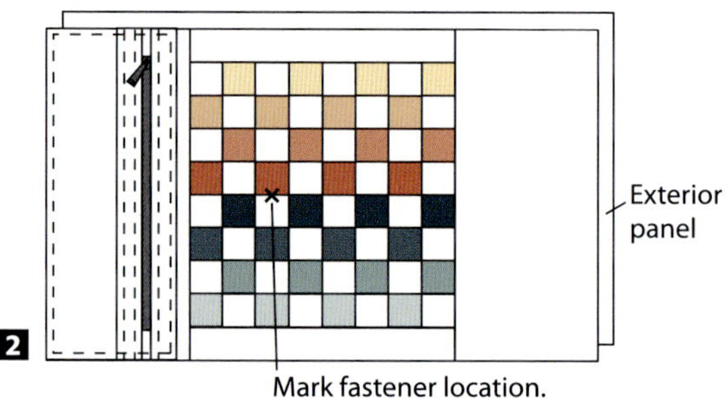

3. Quilt the game board portion of the panel as desired, taking care to avoid stitching over the fastener.

4. Mark the center of the right edge on the interior (game board) side of the panel. Along the top and bottom edges, measure 2˝ from the right edge, and mark. Draw a line to connect the center of the right edge with the marks on the top and bottom.

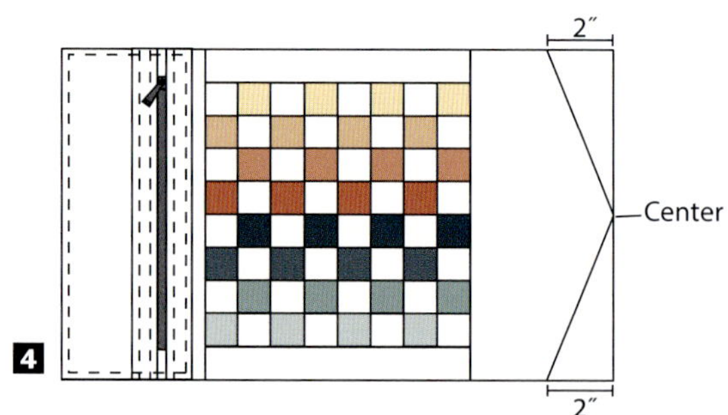

5. Trim away the corners of the right edge of the panel on the marked lines.

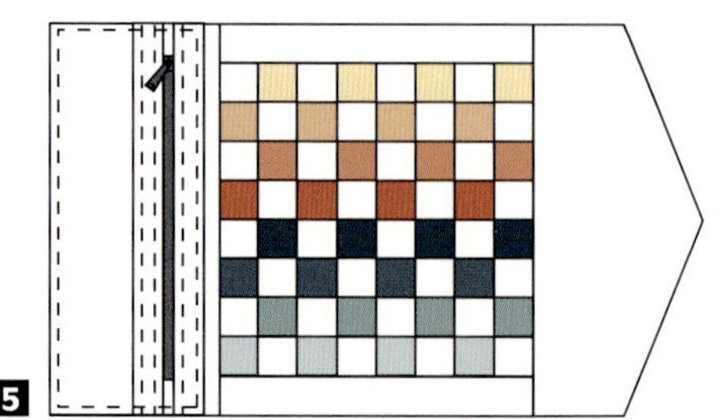

6. Press the J5 binding in half lengthwise, WST. Open one short end of the binding, and press ½˝ over to the wrong side.

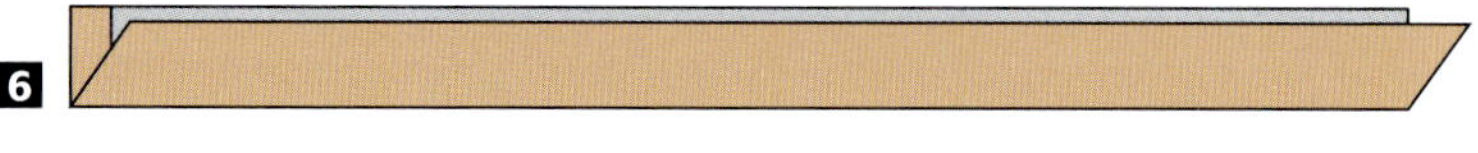

7. Align the raw edge of the binding with the raw edge of the interior (game board) side of the panel starting with the end of the binding that is folded over. Pin or clip the binding in place around the perimeter of the panel. Overlap the binding by approximately 1½˝ when you reach the starting point and trim the excess. Sew the binding in place with a scant ¼˝ seam allowance. Fold the binding over to the exterior side and sew ⅛˝ from the folded edge.

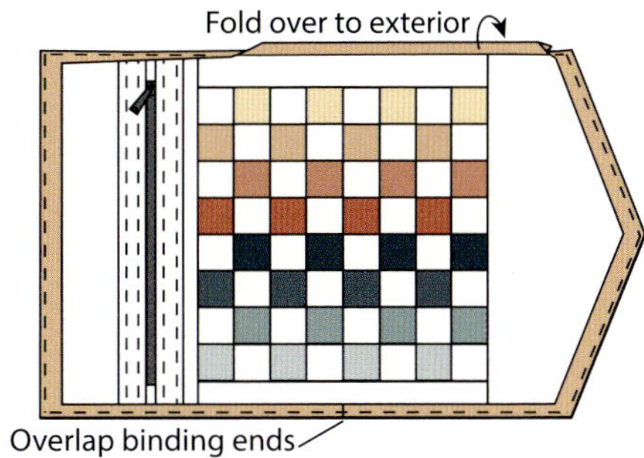

8. Mark a point approximately ½˝ from the pointed corner of the right panel, as shown.

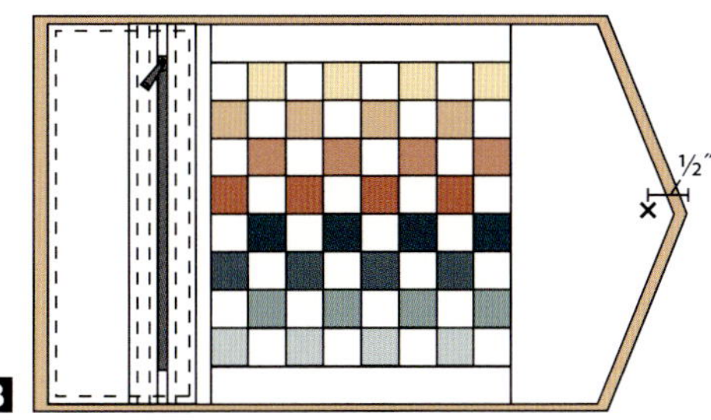

9. Follow manufacturer's instructions included with the metal prong snap fastener to install the stud side of the fastener on the marked point, with the open prong on the exterior side of the game board.

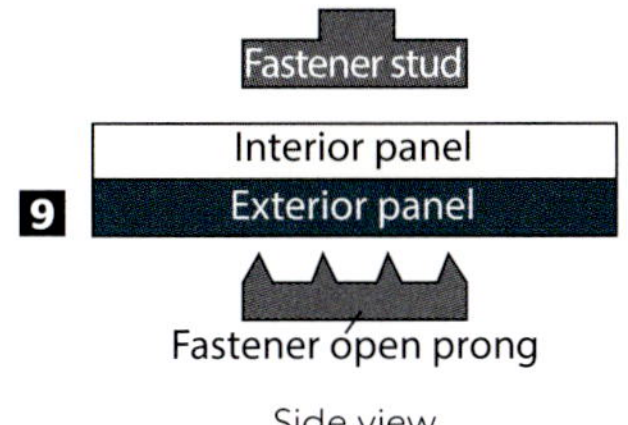

Side view

10. Add game pieces to the zipper pocket, roll the pocket side of the game board in, and secure the fastener to store the Cabin Game Board.

WINTER

Winter is a season of rest and anticipation as nature slumbers under a blanket of soft snow and holiday celebrations brighten gray days. The projects in this chapter are designed to bring comfort and cheer to keep you cozy all season long. The Woodsy Quilt (page 102) marks the transition from fall to winter with its richly colored ombré stripes dotted with snowy evergreens that create a wintery woodland scene. The Nordic Star Tree Skirt (page 106) brings a contemporary handmade touch to holiday decor with its clean lines and oversized star motif. The January Quilt (page 112) celebrates the delicate beauty of snowflakes in the winter air. And the Watercolor Hearts Quilt (page 118) celebrates the love that warms us with a motif of overlapping hearts that make a beautiful transparency effect.

WOODSY QUILT

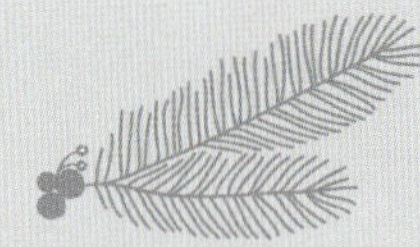

Finished Quilt: 60˝ × 72˝

The Woodsy Quilt is inspired by the beauty of snow-covered evergreen trees. The ombré effect of the colors mirrors the change in seasons from the rich reds and browns of fall to the greens and blues of winter. Be sure to share your project online with the hashtag **#woodsyquilt**

FABRICS & SUPPLIES

Yardages are based on 42˝ wide fabric.

Dark blue (Fabric A): ¾ yard

Dusty green (Fabric B): ½ yard

Light blue (Fabric C): ½ yard

Tan (Fabric D): ⅝ yard

Light pink (Fabric E): ¾ yard

Medium pink (Fabric F): ⅝ yard

Orange (Fabric G): ⅝ yard

Brown (Fabric H):⅝ yard

Cream (Fabric I): 1⅛ yards

Binding: ⅝ yard

Backing: 3⅞ yards (using a horizontal seam)

Material Notes

The fabrics used in this quilt are Art Gallery Fabrics Northern Waters, Spruce, Ocean Fog, Sandstone, Blushing, Cinnamon, Sienna Brick, Teak, White Linen, and Great Plains Big Sky.

CUTTING INSTRUCTIONS

Label each piece as specified in the parenthesis in the cutting lists.

Fabric A

Cut 1 strip 3˝ × WOF; subcut into:

- 4 squares 3˝ × 3˝ (A1)

Cut 8 strips 2½˝ × WOF; subcut into:

- 8 strips 2½˝ × 28½˝ (A2)

Fabric B

Cut 1 strip 3˝ × WOF; subcut into:

- 12 squares 3˝ × 3˝ (B1)

Cut 5 strips 2½˝ × WOF; subcut into:

- 8 strips 2½˝ × 16½˝ (B2)
- 8 strips 2½˝ × 8½˝ (B3)

Fabric C

Cut 1 strip 3˝ × WOF; subcut into:

- 12 squares 3˝ × 3˝ (C1)

Cut 5 strips 2½˝ × WOF; subcut into:

- 8 strips 2½˝ × 16½˝ (C2)
- 8 strips 2½˝ × 8½˝ (C3)

Fabric D

Cut 1 strip 3˝ × WOF; subcut into:

- 8 squares 3˝ × 3˝ (D1)

Cut 6 strips 2½˝ × WOF; subcut into:

- 4 strips 2½˝ × 20½˝ (D2)
- 8 strips 2½˝ × 16½˝ (D3)

Fabric E

Cut 1 strip 3˝ × WOF; subcut into:

- 8 squares 3˝ × 3˝ (E1)

Cut 8 strips 2½˝ × WOF; subcut into:

- 8 strips 2½˝ × 22½˝ (E2)
- 4 strips 2½˝ × 8½˝ (E3)

Fabric F

Cut 2 strips 3˝ × WOF; subcut into:

- 16 squares 3˝ × 3˝ (F1)

Cut 5 strips 2½˝ × WOF; subcut into:

- 8 strips 2½˝ × 10½˝ (F2)
- 12 strips 2½˝ × 8½˝ (F3)

Fabric G

Cut 2 strips 3˝ × WOF; subcut into:

- 16 square 3˝ × 3˝ (G1)

Cut 5 strips 2½˝ × WOF; subcut into:

- 8 strips 2½˝ × 10½˝ (G2)
- 12 strips 2½˝ × 8½˝ (G3)

Fabric H

Cut 1 strip 3˝ × WOF; subcut into:

- 8 squares 3˝ × 3˝ (H1)

Cut 6 strips 2½˝ × WOF; sew together end-to-end and subcut into:

- 4 strips 2½˝ × 32½˝ (H2)
- 8 strips 2½˝ × 10½˝ (H3)

Fabric I

Cut 3 strips 5½˝ × WOF; subcut into:

- 21 squares 5½˝ × 5½˝ (I1)

Cut 12 strips 1½˝ × WOF; sew together end-to-end and subcut into:

- 8 strips 1½˝ × 60½˝ (I2)

Binding

Cut 7 strips 2½˝ × WOF

Quilted by Tamara Darragh
of Remi Vail Studio

Flying Geese

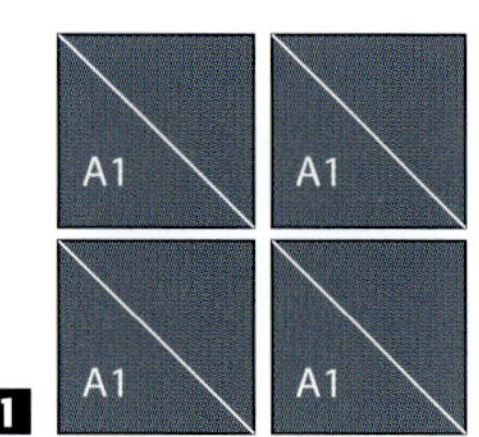

Seam allowances are ¼˝ unless otherwise noted. Pressing direction is indicated by the arrows in the diagrams.

1. Mark a diagonal line on the wrong side of all A1, B1, C1, D1, E1, F1, G1, and H1 squares.

2. Pair 1 I1 square with 4 marked A1 squares and follow the directions for 4-at-a-Time Flying Geese (page 14) to make 4 A/I flying geese. Trim each to 2½˝ × 4½˝, making sure to leave ¼˝ seam allowance at the center point.

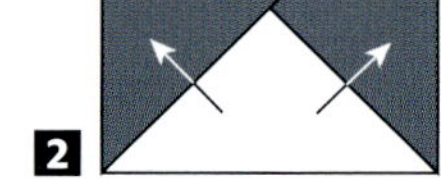

3. Repeat Step 2 with all B1, C1, D1, E1, F1, G1, and H1 squares paired with the remaining I1 squares to make the following total number of flying geese: 4 A/I FG, 12 B/I FG, 12 C/I FG, 8 D/I FG, 8 E/I FG, 16 F/I FG, 16 G/I FG, and 8 H/I FG.

Row Assembly

1. Row 1: Sew A2 strips to the left and right sides of 1 A/I flying geese. Press the seams toward the A2 strips. Repeat to make 4 total Row 1s.

2. Row 2: Arrange the following pieces in order: B2 + B/I FG + B3 + B/I FG + B3 + B/I FG + B2. Sew together and press the seams away from the flying geese to complete Row 2. Repeat to make 4 total Row 2s.

3. Row 3: Arrange the following pieces in order: C2 + C/I FG + C3 + C/I FG + C3 + C/I FG + C2. Sew together and press the seams away from the flying geese to complete Row 3. Repeat to make 4 total Row 3s.

4. Row 4: Arrange the following pieces in order: D3 + D/I FG + D2 + D/I FG + D3. Sew together and press the seams away from the flying geese to complete Row 4. Repeat to make 4 total Row 4s.

5. Row 5: Arrange the following pieces in order: E2 + E/I FG + E3 + E/I FG + E2. Sew together and press the seams away from the flying geese to complete Row 5. Repeat to make 4 total Row 5s.

ROW ASSEMBLY

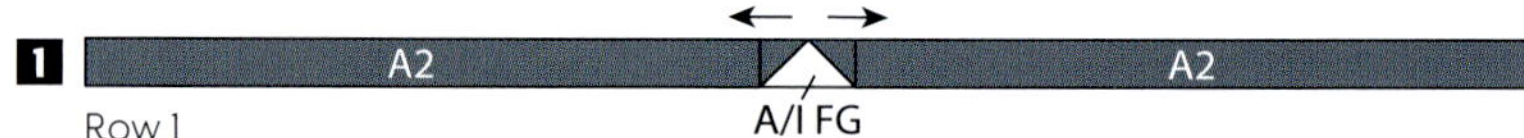

Row 1

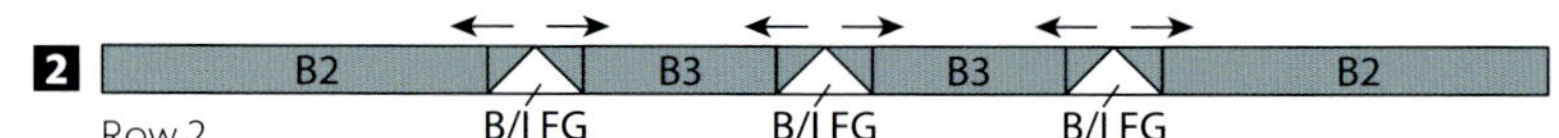

Row 2

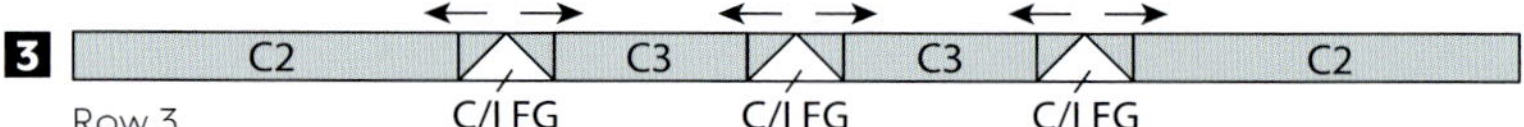

Row 3

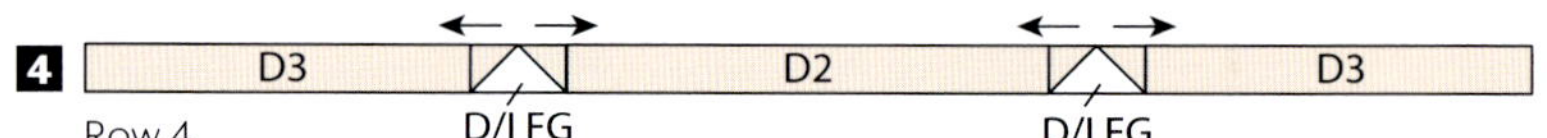

Row 4

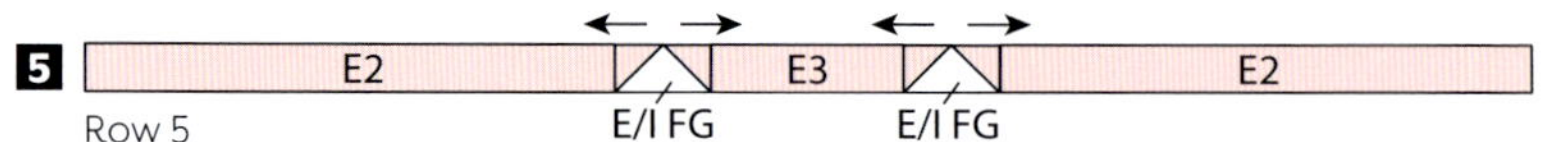

Row 5

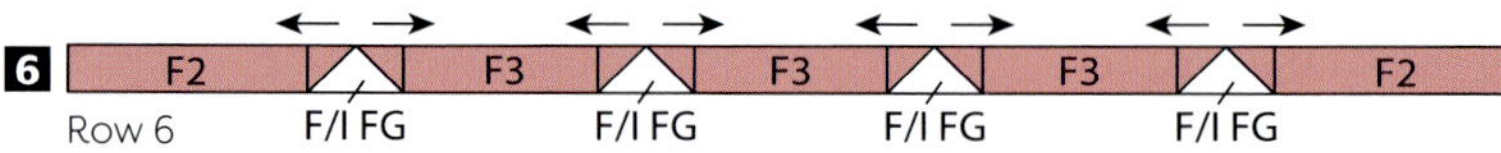

Row 6

6. Row 6: Arrange the following pieces in order: F2 + F/I FG + F3 + F/I FG + F3 + F/I FG + F3 + F/I FG + F2. Sew together and press the seams away from the flying geese to complete Row 6. Repeat to make 4 total Row 6s.

7. Row 7: Arrange the following pieces in order: G2 + G/I FG + G3 + G/I FG + G3 + G/I FG + G3 + G/I FG + G2. Sew together and press the seams away from the flying geese to complete Row 7. Repeat to make 4 total Row 7s.

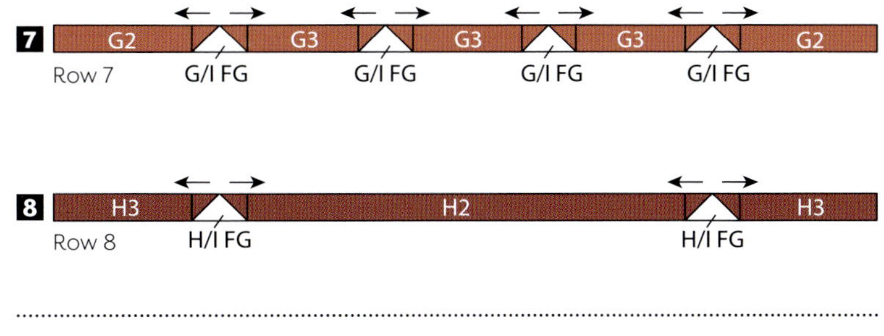

8. Row 8: Arrange the following pieces in order: H3 + H/I FG + H2 + H/I FG + H3. Sew together and press the seams away from the flying geese to complete Row 8. Repeat to make 4 total Row 8s.

QUILT ASSEMBLY

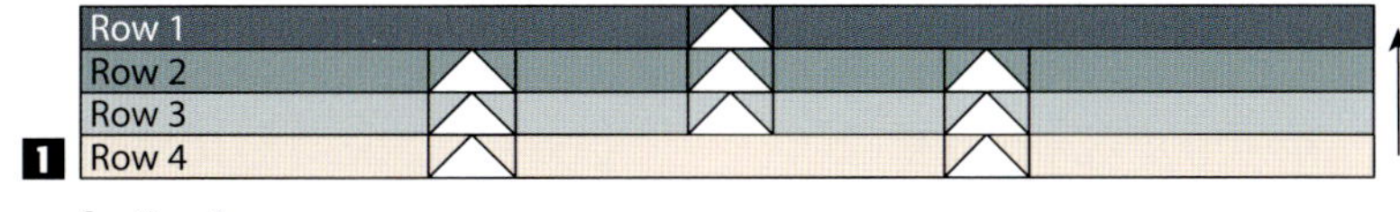

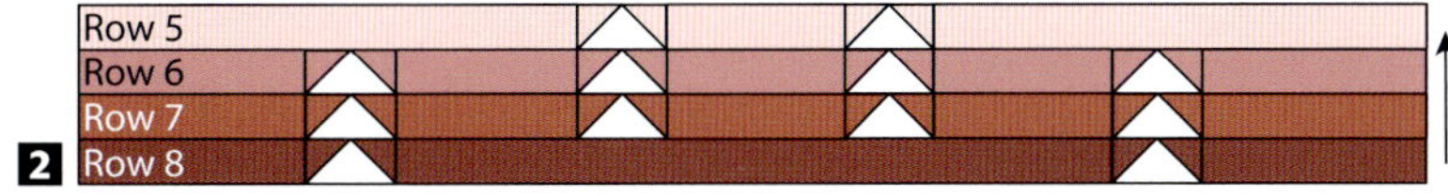

Quilt Assembly

1. Arrange 1 of each Rows 1, 2, 3, and 4 in order, and sew together. Press all seams up toward Row 1 to complete section A. Repeat to make a total of 4 section As.

2. Arrange 1 of each Rows 5, 6, 7, and 8 in order, and sew together. Press all the seams up toward Row 5 to complete section B. Repeat to make a total of 4 section Bs.

3. Arrange the A and B sections in alternating order, starting with section A, with an I2 strip in between each section and at the bottom of the quilt. Sew together and press the seams toward the I2 strips to complete the Woodsy Quilt top.

4. Finish the quilt as desired (see Quilt Finishing, page 17).

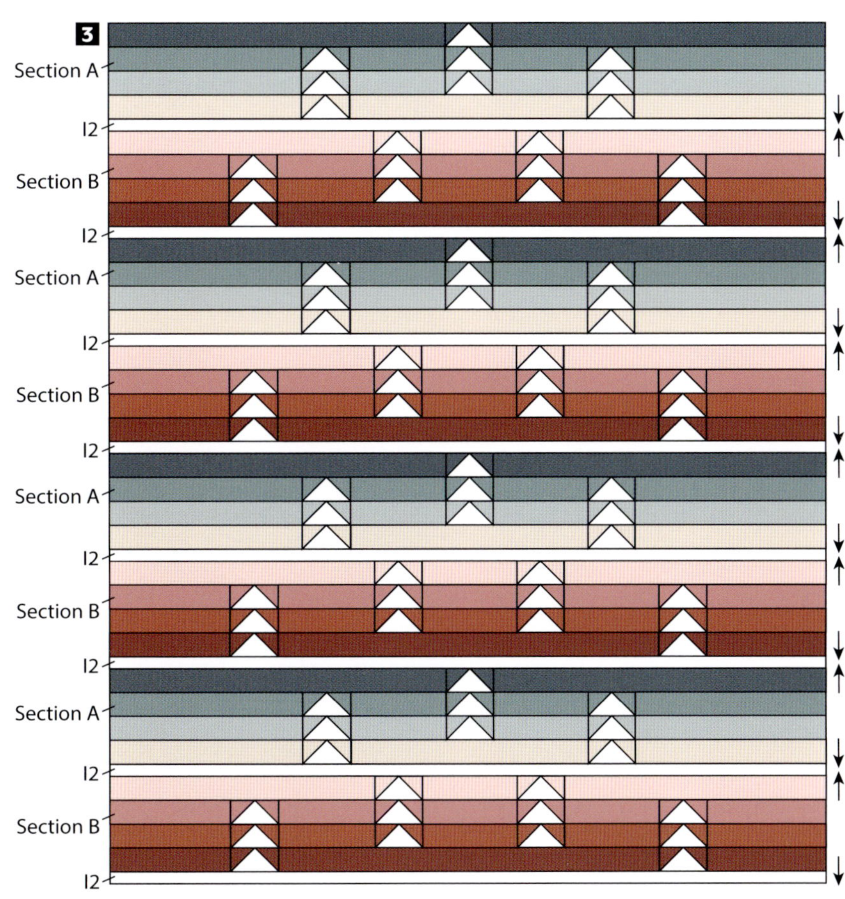

NORDIC STAR TREE SKIRT

Finished Quilt: 49″ × 49″

The Nordic Star Tree Skirt is inspired by my own Scandinavian heritage and its influence in western Wisconsin. My grandpa was Norwegian, and as a child, I grew up enjoying Norwegian treats like lefse and rosettes around the holidays. This classic Scandinavian-style star design preserves and honors those sweet memories and shares this cultural heritage with the next generation as my own children now get to experience those same long-held traditions. Be sure to share your project online with the hashtag **#nordicstartreeskirt**

FABRICS & SUPPLIES

Yardages are based on 42″ wide fabric.

Cream star print (Fabric A): ⅝ yard

Red (Fabric B):⅛ yard

Red gingham print (Fabric C): 1½ yards

Binding: ½ yard

Backing: 3¼ yards

Ribbon: 1¾ yards

Nordic Star Tree Skirt Template (page 127)

Material Notes

The fabrics used in this quilt are Art Gallery Fabrics Twinkle Skies Sugar, London Red, Checkered Charm, and Festive Twinkle.

CUTTING INSTRUCTIONS

Prepare the Nordic Star Tree Skirt Template for this project (see Templates, page 127). Label each cut piece as specified in the parenthesis in the cutting lists.

Fabric A

Cut 2 strips 10″ × WOF; subcut into:

- 4 squares 10″ × 10″ (A1)
- 4 squares 10″ × 10″ (A2)

Fabric B

Cut 1 strip 2″ × WOF; subcut into:

- 1 strip 2″ × 26″ (B1)
- 4 squares 2″ × 2″ (B2)

Fabric C

Cut 1 strip 13½″ × WOF; subcut into:

- 8 rectangles 13½″ × 5″ (C5)

Cut 2 strips 10″ × WOF; subcut into:

- 4 squares 10″ × 10″ (C1)
- 4 squares 10″ × 10″ (C2)

Cut 4 strips 2⅛″ × WOF; subcut into:

- 4 rectangles 2⅛″ × 29″ (C7)

Cut 3 strips 2″ × WOF; subcut into:

- 1 strip 2″ × 26″ (C3)
- 4 rectangles 2″ × 17″ (C6)
- 4 rectangles 2″ × 5″ (C4)

Binding

Cut 6 strips 2½″ × WOF and sew together

Ribbon

Cut 6 strips each 10″ long

Corner Units

Seam allowances are ¼˝ unless otherwise noted. Pressing direction is indicated by the arrows in the diagrams.

1. Mark a diagonal line, corner-to-corner, on the wrong side of 4 A1 squares.

2. Pair each A1 square with a C1 square and use the directions for 2-at-a-Time Half-Square Triangles (page 12) to make each pair into 2 HSTs. Trim all 8 A/C HSTs to 9½˝ × 9½˝.

3. Mark a diagonal line, corner-to-corner, on the wrong side of all A2 and C2 squares. Cut on the lines to make each square into 2 triangles.

4. Arrange an A/C HST, 1 A2 triangle, and 1 C2 triangle as shown. Sew the triangles to the top and right side of the HST and press the seams toward the triangles. Repeat to make a second mirrored unit.

5. Fold 1 C7 rectangle in half matching short ends and mark the center. Arrange the C7 rectangle between the two triangle units from Step 4. Align the center mark with the centers of the HSTs. Sew together and press the seams toward the C7 rectangle. Trim the ends of the C7 rectangle even with the edges of the unit. This completes 1 corner unit measuring 19⅝˝ × 19⅝˝.

6. Repeat Steps 4–5 to make a total of 4 corner units.

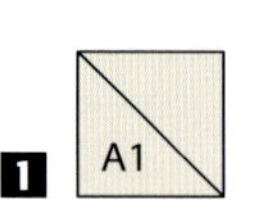

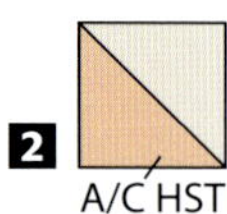

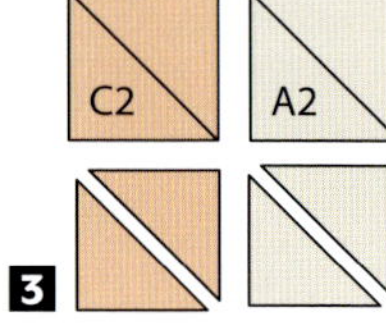

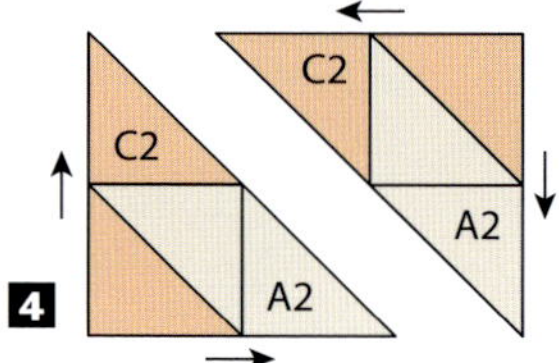

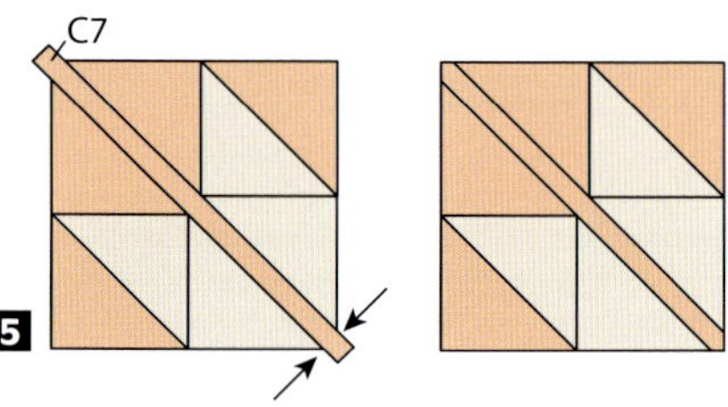

Sashing and Borders

1. Sew 1 B2 square to the end of 1 C6 rectangle. Press the seam towards the B2 square. Repeat to make a total of 4 sashing units.

2. Sew 1 B1 strip and 1 C3 strip together lengthwise. Press the seam toward Fabric B.

3. Cut the strip unit into 12 segments each 2˝ × 3½˝.

4. Arrange 3 segments with the colors alternating as shown and sew together. Press the seams open. Repeat to make a total of 4 units.

SASHING AND BORDERS

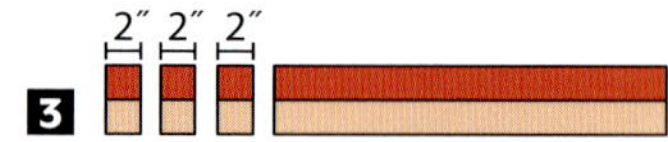

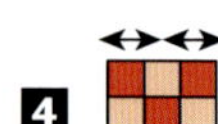

5. Sew 1 C4 rectangle to the bottom of each Step 4 unit and press the seams toward the C4 rectangles.

6. Sew 1 C5 rectangle to both sides of each Step 5 unit and press the seams towards the C5 rectangles to complete the 4 border units.

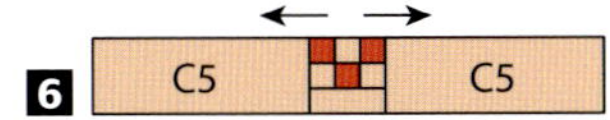

Final Assembly

1. Arrange 1 sashing unit between 2 corner units with the Fabric B end of the sashing at the top. Sew together and press the seams toward the sashing unit to make half of the star. Repeat to make a second half of the star.

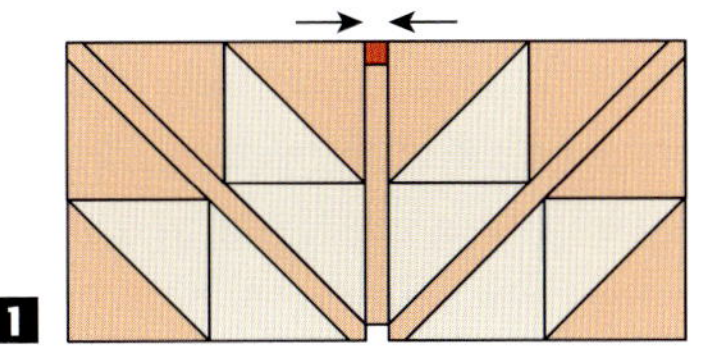

2. Arrange the remaining 2 sashing units between the 2 star halves with the Fabric B ends on the edges. Sew together and press the seams toward the sashing units to complete the star.

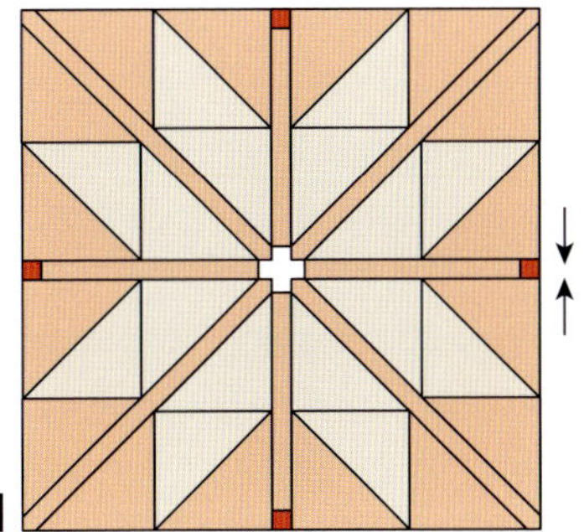

3. Arrange the border units on all 4 sides of the star with the center of the border unit matched to the Fabric B end of the sashing pieces in the star. Sew together and press the seams toward the border units.

4. In the top left corner of the top border unit, measure 5″ toward the center of the border unit and make a mark. Repeat on each outer corner of each border unit. Connect the marks across each corner. Cut on the marked lines to trim away the corner fabric.

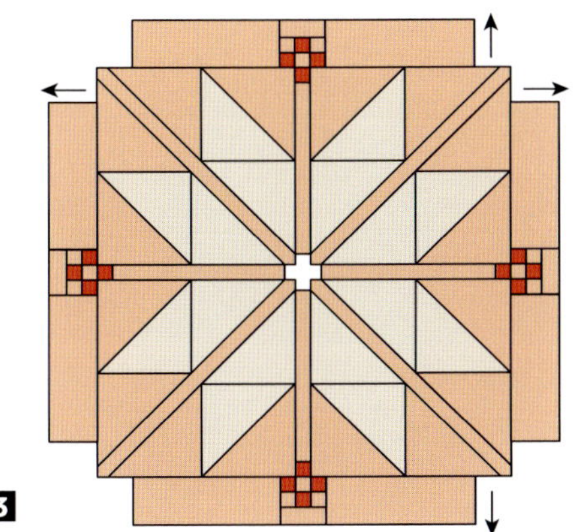

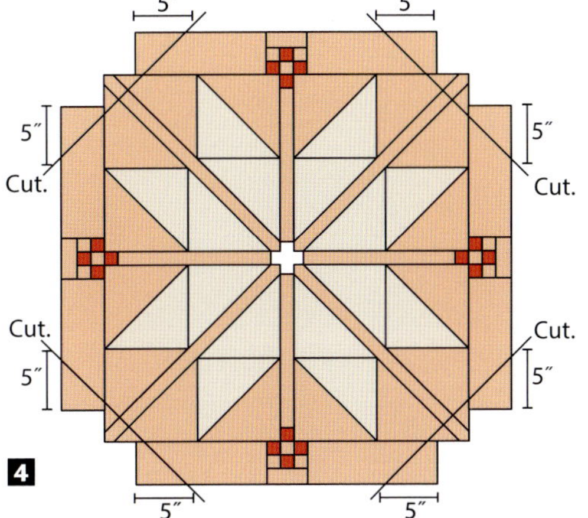

5. Piece the tree skirt backing as needed so that it measures 57˝ × 57˝. Make a quilt sandwich with the backing (right side down), a layer of batting, and the Step 4 quilt top (right side up). Baste the layers together with safety pins or basting spray and quilt as desired. Trim away the excess batting and backing from the quilt top.

6. Place the Nordic Star Tree Skirt Template in the center of the tree skirt and align the marks on the sides of the template with the centers of the sashing on the top, bottom, and sides of the star. Trace around the template. Mark a diagonal line from the center of the tree skirt through the middle of one of the corner units as shown. Cut on the line to the center of the tree skirt and then cut out the templated circle on the marked line.

7. Divide the ribbon pieces into 3 pairs and arrange the pairs along the cut line from Step 6, matching raw edges. The first set should be 1˝ from the circular center cut out, and the last pair should be 3˝ from the outside edge, with the middle set evenly spaced between the two other sets (approximately 8½˝ away from both), as shown. Sew the ends of the ribbons in place using a ⅛˝ seam.

8. Press the binding in half lengthwise WST. Open one short end of the binding and press ½˝ to the wrong side.

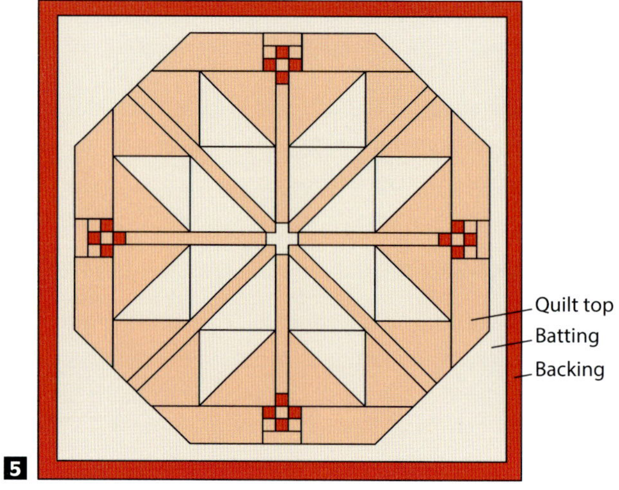

Sandwich before quilting

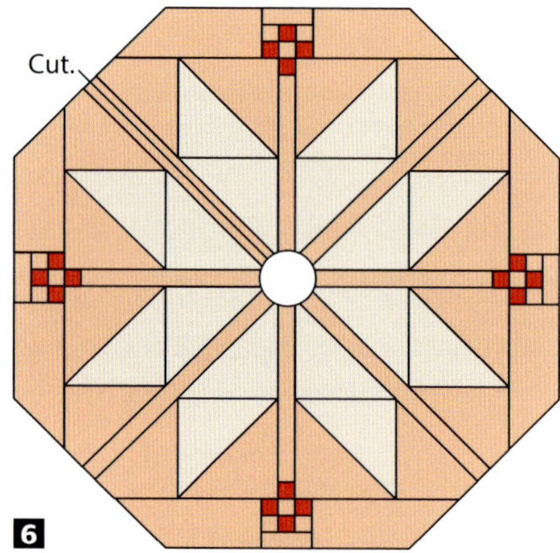

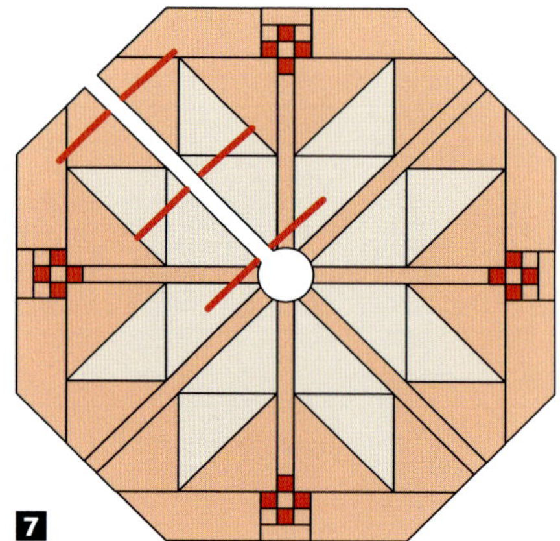

9. Align the raw edge of the binding with the raw edge of the tree skirt backing, starting with the end that is folded over. Pin the binding in place around the entire perimeter of the tree skirt and the cut into the center, around the center circle, and back out to the perimeter. Overlap the binding when you reach the starting point by approximately 1½˝. Trim the excess.

10. Sew the binding in place with a scant ¼˝ seam allowance. Fold the binding over to the front side of the tree skirt and sew ⅛˝ from the folded edge to secure and complete the Nordic Star Tree Skirt.

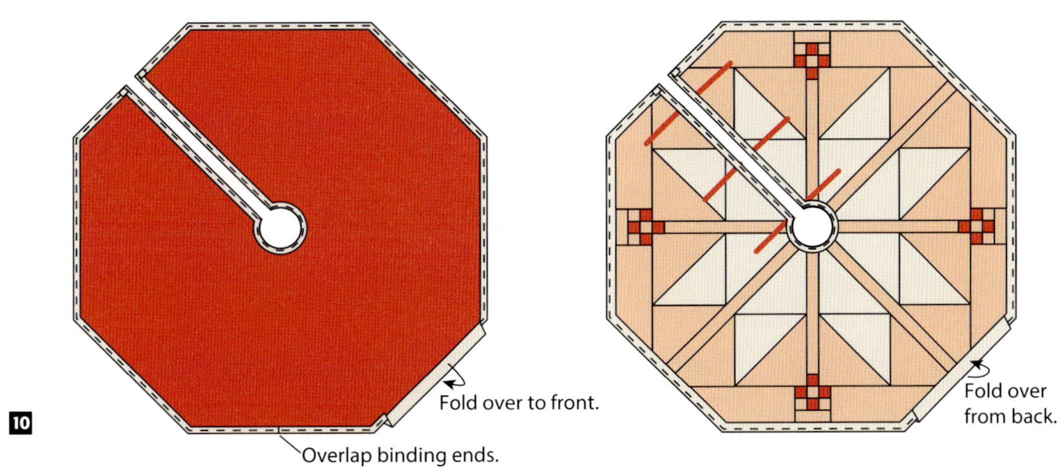

JANUARY QUILT

Finished Quilt: 63˝ × 63˝

The January Quilt is inspired by fresh winter snow and the delicate beauty of snowflakes. This modern nostalgic design is a celebration of the winter season and the sweet memories made on snowy days of a lifetime of winters. From building snowmen, to sledding down the neighborhood hill, to the simple joy of cozying up and watching tiny ice crystals create a winter wonderland outside of the window, winter is a time to slow down and cherish. Be sure to share your project online with the hashtag **#januaryquilt**

FABRICS & SUPPLIES

Yardages are based on 42˝ wide fabric.

Cream (Fabric A): 1¼ yards

Charcoal floral print (Fabric B): 3 yards

Binding: ⅝ yard

Backing: 4 yards

Material Notes

The fabrics used in this quilt are Art Gallery Fabrics Creme de la Creme, Delicate Balance Coal, and Snowglobe.

CUTTING INSTRUCTIONS

Label each piece as specified in the parenthesis in the cutting lists.

Fabric A

Cut 4 strips 3½˝ × WOF; subcut into:

- 4 rectangles 3½˝ × 24½˝ (A5)
- 4 squares 3½˝ × 3½˝ (A4)

Cut 4 strips 3½˝ × WOF (A1)

Cut 2 strips 3½˝ × WOF (A2)

Cut 1 strip 3½˝ × WOF (A3)

Fabric B

Cut 5 strips 6½˝ × WOF; sew together, and subcut into:

- 4 strips 6½˝ × 45½˝ (B8)

Cut 4 strips 6½˝ × WOF; subcut into:

- 4 rectangles 6½˝ × 15½˝ (B7)
- 4 rectangles 6½˝ × 9½˝ (B6)
- 12 rectangles 3½˝ × 6½˝ (B4)

Cut 4 strips 3½˝ × WOF (B1)

Cut 1 strip 3½˝ × WOF (B2)

Cut 2 strips 3½˝ × WOF (B3)

Cut 4 strips 3½˝ × WOF; subcut into:

- 8 rectangles 3½˝ × 15½˝ (B5)
- 4 rectangles 3½˝ × 6½˝ (B4)
- 1 square 3½˝ × 3½˝ (B9)

Binding

Cut 7 strips 2½˝ × WOF

Quilted by Sandy Saengsuk of
Thai Charm LLC

Strip Pieced Units

Seam allowances are ¼″ unless otherwise noted. Pressing direction is indicated by the arrows in the diagram.

1. Pair each A1 strip with a B1 strip and sew together along the long sides to make a total of 4 strip sets. Press the seams toward B1.

2. Cut each Step 1 strip set into 11 segments measuring 3½″ × 6½″ (totaling 44 segments). Set aside 4 segments.

3. Arrange 2 segments opposite one another and sew together. Press the seam open to make one 4-patch unit measuring 6½″ × 6½″. Repeat to make a total of twenty 4-patch units.

4. Sew an A2 strip to the top and bottom of a B2 strip. Press the seams toward the B2 strip.

5. Cut the Step 4 strip set into 12 ABA units measuring 3½″ × 9½″.

6. Sew an A3 strip between 2 B3 strips. Press the seams toward the B3 strips.

7. Cut the Step 6 strip set into 8 BAB units 3½″ × 9½″.

8. Sew 1 BAB unit between 2 ABA units to make one 9-patch unit measuring 9½″ × 9½″. Press the seams open. Repeat to make a total of four 9-patch units.

9. Sew 1 ABA unit and 1 BAB unit together and press the seam open to make one 6-patch unit measuring 6½″ × 9½″. Repeat to make a total of four 6-patch units.

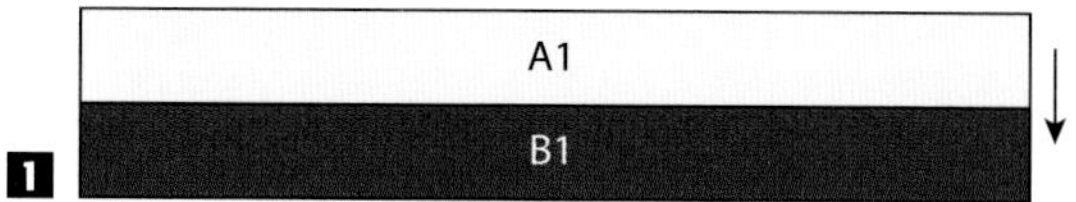

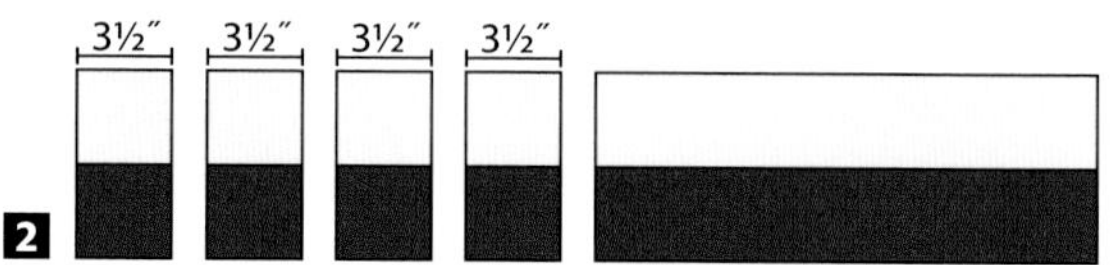

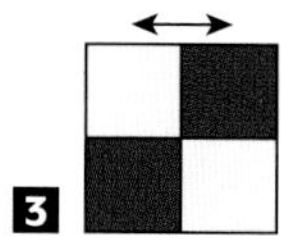

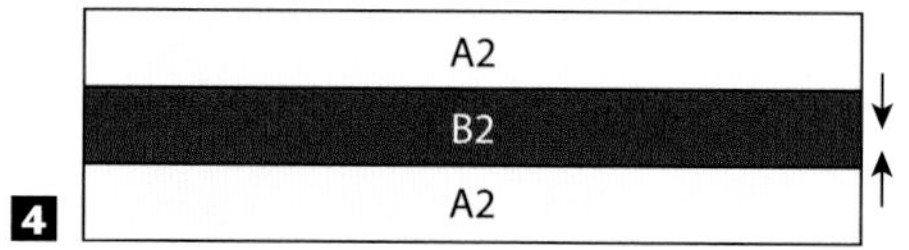

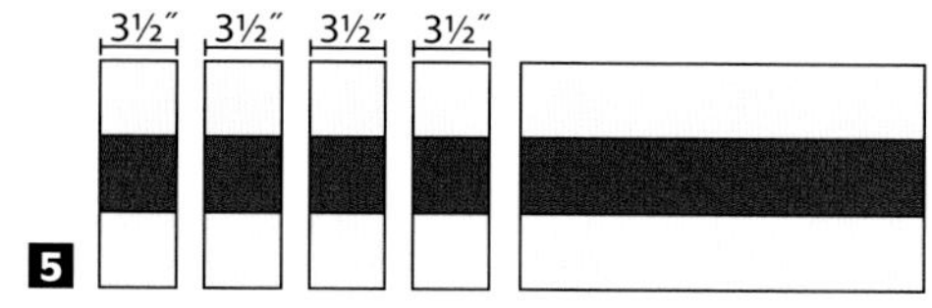

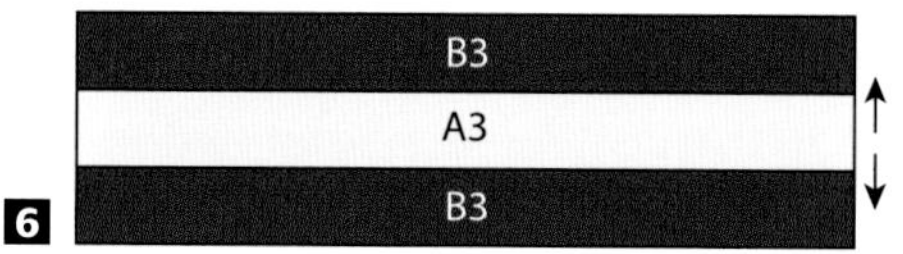

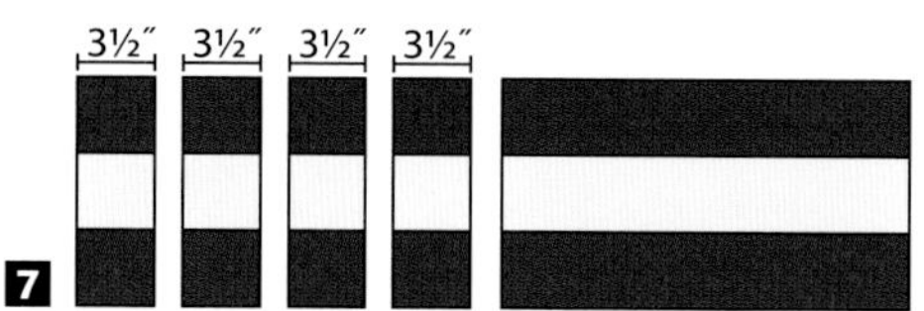

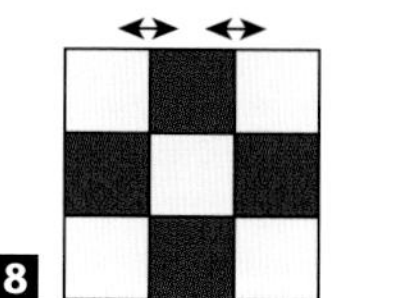

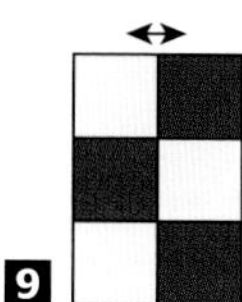

Other Units

1. Sew four 4-patch units into 2 columns as shown. Press the seams open to make 2 mirrored 8-patch units (8P/A and 8P/B).

2. Sew 1 B4 rectangle to the top of each 8-patch unit and press the seam toward B4.

3. Sew 1 B5 rectangle to the right of the 8P/A unit and sew 1 B5 rectangle to the left of the 8P/B unit. Press the seams toward B5 to complete 1 8P/A unit and 1 8P/B unit, each measuring 9½″ × 15½″.

4. Repeat Steps 1–3 to make a total of 4 8P/A units and 4 8P/B units.

5. Sew one 4-patch unit, 2 B4 rectangles, and 1 A4 square into rows as shown. Press the seams toward the B4 rectangles.

6. Sew the rows together and press the seam open to make 1 square unit.

7. Repeat Steps 5–6 to make a total of 4 square units.

8. Sew 1 B6 rectangle to the left side of a 9-patch unit and press the seam toward B6.

9. Sew 1 B7 rectangle to the top of the Step 8 unit and press the seam toward B7 to complete 1 corner unit.

10. Repeat Steps 8–9 to make a total of 4 corner units.

11. Sew 1 each of the corner, 8P/B, 8P/A, and square units into 2 rows as shown. Press the seams toward the 8P/B and 8P/A units.

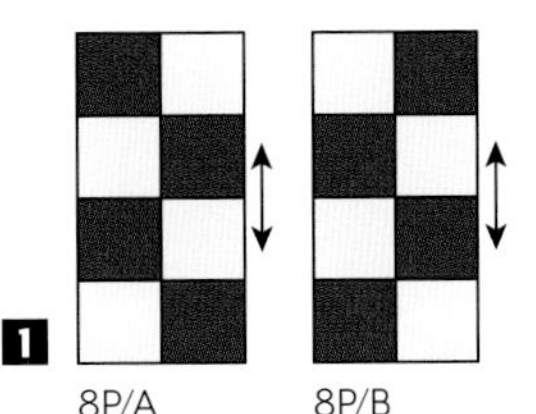

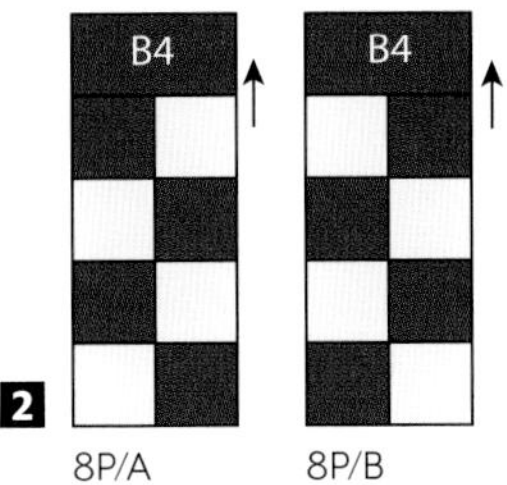

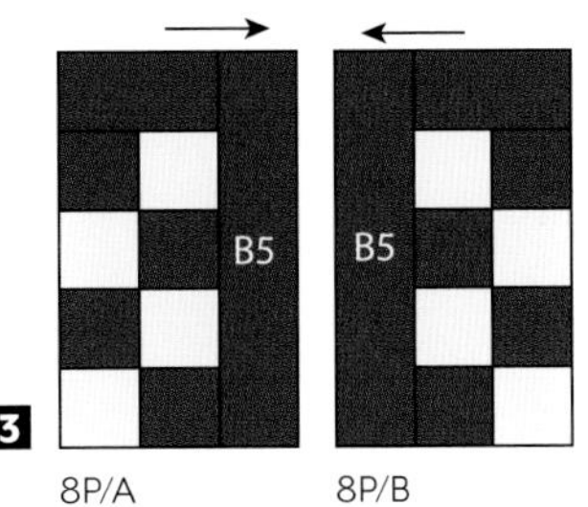

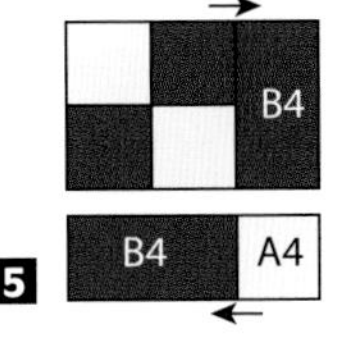

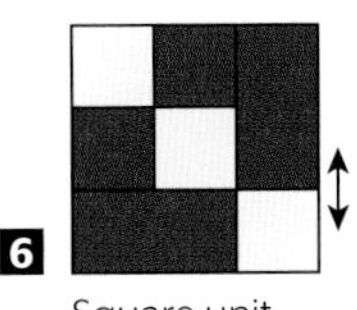

Square unit

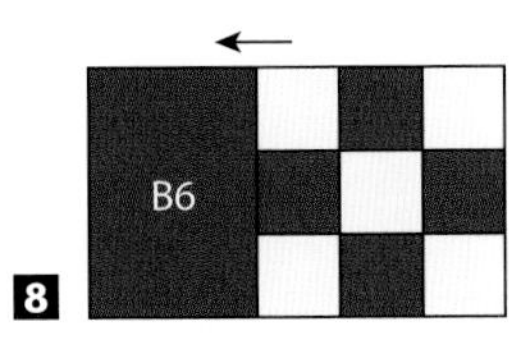

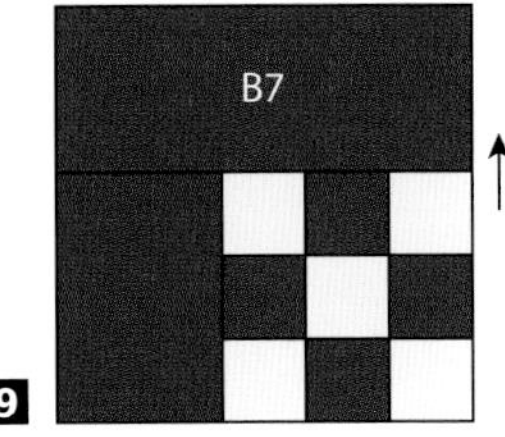

Corner unit

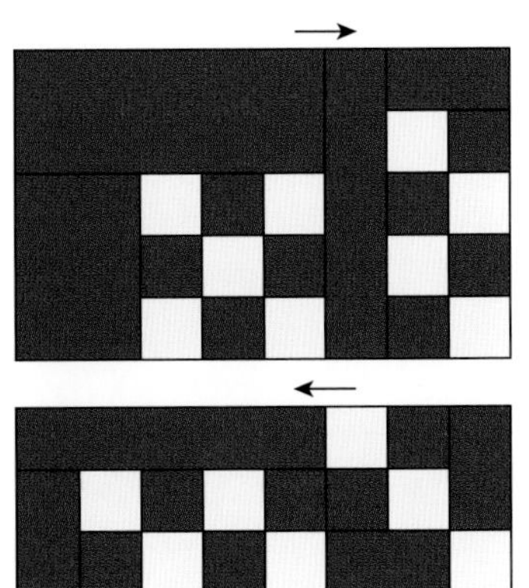

12. Sew the rows together and press the seam open to create a quarter snowflake.

13. Repeat Steps 11–12 to make a total of 4 quarter snowflakes.

14. Sew strip pieced Step 2 segments to the ends of a B8 rectangle. Note the orientation of the segments. Press the seams toward B8 to make 1 side border (S1) measuring 6½″ × 51½″. Repeat to make a second S1 border.

15. Sew 6-patch units to the ends of a B8 rectangle. Note the orientation of the 6-patch units. Press the seams toward B8 to make 1 top/bottom border (S2) measuring 6½″ × 63½″. Repeat to make a second S2 border.

Quarter snowflake

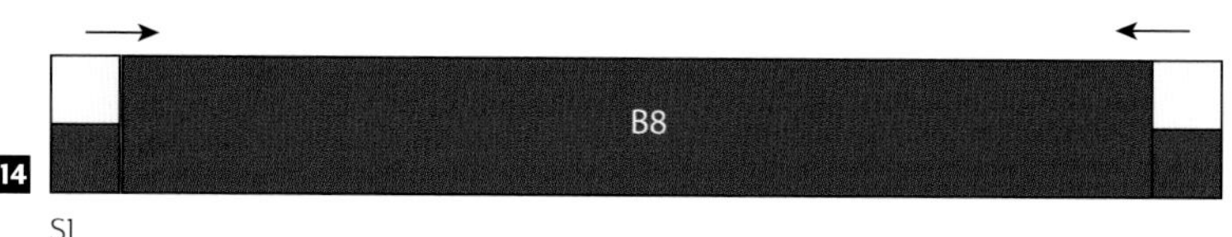

S1

S2

Quilt Top Assembly

1. Arrange 4 quarter snowflakes, 4 A5 rectangles, and 1 B9 square as shown.

2. Sew the pieces into rows. Press the seams toward the A5 rectangles.

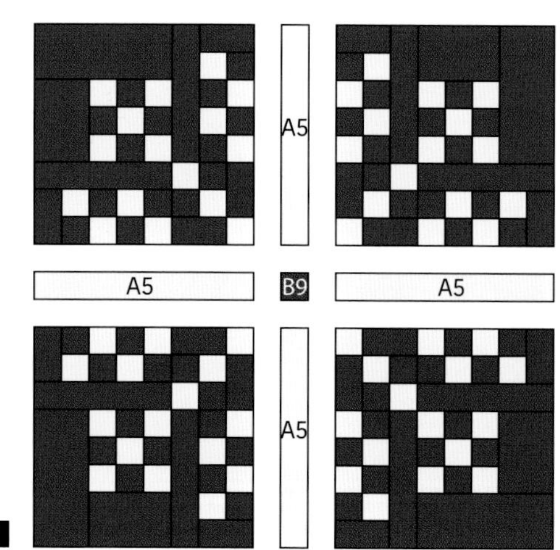

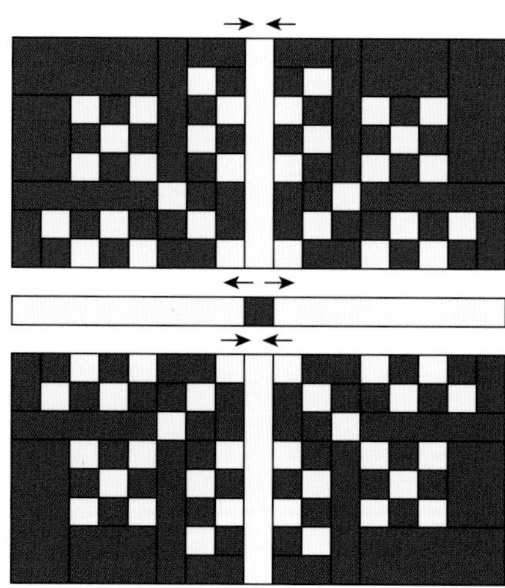

3. Sew the rows together and press the seams toward the center row to make the Snowflake unit.

4. Sew S1 borders on the left and right sides of the Snowflake unit, taking care to note the orientation of the 2-patch segments. Press the seams toward the S1 borders.

5. Sew S2 borders to the top and bottom of the Snowflake unit as shown, taking care to note the orientation of the 6-patch units. Press the seams toward the S2 borders to complete the January Quilt top.

6. Finish the quilt as desired (see Quilt Finishing, page 17).

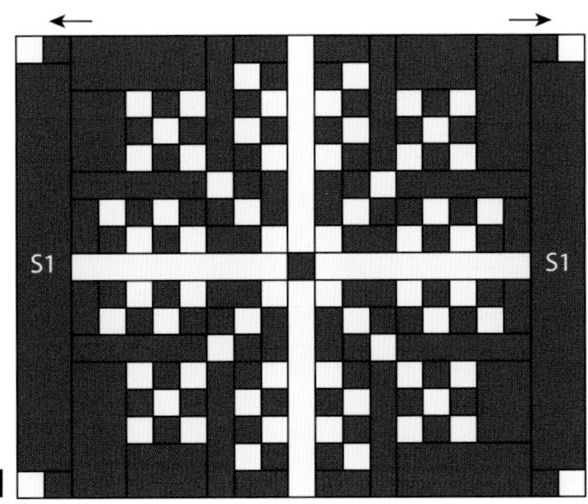

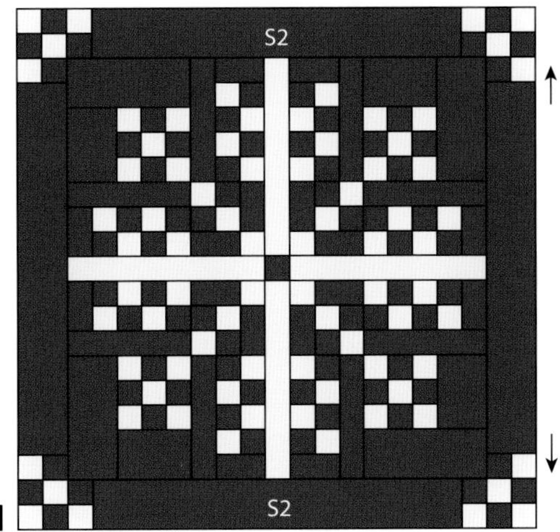

WATERCOLOR HEARTS QUILT

Finished Heart Block Size: 12˝ × 12˝ || **Finished Triple Heart Block Size:** 12˝ × 24˝ || **Finished Quilt:** 63˝ × 72˝

Watercolor Hearts features a unique overlapping heart motif that appears transparent as though it has been painted with watercolors. This design is inspired by the idea that our relationships create touch points for our hearts to connect to one another and be colored vibrantly by those we love. Be sure to share your project online with the hashtag **#watercolorheartsquilt**

FABRICS & SUPPLIES

Yardages are based on 42˝ wide fabric.

Plum (Fabric A): ½ yard

Mauve: (Fabric B): ¼ yard

Light peach (Fabric C): ½ yard

Medium peach (Fabric D): ¼ yard

Red orange (Fabric E): ½ yard

Dark gold (Fabric F): ½ yard

Light gold (Fabric G): ¼ yard

Light teal blue (Fabric H): ¼ yard

Dark green (Fabric I): ½ yard

Cream (Fabric J): 2¼ yards

Binding: ⅝ yard

Backing: 4 yards (using a horizontal seam)

Material Notes

The fabrics used in this quilt are Art Gallery Fabrics Flights of Fancy in Plumwood, Mauve, Shell, Peach, Cinnabar, Gilded, Amber, Celeste, and Spruce, White Linen, and Fleuron Six.

CUTTING INSTRUCTIONS

Label each piece as specified in the parenthesis in the cutting lists. For each color, label the pieces with the fabric color letter and the number in parenthesis. For example, a 7˝ × 7˝ square from Fabric F should be labeled F1.

Fabrics A and F

Cut 1 strip 7˝ × WOF; subcut into:

- 1 square 7˝ × 7˝ (1)
- 4 squares 6½˝ × 6½˝ (4)
- 1 square 5½˝ × 5½˝ (3)
- 2 squares 3½˝ × 3½˝ (2)

Cut 1 strip 6½˝ × WOF; subcut into:

- 6 squares 6½˝ × 6½˝ (4)

Fabrics B, D, G, and H

Cut 1 strip 5˝ × WOF; subcut into:

- 4 squares 5˝ × 5˝ (1)
- 2 squares 3½˝ × 3½˝ (2)
- 4 squares 3˝ × 3˝ (3)

Cut 1 strip 2½˝ × WOF; subcut into:

- 8 squares 2½˝ × 2½˝ (4)

Fabric C

Cut 1 strip 5½˝ × WOF; subcut into:

- 2 squares 5½˝ × 5½˝ (C3)
- 12 rectangles 4½˝ × 2½˝ (C4)

Cut 1 strip 4½˝ × WOF; subcut into:

- 4 rectangles 4½˝ × 2½˝ (C4)
- 8 squares 3½˝ × 3½˝ (C2)

Cut 1 strip 5˝ × WOF; subcut into:

- 8 squares 5˝ × 5˝ (C1)

Fabrics E and I

Cut 1 strip 7˝ × WOF; subcut into:

- 5 squares 7˝ × 7˝ (1)
- 2 squares 3½˝ × 3½˝ (3)

Cut 1 strip 6½˝ × WOF; subcut into:

- 2 squares 6½˝ × 6½˝ (4)
- 4 squares 5˝ × 5˝ (2)

Cut 1 strip 2½˝ × WOF; subcut into:

- 8 rectangles 2½˝ × 4½˝ (5)

Fabric J

Cut 2 strips 7˝ × WOF; subcut into:

- 12 squares 7˝ × 7˝ (J1)

Cut 4 strips 6½˝ × WOF; sew together end to end, and cut into:

- 2 strips 6½˝ × 63½˝ (J5)

Cut 8 strips 3½˝ × WOF; sew together end to end, and cut into:

- 5 strips 3½˝ × 60½˝ (J4)

Cut 1 strip 3½˝ × WOF; subcut into:

- 8 squares 3½˝ × 3½˝ (J2)

Cut 3 strips 2½˝ × WOF; subcut into:

- 48 squares 2½˝ × 2½˝ (J3)

Binding

Cut 7 strips 2½˝ × WOF

Quilted by Tamara Darragh of Remi Vail Studio

Basic Assembly

Seam allowances are ¼″ unless otherwise noted. Pressing direction is indicated by the arrows in the diagrams.

HALF-SQUARE AND QUARTER-SQUARE TRIANGLES

1. Mark a diagonal line, corner-to-corner, on the wrong side of all J1 squares.

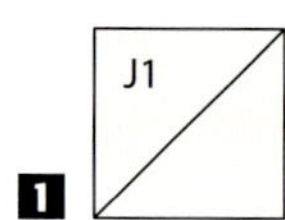

2. Pair 1 J1 square with 1 A1 square and follow the instructions in 2-at-a-Time Half-Square Triangles (page 12) to make 2 A/J HSTs. Trim to 6½″ × 6½″.

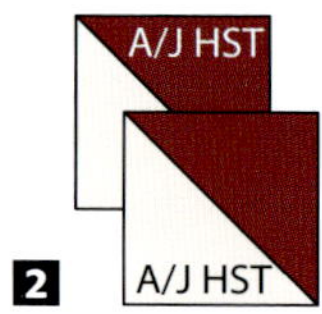

3. Repeat Step 2 with all E1, F1, and I1 squares paired with J1 squares to make a total of 10 E/J HSTs, 2 F/J HSTs, and 10 I/J HSTs. Trim all to 6½″ × 6½″.

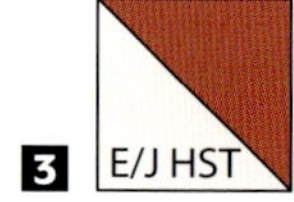

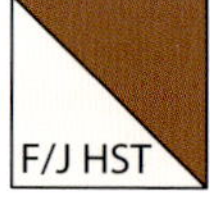

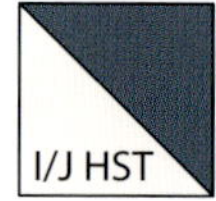

4. Sew 2 A/J HSTs together, as shown, and press the seam open to make 1 heart bottom.

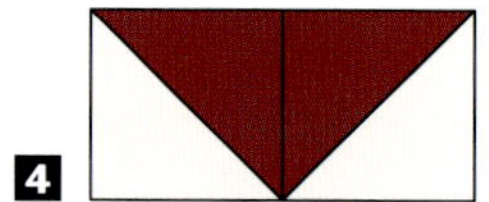
Heart bottom A

5. Repeat Step 4 with all HSTs from Step 3 in matched pairs to make a total of 1 heart bottom A, 5 heart bottom Es, 1 heart bottom F, and 5 heart bottom Is.

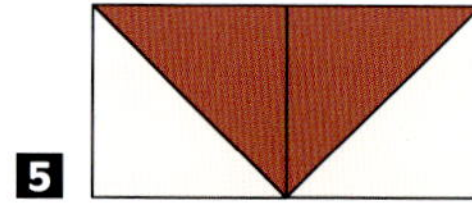
Heart bottom E

Heart bottom F

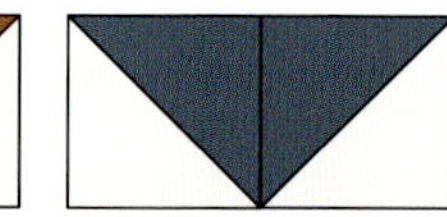
Heart bottom I

6. Mark a diagonal line, corner-to-corner, on the wrong side of all C1, D1, and H1 squares.

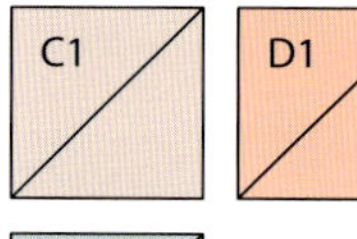

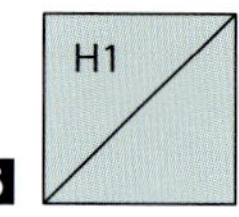

7. Pair each C1 square with a B1 square and use the directions for 2-at-a-Time Half-Square Triangles (page 12) to make a total of 8 B/C HSTs. Trim to 4½″ × 4½″.

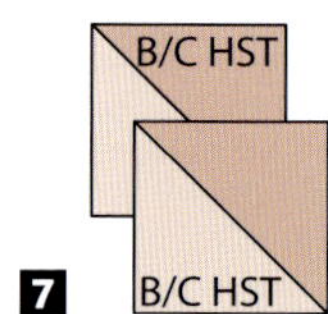

8. Repeat Step 7, pairing all D1 squares with E2 squares, all G1 squares with C1 squares, and all H1 squares with I2 squares to make a total of 8 HSTs in each combination D/E, G/C, and H/I. Trim each HST to 4½″ × 4½″.

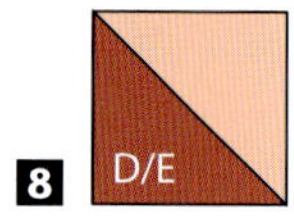

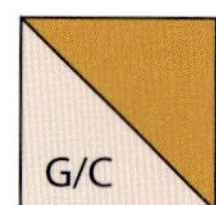

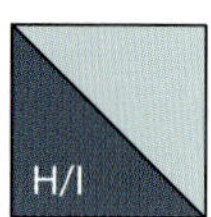

9. Mark a diagonal line, corner-to-corner, on the wrong side of all C2 and J2 squares.

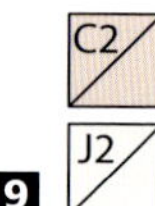

10. Pair each A2 square with a J2 square and follow the instructions for 2-at-a-Time Half-Square Triangles (page 12) to make a total of 4 A/J HSTs. Trim to 3″ × 3″.

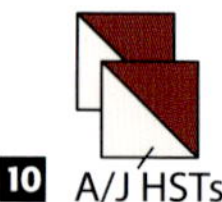

11. Repeat Step 10, pairing all B2 squares with C2 squares, all D2 squares with C2 squares, all E3 squares with J2 squares, all F2 squares with J2 squares, all G2 squares with C2 squares, all H2 squares with C2 squares, and all I3 squares with J2 squares. Make a total of 4 HSTs in each combination B/C, D/C, E/J, F/J, G/C, H/C, and I/J. Trim to 3″ × 3″. Press the seams toward Fabric C and away from Fabric J.

12. Mark a diagonal line, corner-to-corner, perpendicular to the center seam, on the wrong side of all A/J, E/J, F/J, and I/J HSTs.

13. Pair each A/J HST with a B/C HST, RST, with the center seams aligned. Pair the E/J HSTs with the D/C HSTs, the F/J HSTs with the G/C HSTs, and the I/J HSTs with the H/C HSTs.

14. Follow the instructions for 2-at-a-Time Half-Square Triangles (page 12) to make each pair from Step 13 into 2 quarter-square triangles (QSTs). Trim to 2½″ × 2½″. Press the seams open. This will yield a total of 8 QSTs in each combination A/B/C/J, C/D/E/J, C/F/G/J, and C/H/I/J.

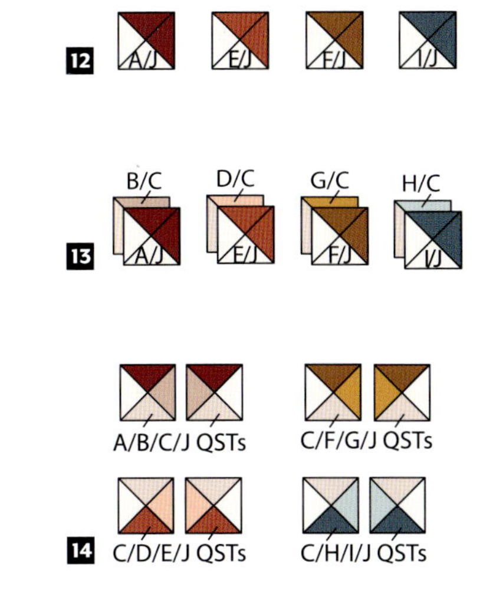

FLYING GEESE

1. Mark a diagonal line, corner-to-corner, on the wrong side of all B3, D3, G3, and H3 squares.

2. Pair 1 A3 square with 4 B3 squares and follow the directions for 4-at-a-Time Flying Geese (page 14) to make 4 A/B flying geese (A/B FG). Trim each to 2½″ × 4½″, making sure to leave ¼″ seam allowance at the center point.

3. Repeat Step 2, pairing 4 D3 squares with 1 C3 square, 4 G3 squares with 1 F3 square, and 4 H3 squares with 1 C3 square to make a total of 4 flying geese in each combination: C/D FG, F/G FG, and C/H FG.

FLYING GEESE

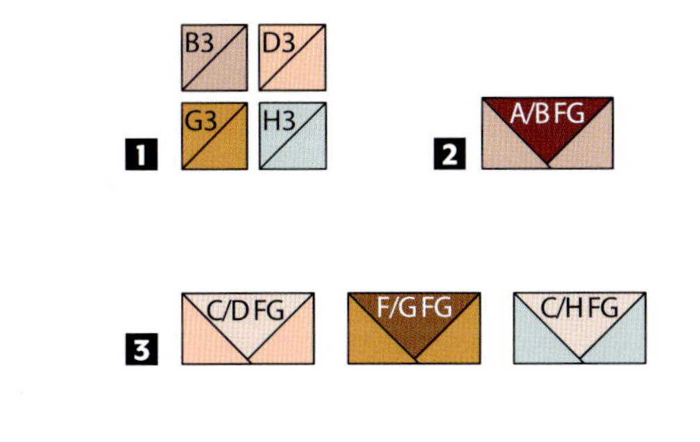

Heart Blocks

1. Mark a diagonal line, corner-to-corner, on the wrong side of all J3 squares.

2. Pin 1 J3 square RST on both upper corners of 1 A4 square as shown.

HEART BLOCKS

3. Sew on the marked lines and cut away the excess corner fabric ¼˝ from the seam. Press the seams toward Fabric J to complete 1 Corner A measuring 6½˝ × 6½˝.

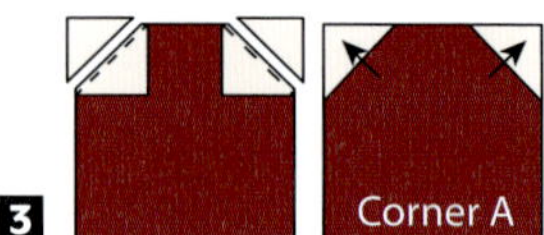

4. Repeat Steps 2–3, pairing 2 J3 squares with all A4, E4, F4, and I4 squares to make the following totals of each corner unit: 10 Corner A, 2 Corner E, 10 Corner F, and 2 Corner I.

5. Sew 2 corner unit As together and press the seam open to make 1 heart top A.

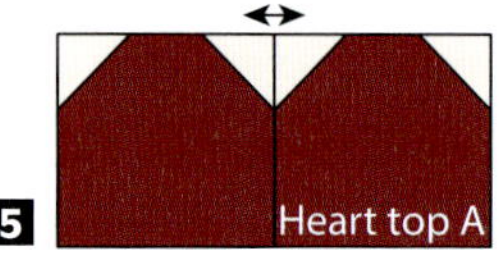

6. Repeat Step 5 with all corner units in matched pairs to make a total of 5 heart top As, 1 heart top E, 5 heart top Fs, and 1 heart top I.

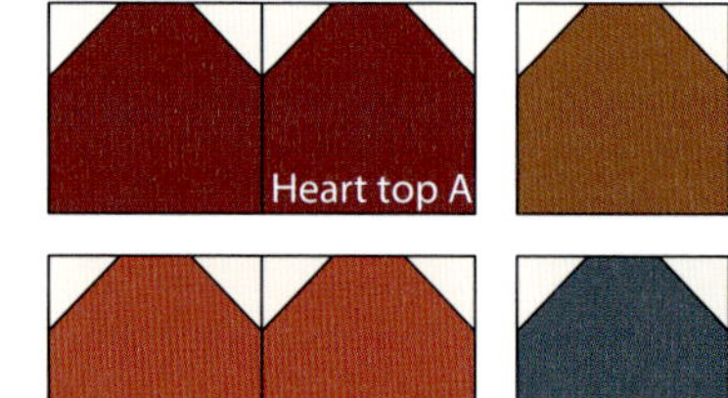

7. Pair 1 heart top in each fabric color with a matching heart bottom. Sew together, and press the seams toward the top to make 1 Heart block measuring 12½˝ × 12½˝ in each color A, E, F, and I.

8. Set the remaining heart tops aside.

Triple Heart Blocks

1. Arrange the pieces as shown in the row diagrams and sew together. Press the seams toward the squares to make 1 flying geese (FG) row. Repeat to make a total of 4 of each FG row 1 through 4.

2. Arrange the pieces as shown in the row diagrams and sew together. Press the center seam open and the outer seams toward the rectangles to make 1 HST row. Repeat to make a total of 4 of each HST row 1 through 4.

3. Arrange the following units in a column: Heart Top A + FG Row 1 + HST Row 1 + FG Row 2 + HST Row 2 + Heart Bottom E

Sew together, and press the seams as shown to complete 1 Triple Heart block A. Repeat to make a total of 4 Triple Heart block As.

4. Arrange the following units in a column: Heart Top F + FG Row 3 + HST Row 3 + FG Row 4 + HST Row 4 + Heart Bottom I

Sew together, and press the seams as shown to complete 1 Triple Heart block B. Repeat to make a total of 4 Triple Heart block Bs.

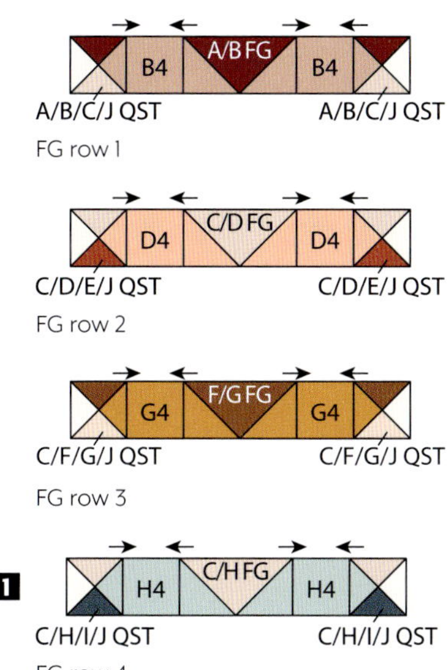

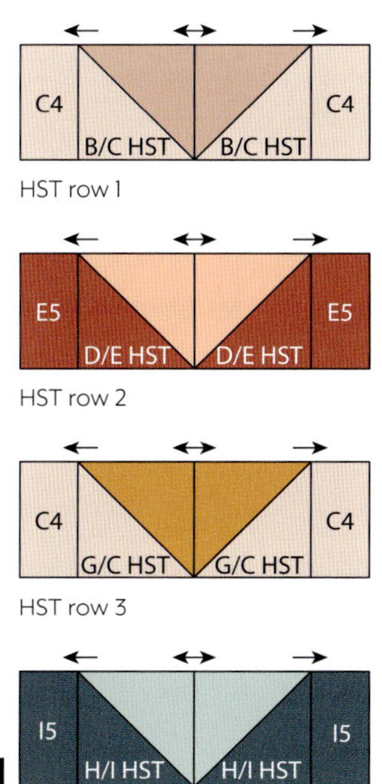

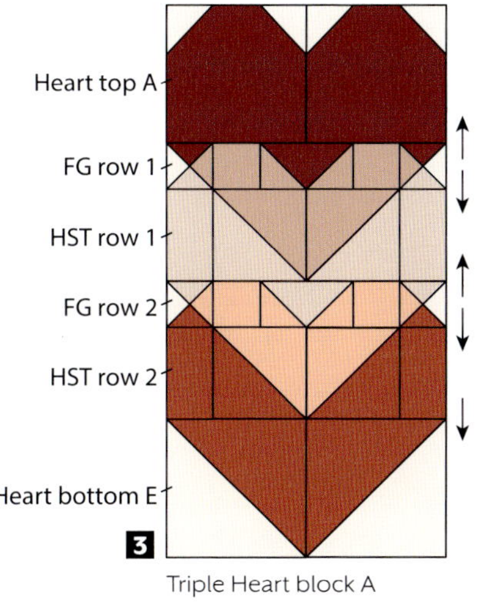

Triple Heart block A

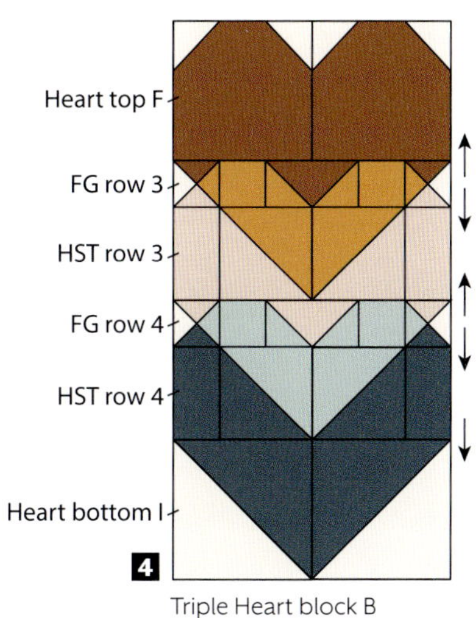

Triple Heart block B

Quilt Assembly

1. Arrange the Heart blocks and Triple Heart blocks into 4 columns, as shown, and sew each column together. Press the seams down toward the bottom of each column.

Column 1: Triple Heart A + Triple Heart B + Heart A

Column 2: Heart E + Triple Heart B + Triple Heart A

Column 3: Triple Heart B + Triple Heart A + Heart F

Column 4: Heart I + Triple Heart A + Triple Heart B

2. Arrange 5 J4 sashing strips and the 4 columns as shown. Sew the J4 sashing and the columns together. Press the seams toward the J4 sashing.

3. Sew the J5 border strips to the top and bottom of the quilt top. Press the seams toward the border strips to complete the Watercolor Hearts Quilt top.

4. Finish the quilt as desired (see Quilt Finishing, page 17).

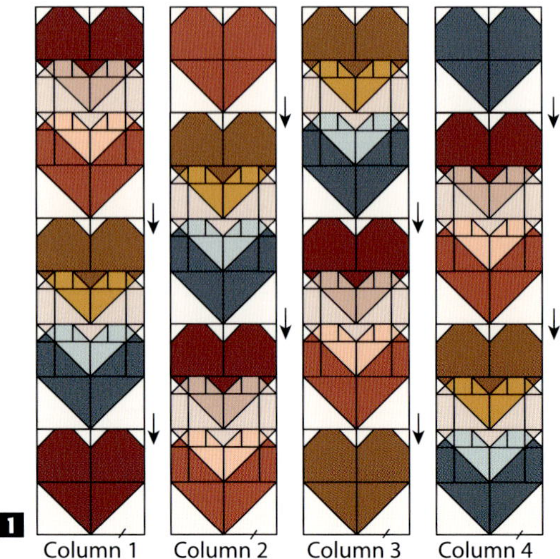

About the Author

Abby Luchsinger is a Wisconsin native and third-generation quilter who has been sewing and crafting for as long as she can remember. She started learning to sew from her grandmother as a little girl and she now enjoys quilting with her mom and teaching her own little girls.

Abby attended the University of Wisconsin and graduated with degrees in Political Science, French, and International Studies, aspiring to work in politics. She started her professional career as a policy advisor in the state senate, and also worked as a campaign coordinator for several state and federal campaigns before she and her husband moved to Oregon for his continuing education. While on the West Coast, she worked at a university coordinating events, communications, and continuing education. Following the arrival of her first baby, she and her family returned to Wisconsin and her focus transitioned to caring for her growing family as she welcomed a son and three daughters in just over five years. Abby launched her own quilt pattern design business, Abby Maed, in 2022, named with a clever play on her middle name, Mae, which she shares with her grandmother.

Since then, Abby has built a quilt pattern collection of her original designs imbued with her distinct style, featuring soft earthy colors and modern motifs that are simultaneously fresh, cozy, and timeless. Abby was a 2023 Art Gallery Fabrics Sewcialite and is now an Art Gallery Fabrics fabric designer. Her first fabric collection, as a member of the Sewcial Bee Collective, released in 2025. Abby is also a member of the Nine Patch Quilt Collective, the group of pattern designers behind the popular annual Sweater Weather Sampler. She lives outside of Madison, Wisconsin with her family, and when she's not quilting you can find her dabbling in other arts and crafts, hiking, traveling, volunteering with her church and in her community, and adventuring with her kids. Abby's designs and more of her quilting journey can be found at **abbymaed.com** and on social media **@AbbyMaed**

TEMPLATES

Scan the QR codes or visit the websites at right to access the templates for this book. The templates are available on US-Letter size sheets for printing at home, or on full-size sheets for printing at a copy shop.

US-Letter size
tinyurl.com/11623-pattern1-download

Full size
tinyurl.com/11623-pattern2-download

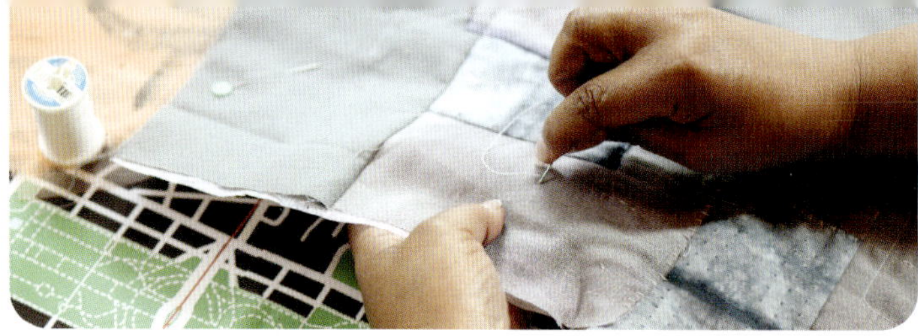